THE MEDICAL KNOWLEDGE
OF SHAKESPEARE

AMS PRESS
NEW YORK

THE

MEDICAL KNOWLEDGE

OF

SHAKESPEARE.

BY

JOHN CHARLES BUCKNILL, M.D., LOND.,

FELLOW OF THE ROYAL COLLEGE OF PHYSICIANS; FELLOW OF UNIVERSITY COLLEGE, LONDON;
SUPERINTENDENT OF THE DEVON COUNTY LUNATIC ASYLUM; EDITOR OF "THE JOURNAL
OF MENTAL SCIENCE"; AUTHOR OF "THE PSYCHOLOGY OF SHAKESPEARE",
AND JOINT AUTHOR OF "THE MANUAL OF PSYCHOLOGICAL MEDICINE."

LONDON:
LONGMAN & CO., PATERNOSTER ROW.
1860.

Reprinted from the edition of 1860, London

First AMS EDITION published 1971

Manufactured in the United States of America

International Standard Book Number: 0-404-01146-2

Library of Congress Catalog Number: 72-155634

AMS PRESS INC.
NEW YORK, N.Y. 10003

TO THE RIGHT HONOURABLE LORD CAMPBELL,

LORD HIGH CHANCELLOR,

&c., &c.

My Lord,

Some months have elapsed since your Lordship kindly gave me permission to dedicate to you the following pages, which, in great measure, owe their origin to your Lordship's interesting work on "*Shakespeare's Legal Acquirements.*"

In the meanwhile, your Lordship's merits have placed you on the very summit of professional honour, from which you reflect augmented lustre on the republic of letters, of which you are so eminent a citizen.

I feel the highest satisfaction in presenting this work to the public under the sanction of your Lordship's name, as a testimony of my admiration of your Lordship's character, and of our common reverence for him who stands in literature "the foremost man of all this world."

I remain,

Your Lordship's most obedient Servant,

THE AUTHOR.

Exeter, April 16th, 1860.

CONTENTS.

Introduction	Page 1
The Tempest	57
Two Gentlemen of Verona	61
Merry Wives of Windsor	66
Measure for Measure	68
Comedy of Errors	75
Love's Labour Lost	78
Taming of the Shrew	84
Midsummer Night's Dream	89
Merchant of Venice	92
All's Well that Ends Well	95
As You Like It	107
Much Ado about Nothing	112
Twelfth Night	118
Winter's Tale	125
King John	132
King Richard II.	139
King Henry IV., First Part	144
King Henry IV., Second Part	148
King Henry V.	165

KING HENRY VI., FIRST PART	PAGE 170
KING HENRY VI., SECOND PART	173
KING HENRY VI., THIRD PART	180
RICHARD III.	182
KING HENRY VIII.	188
MACBETH	191
CORIOLANUS	201
JULIUS CÆSAR	212
ANTONY AND CLEOPATRA	217
CYMBELINE	222
TROILUS AND CRESSIDA	228
ROMEO AND JULIET	238
TIMON OF ATHENS	245
HAMLET	259
LEAR	266
OTHELLO	269
PERICLES	275
TITUS ANDRONICUS	278
VENUS AND ADONIS	278
THE RAPE OF LUCRECE	281
SONNETS	285
THE LOVER'S COMPLAINT	289

SHAKESPEARE'S MEDICAL KNOWLEDGE.

SHAKESPEARE'S MEDICAL KNOWLEDGE.

The perusal of Lord Campbell's interesting work on Shakespeare's legal attainments, brought to the author of the following pages the conviction, that the knowledge of the great dramatist was in each department so extensive and exact, that it required the skilled observation of a professional mind fully and fairly to appreciate and set it forth. He found many passages cited in Lord Campbell's able criticism in proof of Shakespeare's legal acquirements, which, in an ignorance of legal phraseology, certainly not greater than common, he had mistaken for phrases of vulgar significance having no legal import; and, reasoning from analogy, he was led to the belief that passages of medical significance would be overlooked unless they were expressly sought for by some one whom the bias of a medical education had qualified to execute the task.

Although the author desires explicitly to disavow the intention to put forward in behalf of his own profession, any rival claims for the honor of having occupied the unaccounted-for period of Shakespeare's early manhood, he must confess, that it would be gratifying to professional self-esteem, if he were able to shew that the immortal dramatist, who bears, as Hallam says, " the greatest name in all literature," paid an amount of attention to subjects of medical interest, scarcely if at all inferior to that which has served as the basis of the learned and ingenious argument, that this intellectual king of men had devoted seven good years of his life to the practice of the law. The honor of medicine would appear somewhat abated, if Shakespeare had made no further references to it than those contained in the contemptuous description of Romeo's starved apothecary and his shop, and in Macbeth's impatient exclamation, " throw physic to the dogs."

The truth, however, when eliminated, appears to be so contrary to so slighting a regard, that it would be difficult to point to any great author, not himself a physician, in whose works the healing art is referred to more frequently and more respectfully than in those of Shakespeare; the sacred writings alone being excepted, for in these the calling of the physician certainly receives its highest expression of honor. The motive, however, for writing, and the excuse for publishing the following pages, is not to exalt the medical profession by citing in its glorification the favourable opinion and special knowledge of the great bard, but to contribute to the elucidation of his universal genius, and to prove that, among others, " the myriad-mind" had paid close attention to this most important and personally interesting subject of study.

In criticisms on Shakespeare, the judgment is often blinded by the incense of indiscriminating adulation. To insist that every trivial reference to the common ailments of mankind is a proof of medical study, would be to fall into this error, since there are few who have not had personal experience of disease, and there are none who have not heard the subject descanted upon by others ; and the very existence of disease implies the application of remedies, though, it may be, not by doctors, since what Tacitus says of nations is true of individuals, that none have been without medicine, though many without medical men. The causes of law are, in the social state, as common as the causes of medicine, but its practice is more rare ; and, it is not every quarrelsome fellow who even knows, like the Capulet swash-buckler, that, by forcing his adversary to begin the fray, he will have the law on his side. Now although it must be granted, that technical expressions are the trade marks of the mind, and that their frequent and appropriate use can only be accounted for by their having been stamped upon the memory by some pressure more urgent than casual and general conversation, it must be remembered that Shakespeare's father was engaged in legal transactions, from which the son might have garnered many technicalities which his infallible memory would afterwards reproduce. But the use of technical expressions may appropriately be acquired by poets for the purpose of their art, and by means of special study undertaken for that end. This is remarkably the case in the abundance of nautical expressions made use of in the second Canto of Don Juan, numbers of which are purely technical, and derived from professional sources which have been carefully noted. In the olden time, however, these signs of peculiar mental training would have less value than at present, when every calling is so defined, and separated from every other calling. In the olden time, a man might be an admiral, and a general, and a statesman, and a country

B²

gentleman, and somewhat of a lawyer, doctor, and divine into the bargain; and this universality of education stamped itself upon the works of the old authors; upon those of Montaigne, for instance; and, above all, upon those of Shakespeare. Hence arises the easy possibility of misjudging the calling of an old writer, from the professional knowledge indicated in his works. There is more of medicine than of law in Bacon's *Essays* and *Advancement of Learning*, and nearly as much of law as of medicine in Rabelais; yet the former was a practising lawyer and judge; while the latter was a practising physician, and a medical, as well as a general author; who, in addition to his immortal biography of Pantagruel and Panurge, translated the aphorisms of Hippocrates, and some of Galen's works. There is, perhaps, no author who so profusely employs technical terms as Rabelais, and this not only in medicine and in law, but in maritime and other professional business; so that this readiness of one author to use the terms of art proper to several callings, greatly decreases the value of such wordsigns, as an indication of the calling of the author himself.

Another indication of professional training, less obvious, but less deceptive than the employment of professional language, is to be found in the existence of a professional habit of mind. No one has represented this habitude of thought with more truthfulness, and with less exaggeration than Shakespeare himself. The formalism of the lawyer in Escalus, and the self-possession of the doctor in Cordelia's physician, the pedantic strategist in Fluellen, the scheming statist in Polonius, and many other forms of professional characterization, bear the impression, not more of individual differences of disposition, than of the sidelong growth of mind which special education impresses.

The intellectual and moral influences of the professions, are treated of, systematically, by Archbishop Whately, in his work on *Rhetoric*, and it will be worth while to consider, whether the mental peculiarities which he indicates as incidental to the studies of law and medicine, are to be found in Shakespeare. The Archbishop imputes to the medical profession a tendency to infidelity, and even to atheism, as its most important and prevailing bias; an opinion, which he says, is common even to a proverb—the old Latin proverb we presume: "*Ubi tres medici duo athei.*" The Archbishop can scarcely be called unjust in this imputation, for it is accepted by one of the most pious of physicians, the author of the *Religio Medici* himself. He, however, finds a curious argument against its truth, namely, that "though in point of devotion and piety, physicians do meet with common obloquy; yet, in the Roman *Calendar*, we find no less than twenty-nine saints and martyrs of that profession." The Archbishop's opinion, however, is as old as Chaucer, who, describing the Doctour of Physike, says, that

"His studie was but litel on the Bible."

If this imputation be in any degree just, it cannot be said that Shakespeare partakes of the characteristic; for, although the sceptical doubts of Hamlet probably indicate a phase in the poet's own mind, his writings as a whole are pervaded by an unquestionable and sincere spirit of reverence, the more remarkable in his age, as it is entirely divested of the bigotry which distinguished each of the two religious parties, which then divided society in the fierce war of opinion.

The second great mental peculiarity which the Archbishop attributes to the physician is that of indifference to death. By this of course he means, sentimental indifference; for he cannot and does not attribute to the physician a reasoning indifference to the 'fell anatomy', whose victory is the physician's defeat. The medical man becomes familiar with the sight and the idea of death, and from thence arises an absence of emotion in the contemplation of this fearful event, which the Archbishop points to as a mental characteristic. If this be true, which we somewhat doubt, the writings of Shakespeare indicate no parallel bias as existing in his mind. Death had a basilisk charm for his imagination, and in a variety of most eloquent passages he turns the subject over, and contemplates it from every side. "To lie in cold obstruction and to rot," or "to bathe in fiery floods," are to him painfully obtrusive ideas, so that he cannot even face the drunken caricature of death's image without a shudder.

The great mental peculiarity which Archbishop Whately attributes to the legal profession, is one which at first sight will appear far less important than the evils which he alleges against the tendency of medical education; but inasmuch as it imputes to the lawyers a peculiarity in the use of man's highest attribute, it will in truth be found to imply a mental warp even more radical than that which is laid to the charge of the doctors. The charge amounts to this, that the lawyer habitually employs his intellect for the purpose of proving a certain proposition which he assumes to be true. On this point, Whately, quoting from

Bishop Coplestone, says, "Reasoning comprehends inferring and proving, which are not two different things, but the same regarded in two different points of view; he who infers proves, and he who proves infers; but the word 'infer' fixes the mind first in the premise, and then on the conclusion. The word 'prove,' on the contrary, leads the mind from the conclusion to the premise.—To infer is the business of the Philosopher, to prove of the Advocate. The former, from the great mass of known and admitted truths, wishes to elicit any valuable additional truth whatever that has been hitherto unperceived, and, perhaps, without knowing with certainty what will be the terms of his conclusion. Thus, the Mathematician, *e. g.*, seeks to ascertain what is the ratio of circles to each other, or what is the line whose square will be equal to a given circle. The Advocate, on the other hand, has a proposition put before him, which he is to maintain as well as he can. His business, therefore, is to find middle terms (which is the invention of Cicero); the Philosopher's to combine and select known facts or principles, suitably for gaining from them conclusions which, though implied in the premises, were before unperceived; in other words, for making 'logical discoveries.'"

Now it cannot be doubted that the tendency of Shakespeare's mind was strongly bent against this professional mode of reasoning. He may, indeed, briefly have adopted it on one or two occasions to serve a particular purpose, as where Warwick reasons so like a lawyer, to prove that Gloster was murdered by Suffolk and Beaufort; but the prevailing tendency of Shakespeare's mind was eminently adverse to this proving process of reason. His intellect was in the widest sense philosophic, embracing known truths, and stretching forward to grasp the unknown by bold and subtle inference.

Shakespeare appears, therefore, to have had no professional warp of mind. The well-balanced strength of his intellect would either indicate that he had exercised it in some gymnasium of thought, like that which "sweet philosophy" affords; or if this Pegasus had indeed been in professional harness, it would seem most probable that he had not strained in one direction for seven years, since he could scarcely have done so without contracting some mental distortion, which would have injured the beautiful symmetry of his powers; and, therefore, if in harness at all, the likelihood is that he had changed from one to another employment, picking up terms of art and knowledge of men in many different phases of life. Altering the words of his own sly philosopher, might he not say, "What, would you tie me down to law, to physic, or to the ferula? Am I not William Shakespeare, old Shakespeare's son of Stratford? By birth a wool-comber, by education a clerk, by transmutation an actor, and now by present profession a play-wright?"

But, whatever changes he may have undergone, however various the points of view from which he may have looked upon life, one thing is certain, that he must have been a keen observer of men, and an insatiable devourer of books. According to Bacon's dictum he could not have been full without the one, or ready without the other. He is both the fullest and the readiest of men, and, therefore, must have been a student, living in the world.

In commenting upon Shakespeare's description of diseases of the mind, it has been possible to compare his knowledge with the most advanced science of the present day. The study of the laws which govern the moral and intellectual part of man, had even in ancient times attained to a degree of perfection that makes all modern metaphysics appear like a twice told tale. Metaphysical science is as old as Aristotle and Plato, but physical science, upon which modern medicine is founded, traces its parentage no higher than to Shakespeare's great contemporary, Bacon. Shakespeare, therefore, wrote in the mere infancy of medicine as a physical science; and it would be as unfair to compare his medical knowledge with that of the present day, as it would be to compare Lord Bacon's own chemical absurdities in his *Natural History of the Form of Hot Things*, with the mature enlightenment of Liebig, or of Faraday.

This view of the right method of conducting the professional criticism of an old author, did not at first present itself. The easy and pleasant task of re-perusing the plays, marking all passages of medical significance, and estimating their import by the light of the knowledge we at present possess, appeared sufficient for the end in view. But the unfairness and inadequacy of this mode of estimating Shakespeare's medical knowledge quickly became apparent; and, in attempting to form an opinion of the degree in which an old author was acquainted with an old subject, it became evident that the operation of time must carefully be borne in mind; which, as Shakespeare himself says:

"Doth blot old books, and alter their contents."

Dr. Willis, in his *Preface* to the *Works of Harvey*, commenting upon the meaning to be attached to a passage in Cæsalpinus, gives a caution eminently needful in the execution of the task we have in hand.

"The interpretation which successive generations of men

give to a passage in a writer some century or two old,
is very apt to be in consonance with the state of knowledge
at the time, in harmony with the prevailing ideas of the
day; and, doubtless, often differs signally from the meaning
that was in the mind of the man who composed it. The
world saw nothing of the circulation of the blood in Servetus,
Columbus, Cæsalpinus, or Shakespeare, until after William
Harvey had taught and written."

In order to give to medical passages in Shakespeare a just
critical interpretation, that is an interpretation in consonance with the medical knowledge of his own time, it will be
needful to give a brief sketch of the state of medicine in the
sixteenth and seventeenth centuries. It may be thought that
the various histories of medicine would give the needful
information on this point, but reference to them has resulted
in disappointment. *Le Clerc's History of Physick, made
English by Drs. Drake and Baden in* 1699, might be
expected to give a satisfactory statement of the condition
of physick in the age immediately antecedent to its publication, but it is unfortunately monopolized by dissertations
on the medicine of the Greeks and Arabians; a fault
which does not escape the observation of the first English
historian of Physick, Dr. Friend; who, although expressing
his high opinion of Le Clerc's learning and judgment
on the medical history of the ancients, says, that the
fifty-six pages which he designed should serve for a continuation of the history down to the middle of the sixteenth
century, " is not only a very imperfect and superficial performance, but in many particulars inaccurate and erroneous."

Dr. Friend, shortly after Le Clerc, wrote a really original
account of the progress of his science which even now

well merits perusal, and which has evidently served as stock for the soups and sauces of his successors, Dr. Lettsom and Dr. Hamilton. The latter's *History of Medicine and Surgery* is an excellent work on the subject, possessing the immense advantage of having been written after Sprengel had given to the world his learned *Geschichte der Artzneikunde*, the first work which really grappled with the subject. All these works however on the history of medicine have the common characteristic, that they describe the successive improvements and the progress of knowledge, but do not dwell upon the actual state of knowledge at any particular time ; they do not describe the degree of ignorance as well as that of knowledge ; and with slight exceptions they do not indicate the social state and position of the men who practised the art while they studied the science of medicine. The history of a great discovery or the growth of an important opinion is given by them with more or less exactness, but there is no history of medicine which can be referred to, with any probability of discovering whether Shakespeare uttered the professional opinion of his day, when he affirms that

"The sovereign'st thing on earth
Was parmaceti for an inward bruise,"

or whether Romeo's description of the starved apothecary and his shop is in any degree a fair representation of the social state of the drug-vendors of Shakespeare's time. Now a reference to Woodall's *Surgeon's Chest* proves that the virtue attributed to the internal administration of spermaceti, which we should now laugh at, exactly tallies with the opinion of one of Shakespeare's professional contemporaries ; and a reference to the numerous books of medical politics which abound about that period, would shew that the apothecaries, instead of being lean and starved, were stigmatized by the physicians for their exorbitant gains and their wealth. Original authorities, therefore, must be referred to in order to compare Shakespeare's medicine with the books and men of his day. This has been attempted; the medical works of that age have been studied, it is hoped with sufficient success to enable the medical passages of the dramatist to be brought to the test of a fair comparison with the opinions of his professional contemporaries. Perhaps, it may be permitted so far to anticipate the proofs, as to state that this research has been rewarded by establishing the fact, that Shakespeare's theoretical knowledge of medicine closely corresponded to that prevailing at his time among its professors, and that he had authority even for his trivialities and most glaring absurdities. Who would have thought that, when he says that toothache is owing to a humour or a worm, he had the authority of John of Gadisden for the opinion? Who would have thought when he describes Queen Mab's charioteer as

" Not half so big as a round little worm
" Pricked from the lazy finger of a maid."

that the curious statement was supported by the authority of an eminent contemporary surgeon?

These, and other instances, to be adduced in their proper place, appear to amount not merely to evidence, but to proof, that Shakespeare had read widely in medical literature.

The author of an *Essay* in the *Censura Literaria* considers that he establishes the fact of Shakespeare's knowledge of French, by the plagiarism of a line from an obscure French poem, thus; Jaques winds up the description of dotage by the singular line,

"Sans teeth, sans eyes, sans taste, sans everything,"

Garnièr describes the ghost of Admiral Coligny,

" Sans pieds, sans mains, sans nez, sans oreilles, sans yeux ;"

and the critic remarks, that if the copy of a single verbal error from Holinshed, viz. " on this side Tiber," instead of " on that side Tiber," is a proof that the dramatist had read that historian, why is not also his copy of this repetition of *sans*, and his parody of Coligny's ghost, an equally good proof of his having read Garnièr in the original French language ?

It must be admitted that the copy of a trivial circumstance or of an error, is better evidence that the original has been seen, than the copy of some important essential would be. The Chinese artist, who copied the crack in a plate, must have seen that individual plate ; while in the absence of the representation of the defect, it could not have been proved that he had not copied from any one of some hundreds of plates having the same form and pattern. On the same principle, therefore, the coincidence of Shakespeare's verbal expression of some medical absurdities with that of the medical works of his day, is better evidence that he had read those works, than the expression of undoubted medical truths, as that the sun breeds agues, or that surfeit is followed by sour digestion.

Not only was medical science raw and young in Shakespeare's time, but even the social foundations of the medical profession were of recent date. In the dark ages the practice of physic had fallen into the hands of monks and women, and so long as its practice consisted mainly in the blind application of a few empirical receipts, the clerical doctors do not appear to have been interfered with by their ecclesiastical superiors. But when the dawn of science rendered secular study needful to the priestly adepts, the Popes interdicted practices and studies which tended to break down the wall of separation between the clergy and the laity.

The union of the two professions in the middle ages is thus noted by Fuller, in his *Worthies of England:*

"The Ancient Brittans, who went without cloathes, may well be presumed to live without physick. Yet, seeing very Beasts know what is good for themselves (the Deer, *Cretan Dictamum;* and Toad, his Antidote of Plantaine); sure they had some experimental receipts used amongst them, and left the rest to nature and temperance to cure. The Saxons had those they termed Leaches, or Bloud-letters, but were little skilled in methodical practise. Under the Normans, they began in England (and would we had fetch'd Physicians only, and not Diseases from France!) Yet three hundred years since it was no distinct profession, by itself, but practised by men in Orders; witness Nicholas de Fernham, the chief English Physician and Bishop of Durham; Hugh of Evesham, a Physician and Cardinal; Grisant, a Physician and Pope. Yea, the word Physician appears not in our Statutes till the days of King Henry the Eight, who incorporated their Colledge at London: since which time they have multiplied and flourished in our Nation, but never more, and more learned, then in our age, wherein that art, and especially the Anatomical part thereof, is much improved, our Civil Wars perchance occasioning the latter."

In the quaint and witty pages of this author, we find many other traces of the extent to which, in old times, "the medicine for soul and body went hand-in-hand together"; a state of affairs which Fuller would wish to see instituted anew, by making "a physician liable to excommunication for visiting a patient thrice before acquainting a priest of his sickness." Thus, among the physicians of Cornwall, he ranks Dr. Attwell, "parson of St. Tue, well seen in the theoricks of physick," who, "although he now and then used blood-letting, he mostly, for all diseases, prescribed milk, and often milk and apples, which, either by virtue of the medicine, or fortune of the physician, or fancy of the patient, recovered many of desperate extremities." Attwell was living in 1602. He also notices Dr. Phreas, of London, who taught and practised physick in Italy, and whom "the Pope rewarded with the Bishoprick of Bath and Wells; he died in 1465. Sir George Ripley, an alchymist physician, in 1450, "who gave yearly to those Knights of Rhodes, a hundred thousand pounds towards maintaining the war against the Turks. This vast donation make some suspect Sir George for a knight, who might, by this, have been eques auratus, though, never more indeed than Sir Priest and Canon of Bridlington." John St. Giles, "physician to Philip, King of France, who, having the care of bodies, took upon him the cure of souls," and became "in his old age, famous for his divinity lectures in Oxford." According to Matthew Paris, "Robert Grosthead, the pious and learned Bishop of Lincoln, being sick on his death bed, sent for this Mr. John Giles, learned in physic and divinity, that from him he might receive comfort both for body and soul." Grosthead died in 1253, so that it would appear that even the recent thunders of the Pope were unable to make it appear to his immediate subordinates, that the practise of physic and the profession of divinity were necessarily inconsistent.

Dr. Millingen, in his *Curiosities of Medical Experience*, explains the origin of barber surgeons, from the decadence of medical practice among the priests. In 1163, at the Council of Tours, Pope Alexander III., maintaining that the devil, to seduce the priesthood from the duties of the altar, involved them in mundane occupations under the plea of humanity, prohibited the study both of medicine and law amongst all who had taken religious vows.

In 1215 Honorius III. " fulminated a fresh anathema," ordaining, that as the church abhorred all cruel and sanguinary practices, not only no priest should be allowed the practice of surgery, but that the priestly benediction should be refused to all those who professed it. Unable to quit their cloisters, in surgical cases, which could not be so easily cured at a distance, sooner than lose the emoluments of the profession, they sent their servants, or rather the barbers of the community, who shaved, and bled, and drew teeth in their neighbourhood ever since the clergy could no longer perform their operations, on the plea of the maxim, '*Ecclesia abhorret à sanguine;*' bleeding and tooth-drawing being, I believe, the only cases where this maxim was noticed. From this circumstance arose the barber craft, or barber-surgeons."

" Surgery, thus degraded, the separation between its practice and that of medicine became unavoidable, and the two branches were formally made distinct by Bulls of Boniface VI. and Clement V."

Primrose, in his *Popular Errours of Physick*, 1651, gives a more charitable, and, probably, a more correct account of the motives which led to the interference of the Popes with the medical occupations of the inferior clergy, than that attributed by the modern doctor, who is sceptical of anything good under the cassock. He says, " Wherefore, the Divine seems to be blameworthy, who, leaving and neglecting the nobler science to which he hath given up his name, and hath gotten to himself a character never to be blotted out, doth addict himself to another so slippery, so hard, so inconstant." The abovementioned decrees of the church, as they are quoted by Primrose, indicate that the real apprehension was neglect of spiritual things. "Because no man, warring for God, doth entangle himself also in secular affairs; let the Laies, who have more leisure, do these works one for another."—p. 16.

But if the Popes in those old times were hostile to medicine, the doctors it appears returned the compliment by excluding priests from their corporation. The statutes of the College of Physicians excluded all persons who were in holy orders. A curious instance of this will be found in the published proceedings of the College of Physicians against empiricks, by Dr. Goodall, in the prosecution of Dr. Alexander Leighton, in 1617, which is thus recorded, p. 401:

"Dr. Alexander Leighton being required by the Censors to give an account by what authority he practised Physick, He told them by virtue of his Doctour's degree, which he had taken at Leyden, under Professor Heurnius. He was charged as being in Presbyter's orders, and asked why he did not stick to his Ordination. He excepted against the Ceremonies, yet owned himself a Preacher, and acknowledged his practising of Physick. In several parts whereof he was examined, but giving no satisfaction, and being perverse as to Ecclesiastical affairs, he was by the President and Censors interdicted practice. After this, *endeavouring to procure a Licence, it was denied him, because in Holy Orders, the Statutes of the College declaring that none such should be admitted into the College, or permitted to practice.* Wherefore he was a second time forbidden practice. But he still persisting to practice in *London* or within seven miles, was arrested, and afterwards censured, *tanquam infamis*, he having been censured in the Star Chamber, and lost his ears."

The church, however, made her power felt in the College of Physicians, although none of her sons were admitted into its corporation. The Act of the 3rd Henry VIII., c. ii., provides that candidates for permission to practice shall be first examined, approved, and admitted by the Bishop of London,

c

or by the Dean of St. Paul's, calling to him or them four doctors of physick ; and, for surgery, other expert persons in that faculty. The second clause enacts, that beyond the seven-mile precinct of London, no person shall exercise or occupy, as a physician or surgeon, but if he be first approved and examined by the Bishop of the diocese, or by his Vicar-General.

The preamble of this first Act of the physicians gives a curious insight into the practice of medicine in the early part of the sixteenth century. It runs thus, "Forasmuch as the science and cunning of physick and surgery (to the perfect knowledge whereof be requisite both great learning and ripe experience) is daily within the realm exercised by a great multitude of ignorant persons, of whom the greater part have no manner of insight in the same, nor in any other kind of learning : some also can no letters on the book, so far forth that common artificers, as smiths, weavers, and women, boldly and accustomably take upon them great cures, and things of great difficulty; in the which they partly use sorcery and witchcraft, partly apply such medicines unto the disease as be very noxious, and nothing meet therefore ; to the high displeasure of God, great infamy to the faculty, and the grievous hurt, damage, and destruction of many of the king's liege people ; most especially of them who cannot discern the uncunning from the cunning."

This Act refers both to physicians and surgeons, and it was not till the 14th and 15th of Henry VIII. that an Act was passed, making a body corporate of the faculty of physick within London and seven miles compass, giving the power of fine and imprisonment to the office-bearers of the college upon persons presuming to practice without their licence. "*Ita quod punicio hujusmodi medicorum utentium dicta facultate Medicine sic in premissis delinquentium per fines amerciamenta & imprisonamenta corporum suorum & per alias vias rationabiles & congruas exequatur.*"

An Act passed in the 32nd of Henry VIII. excepts the physician from keeping watch and ward, or the office of constable, or other office of the kind; it gives the college power to choose four of their body yearly to search the apothecaries' wares in London, and to levy a forfeiture of 100 shillings in case of an apothecary refusing to have his house searched. And "forasmuch as the science of physick doth comprehend, include, and contain the knowledge of surgery, as a special member and part of the same;" it enacts, that any of the company or fellowship of physicians may "practice and exercise the said science of physick in all and every his members and parts." That is, it enacts that any of the physicians may practice surgery.

The college had their charter renewed and extended by James I., and subsequently by Charles II.; and Dr. Goodall's interesting book, "*The Physicians of London,*" 1684, from which the above extracts have been taken, bears ample testimony to the vigour with which the college exercised their powers of fine and imprisonment upon all who invaded their rights.

The barbers and surgeons were made one company by statute of the 22nd of Henry VIII., before which time they had been distinct companies, under statutes of Edward IV. and Henry VII., the barbers being incorporated but the surgeons "not having any manner of corporation." Henry VIII.'s Act, which incorporates both in one company, provides, however, that no barber in London shall use surgery, and no surgeon

c^2

shall use the craft of shaving. The powers given to surgeons under this statute were greatly inferior to those already cited as given to physicians. The four wardens, however, were empowered to inflict upon persons offending against the articles the forfeit of £5 for every month. It would appear from a statute passed in the 34th and 35th of Henry VIII., that the powers of the surgeons had been exercised in an arbitrary and oppressive manner; "Since the making of the said Act (3rd of Henry VIII.), the company and fellowship of the surgeons of London mindful only of their own lucres, and nothing the profit of the diseased or patient, have sued, troubled, and vexed divers honest persons, as well men as women, whom God hath endued with the knowledge of the nature, kind, and operation of certain herbs, roots, and waters, and the using and administration of them to such as being pained with customable diseases, as women's breasts being sore, *a Pin and Web in the eye*, uncomes of hands, scaldings, burnings, sore mouths, the stone, strangury, saucelim and morphew, and such other diseases; and yet the said persons have not taken anything for their pains or cunning, but have ministered the same to poor people only for neighbourhood and God's sake, and of pity and charity. And it is now well known that the surgeons admitted will do no cure to any person but where they shall know to be rewarded with a greater sum than the cure extendeth unto:—Be it enacted, that it shall be lawful to persons having knowledge and experience of the nature of herbs, roots, and waters, to practice, use, and minister to any outward sore, uncome, wound, apostemations, outward swelling, or disease; any herb or herbs, baths, pultes, and emplaisters, according to their cunning, &c.;

or drinks for the stone, or strangury, or agues, without suit, vexation, trouble, penalty, or the loss of their goods; the aforesaid statute, or any Act to the contrary thereof made in any wise notwithstanding."

The apothecaries, or, as Queen Mary's Act has it, the potecaries, forming the third estate of medicine, although their existence was very evident from the penalties to which they were liable in the statutes of the physicians, had no separate corporation of their own, until James the First granted them a charter and corporation in the thirteenth year of his reign. The apothecaries had been made one corporation with the grocers of London in the fourth of this reign; but in the second charter they were separated from the company of the grocers, and constituted into a distinct corporation of their own, with master, wardens, common seal, &c. No grocer was henceforth permitted to keep an apothecary's shop. Great power was given to the apothecaries over the purchase and sale of medicines, and of entering and searching shops and houses, to discover and burn unwholesome and hurtful medicines; but in their orders concerning medicines they were to advise with the President and Censors of the College of Physicians; who, moreover, had special powers of their own, to "execute the search, and view, and the due punishment of the potecaries for any their evil and fawty stuffe, without the assistance of any of the said wardens."

The great powers of the College of Physicians appear to have brought them abundance of litigation, not only with the irregular practitioners, whom they prosecuted and imprisoned, and who now and then got a verdict against them for false imprisonment, but also with the rival corporations of surgeons and apothecaries. Goodall records, that "there happening in the reign of Elizabeth to arise a difference between the physicians and surgeons, whether the surgeons might give inward remedies in the scrofula, French pox, or any kind of ulcer or wound," Dr. Caius so learnedly defended the rights of the physicians, that it was unanimously agreed by the Queen's Commissioners that it was unlawful for the surgeons to practice in the forementioned cases.

At a later date the contentions of the College of Physicians, who were Galenists, with their innovating chemical brethren, and with the apothecaries and irregulars, were frequent, and afforded, as one result, a curious class of old medical literature, which may be called medico polemical.

Goodall himself was the author of a book in 1677, "written in defence of the College of Physicians against a bold and impudent libel, published with design to expose that learned Society to contempt."

An anonymous author, signing himself "M. N.," and who after announced himself to be Dr. Nedham, published in 1666 a well written and learned attack upon the monopoly of the College, under the title of "*Medela Medicinæ, for the free profession and renovation of the art of Physick.*" "The physicians," he says, "are so confident as to attempt an autocracy in the art of physick," in which he claims "a greater latitude in the profession and practice than the interests of some men of the same profession would be willing to allow."

Nedham's attack was answered by Dr. Twisden, a fellow of the college, in his work entitled "*Medicina veterum vindicata,*" or an answer to a book entitled "*Medela Medicinæ,*" 1666, in which he vindicates the profession, by which he means the college, "which, of late, has been struck at by many writers."

This, however, may be considered rather as a war of opinions than of classes, Nedham belonging to the new sect of chemical physicians, while Twisden and the members of the college generally were Galenists or methodists, holding by the old doctrines of the faculty.

But the great medical iconoclast of the century was Dr. Gideon Harvey, Physician in Ordinary to His Majesty. Three of his works are at hand; "*The Family Physician and the House Apothecary*," 1676, is the earliest, and is an attack upon the avarice and the excessive profits of the apothecaries. The body of the book is occupied by receipts for the domestic preparation of medicines; the introduction, however, is instructive on the medical manners of the time. "I have oft seen bills of apothecaries (says he) risen to 20*l.*, and sometimes 30*l.*, in the time of a fortnight; what is more, I have known an apothecary's bill so extravagant that the sum at the bottom of his account amounted to the sum of 50*l.* in the space of thirty days; when the ingredients of the whole course could not be computed to stand him in 40*s*. But that which sounds worse than all this is, that not long since an apothecary of our suburbs brought in bills for less than three quarters of a year's physick to nine patients, amounting to 1,500*l.*" And all this, as he explains, was for "the little diseases, a sweating bolus, or a potion of mithridate, for a pain in your head and limbs, coughs, stuffing in the head," &c., "the furthest point the apothecary can safely steer." For the greater diseases the greater remedies must be employed, for which a physician is necessary, "who is as little capable to cure great diseases with ordinary medicines, as a grainer is able to cut curious figures in steel with the ordinary tools of a carver or stonecutter; or a barber to take off the hair of your beard with a chopping knife."

"Touching these great medicines, it is very fortunate they have not yet arrived to the knowledge of the little apothecaries, or the prescribing surgeons, who, using them without method, though sometimes they might do good, yet, for want of capacity in the applications, would certainly at most times do great mischiefs with them; and, therefore, every physician ought to reserve them secret by preparing them himself; and when necessary to be used, to send them to the apothecary to be exhibited, or to give them to his patients with what directions are requisite."

In the "*Conclave of Physicians detecting their intrigues, plots, and frauds against their patients,*" 1683, Dr. Gideon Harvey flys at higher game, and rises with the occasion to greater piquancy of vituperation. "Know then," says he, "this famous conclave is the eldest quack synagogue, consisting of a physick pope or patriarch, and a competent number of medicinal cardinals, who, being grown ancient, covetous, and through forgetfulness ignorant, are to govern the rest, and whenever they are consulted they are to impose upon the juniors their pretended long experience, which they are to embrace with the same implicit faith the Turks do their Alcoran." "Against those who refuse being admitted into their conclave, and will not conform, they send forth their Bulls and anathemas, declaring them mountebanks, quacks, chymists, barbers, ignorants, &c.; and if such should at any time have a patient die under their hands of an incurable disease, they thunder at it; he killed the patient, poisoned him, applied wrong medicines, and the like. According to the examination of their treasury, once in eight or ten years they proclaim a jubilee, setting open their doors to physicians, barbers, apothecaries, and renegade priests, who, upon the payment of a certain sum of chequeens, are honored with a fop character, and received into the church porch of Æsculapius, being forbidden to enter any further during the time it is occupied by the whole Conclave or Consiglio picolo, though, at other seasons, they have toleration to peep in, or take a turn or two."

This satirical description of the *Year of Grace* in the olden time, is interesting at the present date, when, after long desuetude, the old custom has been once more revived, though under a judicious liberality which would leave no sore even for the venom of Dr. Gideon to rankle in.

Dr. Gideon's abusive book gives a ludicrous picture of the profession in those times from its weak side. The hypocritical physician, punctual at church, that he may be fetched out by his apothecary under the pretence of a professional call, that he may "make an impression on the people—that he is a man of great physick business," p. 109. The virtuoso physician, who, posting to a sick gentleman in a coach-and-four, is arrested by "an unhappy gaudy butterfly," which he hunts while the patient dies, the seed thought of one of Peter Pindar's odes, p. 60. The avaricious physician, to whom the wife of a poor man brings "an urinal of her sick husband's urine" for him to cast; "the doctor having given the round toss to the urinal," asks "whether her husband had forty pound to spend on a physician," and has the conscience to accept her only groat, p. 113. The doctor of undaunted boldness, who gives three hundred and sixty grains of calomel to a patient, whom "a coach keeping apothecary," had handed over to him with nodes on the tibia, &c. The "infant physician, mimicking a decrepit gravity by apuysing his velvet body on his japan crutche, and drawing his broad-brimmed beaver over his eyes," p. 21. All these, and others, are sketched with wonderful quaintness embellished with vigorous abuse.

The third work of this author is in Latin. The title is: "*Gideonis Harvei, M.D., Medici Regis et Reginæ, Ars curandi morbos expectatione, item de vanitatibus dolis et mendaciis medicorum.*" Instead of the printer's name it has the following motto from Celsus, "Multi magni morbi curantur abstimentia et quiete." It is without date, but must have been subsequent to the "Conclave of Physicians;" since he says, "Plures obitus causam potius quam putativæ convalescentiæ gratias medicis debent, uti amplissime et fideliter libello cui *Medicorum Conclave* titulus apponitur exhibui."

This is really a scientific work, and ought not to have been marred by a repetition of the gross abuse which pervades the vernacular satire. It might well have been named "The Fallacies of the Faculty," and is remarkable as the earliest treatise on the subject of expectant medicine, and the enunciation of a partial truth which has recently become developed into the doctrine of a school; the most fair and faithful statement of which is to be found in the recent work of Sir John Forbes.

Although not elaborated into a creed, the principle of expectant medicine had been recognized and its foundations justly indicated, at a still earlier date, as the following good story from Bullein's "*New Boke of Phisicke*, 1559" will shew:—"Once I fel into a great sicknes, and hitherto I am skant recovered of it, the surfite was so great; but counsail was geuen me, that I should not stay myselfe upon the opinion of any one Physition, but rather upon three: then said I: to retain three at once, requireth great charge, for those men to whome lives be committed, ought liberal rewardes to be geuen. Then sayde my frend, they are good gentelmen, and no great takers. What be theyr names, said I: He answered saying: The fyrste was called Doctor Diet, the second, Doctor Quiet, the third, Doctor Merryman."

Dr. Gideon classifies the physicians of the college in his day into six sects, who support the art of medicine, he says, like the six feet of a monster. First, there are the chalybeate doctors, who cure all diseases with preparations of steel or copper; then there are the medical ass-drivers, who put all their patients upon a diet of asses' milk; next come the jesuitical doctors, cheats *a capite ad calcem*, who depend upon bark, Gideon's favourite aversion; then the medical water-bailiffs, who drench their patients at the mineral springs; then the butcher doctors, *lanii doctores*, who always phlebotomize; and lastly, illustrious in their greater numbers, the muck doctors, *stercorarii doctores*, who expel diseases by purgation. He cites an unfortunate instance of his great namesake's treatment, William Harvey, who doubtless belonged to this last illustrious sect, in proof of a pet, but sufficiently false theory, that the practical physician may waste his time in the study of anatomy.

Gideon Harvey says of him that he was: "*Felicissimus anatomicus, licet medicus nequaquam insignissimus;*" and that, in his unlucky judgment, he prescribed a purge for Lord Rainton, half a dose ot which operated eighty times, so that the whole dose would probably have sent the patient to Hades.

Dr. Willis is very angry with Aubrey for reporting of the great Harvey, that "though all the professsion would allow him to be an excellent anatomist, I never heard that any admired his therapeutic way." What will he say to the more specific accusation of the contemporary doctor?

We have seen that the charges made by apothecaries in the olden times were exorbitant beyond anything known in these days. As might be expected, the irregular quacks had still less conscience; thus, Goodall mentions that one George Butler, who gave the College no little trouble in 1633, charged 30s. a piece for 25 pills; £37 10s. for a box of pills! They, however, had something in them, *virus aut virtus*, for three given to Mrs. Style for a sore leg, had the effect of killing her the night she took them. One Dr. Tenant, also prosecuted by the College, in James the First's reign, "was so impudent and unconscionable in the rating of his medicines, that he charged one pill at £6, and an apozeme at the same price."

The reported prosecutions by the College contain many instances of a like character, so that the president and society might claim to have protected the ignorant public not only from poison, but from extortion.

The fee of the physician in the olden time, appears to have been the still customary guinea. Gideon Harvey gives sarcastically the details of a case in which a patient was treated by three physicians, who attended daily, and sometimes twice a day. "This *Repetatur* (he says) at three guineas more, is somewhat dearer than neck-beef." Again: "℞ *Persistat in usu julapii nuper præscript.* Every word in this prescription costs the patient half-a-guinea, but it's no great matter, he will not want the money whither he is going."

These charges, it must be admitted, appear exorbitant, since in Shakespeare's time, the value of money was at least five-fold that which it at present bears. This is well known from other sources, but there is at least one passage in the dramas which marks the change.

"*Shallow.* How a score of ewes now?
Silence. Thereafter as they be: a score of good ewes may be worth ten pounds." *Henry IV., Part II.*

At the present time, a score of good ewes in Warwickshire would be worth fifty pounds.

On the other hand, the now customary six and eight pence of the lawyer appears, in Shakespeare's lifetime, to have been three and four pence, or just half.

"*Clown.* As fit as ten groats is for the hand of an attorney."
All's Well that Ends Well.

The fee of the physician is also referred to:

"Kill thy physician, and thy fee bestow
Upon the foul disease." *Kent, in Lear.*

Its amount, however, is nowhere specified, but it was sufficient to afford the means of rapid wealth. Thus, we find that William Harvey, though in little esteem and moderate practice during a considerable portion of his career, was enabled to bequeath the then great sum of £20,000; and the many foundations of colleges and lectureships which we owe to other physicians of that day, testify both to their wealth and their public spirit.

The wealth and social position of the olden physicians is apparent, even from many passages in the satirical attacks we have referred to. Thus, it is shewn, that they habitually rode in coaches, when to do so was the luxury of the rich and the great; they clothed in velvet, and wore velvet caps of a conceited cut; but, above all, they aimed at maintaining themselves at the highest level of intellectual aristocracy, in their knowledge of the learned and modern languages, and their attainments in the general science and literature of their age. It was for these accomplishments that the earlier physicians were most celebrated, even among the men of their own time. Thus, Fuller, in his *English Worthies*, records of Dr. Linacer, the founder of the College, that, "Returning unto England, he brought languages along with him, and was the first restorer of learning in our nation. It is questionable whether he was a better Latinist or Grecian, a better grammarian or physician, a better scholar or man for his moral deportment." Dr. Caius, contemporary with Shakespeare, and the founder of the College bearing his name at Cambridge, was a man of the same metal. "I may call these two doctors the two phenixes of their profession in our nation," says Fuller. Another Fellow of the College of Physicians, contemporary with Shakespeare's later years, was the Marquis of Dorchester, who, at the age of forty-three, applied himself to the study of physic, and acquired great proficiency therein; "he esteemed his Fellowship in the College, an honour second only to that of his peerage, and maintained that his colleagues were the most learned society in the world, and he bequeathed to them his library of the value of £4,000, being the best at that time in any private hand in the nation."

Classical learning, rather than natural science, the peculiar province of the medical man, appears to have been the characteristic of the physicians in the sixteenth century; but, in the early part of the seventeenth century, medical science took a bound in the discovery of Shakespeare's great contemporary, Harvey; and, somewhat later in the century, in the more numerous and purely professional, though less brilliant achievements of Sydenham, to whom the installation of the rational medicine of modern times may be said to be due. The names of Harvey and of Sydenham would alone be sufficient to make the London College illustrious for ever. It must not, however, be thought that medical knowledge increased in a regularly progressive manner during these times; on the contrary, very eminent members of the College wrote from time to time, incredible nonsense, so that an examination into the tenets of that day would indicate that the march of science was not like the peaceful progress of a great king, but rather like that of a general, whose army gaining here, and beaten back there, after many vicissitudes, remains master of the country; a proof of this may be found in the doctrine of fermentation, published by the celebrated anatomist of the brain, Dr. Willis, in 1659, who maintained that all natural changes in organic bodies depend upon fermentation in their constituent principles, which are spirit, sulphur, salt, water, and earth; and in the works of Sir George Ent, a great man in his day, who maintained that the virus of intermittent fevers and of small pox was not derived from the blood, but from a certain nutritious juice, and that the blood serves, not to nourish the body, but to keep it warm; and, that the urine is not conveyed to the kidneys by the emulgent arteries, which only bring the blood thither to cherish and keep them warm, but by the nerves.

Among the most singular records of the College, published by Goodall, are the letters which passed between the Society, as the members then called themselves, and Elizabeth's great statesman, Walsingham. Walsingham appears to have been a favourer of empirics, and a believer in them, for he had submitted his own health to one of the fraternity; though this evidence of his faith may not be thought worth much by those who are acquainted with the pranks which men play with their own bodies. A humorous disciple of the hydropathic empiricism of the present day acknowledges that he had no faith in Priestnitz, because he treated himself according to his system, but that when this high priest of *Hygeia fontana* had subjected a favorite horse to the same therapeutics, he yielded implicit credence at least to the German's honesty.

The College of Physicians at the present day may care little that those who make the laws of the land may now and then rebel against the laws of nature, and the dictates of sense, by their adhesion to empirical follies; but in Elizabeth's time, statesmen possessed greater powers and exercised them in a more arbitrary manner than they dare to do now. Walsingham wrote to the College in 1551, in behalf of one Margaret Kennix, as he says, by Her Majesty's commandment, "signifying how that it was Her Highness' pleasure that the poore woman shoold be permitted by you quietly to practise and minister to the curing of diseases and wounds by the means of certain simples, in the applieing whereof it seemeth God hath given her an especiall knowledge." In this herb-practice, it appears, she "was restrained by the College, contrary to Her Majesty's pleasure." "I shall, therefore, desire you forthwith (proceeds Walsingham) to take order among yourselves for the re-admitting her into the quiet exercise of her small talent, lest, by the renewing of her complaint to Her Majesty thorough your hard dealing towards her, you procure' further inconvenience therby to yourself, then perhaps you woold be willing shoold fall out." The reply of the physicians is truly courageous, daring, as it does, both the displeasure of the great man, and of his despotic mistress. "We act," they say "under the straight band of our oth and conscience, which we esteem of greater weight than that we can release ourselves thereof at our pleasure." They appeal to the 'holsome lawes,' in the administration of which they are "no whit culpable for not suffering either her or any other whatsoever, to intrude themselves into so great and dangerous a vocation;" and they decline to accede to his honor's request; and as for his threat, they end, "professing ourselves to be more willing and content to abide any inconvenience whatsoever may ensue, rather than to be brought to allow of so disorderly an attempt either in her, or in any other her lyke."

Five years subsequent to this, Walsingham again addressed the College in favour of one *Not*, a practitioner in physick, whom they had committed to prison in the Compter. The College appears to have been too strong for the Secretary, for this *Not* had been his own medical attendant, a fact which he assigns as the reason of his interference. "Forasmuch as both myself have heretofore used him, and divers other gentlemen have also received good by him."

The President and Society of Physicians again deny the great man's request, alleging their oath and the laws. They say, that Not "stubbernly (upon what encouragement we know not,) of purpose infringeth our privileges, and the holsome lawes of this realme, which we by solemn oth are bound to maintain."

Walsingham again tried to bend the College to his views in 1589, when he wrote requesting them to release from prison one Paule Buck, a practitioner in physick and surgerie. He received a reply similar in tenor to the former ones; and upon two members of the College waiting on him, with the letter, he assured them, "that he would never act in anything contrary to the benefit or dignity of their society; and if upon any time by the importunity of friends he did write upon such an occasion, he, notwithstanding, left them to act what they thought most prudent."

It appears, therefore, upon due consideration of the evidence of these old works, that the medical profession in the time of Shakespeare, consisted of physicians, surgeons, and apothecaries. The physicians in London constituted a corporation, yielding great powers. Its members possessed the influence derived from mental superiority, wealth, and high social position. Familiar at courts, and the friends of kings, they maintained their privileges with a high hand. With great learning they possessed little knowledge. Their professional opinions were founded mainly upon the dogmata of Galen; and their practice upon a complcated pharmacy of vegetable substances, interspersed with offensive animal matters, and directed by mixed traditions of experience and superstition. But withal they were the freest intellects of their age, and the first to apply the great mental instrument for the discovery of natural truth bequeathed to them by Bacon; the doctrines of the Novum Organon resulting in the discovery of Harvey, half a century before they culminated in those of Newton. Moreover, the very want of that minute knowledge which is apt to invest the physician of the present day with a crust of pedantry, compelled the physician of olden time to sharpen his intellect in the ways and thoughts of men, so as to derive as much light as possible through the narrow openings of knowledge.

The olden physician, therefore, was a man of the world, whose good taste, and good manners, formed by travel and learning, provided a decent cloak for his scientific ignorance, and whose good sense and keen observation enabled him to look into the secrets of men, when those of nature were still unrevealed. This is the "kind of men" of which a physician ought to be according to Queen Elizabeth, as we see in her letter recommending her physician, Dr. James, to the 'Emperor of Russia:' "Quod hominum genus (medicum) quoniam et plurimarum rerum cognitionem et morum probitatem non vulgarem postulat." Such physicians Shakespeare may have known in this Dr. James, or in Dr. Caius, or in Dr. W. Harvey, and certainly did know in his son-in-law, Dr. Hall. Such physicians he has represented in Lear, Cymbeline, and Macbeth.

As any attempt to delineate the ordinary practice of physic as it existed in Shakespeare's time, during the infancy of the science, must necessarily be of antiquarian rather than of scientific interest, it will best be illustrated in these pages from the case-book of a physician, whose life was intimately bound with that of our great poet, and from the recorded treatment of the poet's own near relatives.

Shakespeare's eldest daughter Susanna, married Dr. John Hall, a physician of great provincial eminence, practising at Stratford upon Avon. The registration of his marriage stands thus:

"1607, June 5, John Hall, Gentleman, and Susanna Shaxspere."

From the terms of this entry, Mr. Collier, in his exact and careful estimate of the meagre accounts which have come down to us of Shakespeare's belongings, appears to arrive at the conclusion that Hall occupied a lower professional grade before he practised as a physician. "The eldest daughter of William and Ann Shakespeare, Susanna, having been born in May, 1583, was rather more than twenty four years old, when she was married on the 5th of June, 1607, to Mr. John Hall, of Stratford. He is styled 'Gentleman' in the register, but he was a professor of medicine, and subsequently practised as a physician." Mr. Collier supposes "that the ceremony was performed in the presence of our great dramatist, during one of his summer excursions to his native town," and he thinks the New Place, otherwise called the Great House at Stratford, was Shakespeare's country residence, and that "Dr. and Mrs. Hall were joint occupiers, and aided in keeping up the vivacity of the family circle." And when Shakespeare went to London, in 1614, on business relating to the enclosure of common lands near Stratford, Hall accompanied him, as we learn from a notice of an interview with the father and son-in-law, by Thomas Greene.

It will be an interesting subject of enquiry, whether such of the Dramas as were written after their author entered into terms of intimate relationship with a physician, well educated in the professional knowledge of his time, bear any impression of the mental contact, since it is scarcely possible, but that some influence should have been exercised upon the impressible mind of the poet, by the husband of his favourite daughter, living with him in the same house.

Speaking of the death of the poet, Mr. Collier remarks, "We need hardly entertain a doubt, that he was attended in his last illness by his son-in-law, Dr. Hall, who had then been married to Susanna Shakespeare more than eight years; we have expressed our opinion that Dr. and Mrs. Hall lived in the same house with our poet, and it is to be recollected, that in his will he leaves New Place to his daughter Susanna. Hall must have been a man of considerable science for the time at which he practised; and he has left behind him proofs of his knowledge and skill, in a number of cases which had come under his own eye, and which he described in Latin; these were afterwards translated from his manuscript, and published in 1657, by James Cooke, with the title of *Select Observations on English Bodies.* But the case of Dr. Hall's father-in-law is not found there, because most unfortunately the observations only began in 1617. One of the earliest of them shews that an epidemic called 'the new fever,' then prevailed in Stratford, and 'invaded many.' Possibly Shakespeare was one of these; though had such been the fact, it is not unlikely that, when speaking of 'the Lady Beaufou' who suffered under it, only July 1st, 1617, Dr. Hall would have referred back to the earlier instance of his father-in-law. He does advert to a certain ague of which, at a period not mentioned, he had cured Michael Drayton, ('an excellent poet,' as Hall terms him,) when he was perhaps, on a visit to Shakespeare. However, Drayton, as formerly remarked, was a native of Warwickshire, and Dr. Hall may have been called in to attend him at Hartshill."

The registration of Dr. Hall's burial is in these terms:

"1635, *Nov.* 26. *Johannes Hall, Medicus peritissimus,*"

a designation which a careful perusal of his work, for the opportunity of which we have to thank Mr. Collier, appears fairly to justify.

The title of the work is as follows: "*Select Observations on English Bodies, or Cures Empirical and Historical Performed on very eminent Persons in Desperate Disorders. First written in Latine by Mr. John Hall, Physician, of Stratford, where he was very famous, as also in the counties adjacent. Now put into English for common benefit, by James Cook, Practitioner in Physick and Chirurgery. London: Printed by John Shirley, at the Golden Pelican in Little Brittain,* 1657."

"OBSERVATION XXXV. A child of Mr. Walker's, of Ilmington, Minister, aged six months, afflicted with the falling sickness, by consent was thus freed: First, I caused round pieces of Piony Roots to be hanged about the Neck. When the Fit afflicted, I commanded to be applied with a spunge to the Nostrils, the Juyce of Rhue, mixed with White-wine Vinegar; by the use of which it was presently recovered; and falling into the fit again, it was removed in the same manner. To the Region of the Heart was applied the following: ℞ *Theriac. ven.* ʒii. *Rad. Pæon. pul.* ʒss. *Misc.* The hair was powdered with the powder of the Roots of Piony. And thus the child was delivered from all its Fits."

"OBSERVATION LX. Talbot, the first-born of the Countess of Salisbury, aged about one year, being miserably afflicted with a Feaver and Worms, so that Death was only expected, was thus cured. There was first injected a Clyster of Milk and Sugar. This gave two stools, and brought away four worms. By the Mouth was given *Hartshorn burnt*, prepared in the form of a Julep. To the Pulse was applied *Ung. Populeon* ʒii *mix'd with Spiders Webs, and a little Powder of Nutshels.* It was put to one Pulse of one Wrist one day, to the other the next. To the Stomach was applied Mithridate; to the Navel, the Emplaster against Worms. And thus he became well in three days, for which the Countess returned me many thanks, and gave me great Reward."

"OBSERVATION LX. [*2nd Cent.* Dr. Hall's own Case.] Thou, O Lord, which hast the power of Life and Death, and drawest from the Gates of Death, I confess, without any Art or Counsel of Man, but only from Thy Goodness and Clemency, thou hast saved me from the bitter and deadly symptoms of deadly Fever, beyond the expectation of all about me, restoring me, as it were, from the very jaws of Death to former health; for which I praise Thy name, O most merciful God and Father of our Lord Jesus Christ, praying Thee to give me a most thankful heart for this great favour, for which I have cause to admire Thee. About the 57th year of my age, August 27, 1632, to Septemb. 29, I was much debilitated with an *immoderate Flux of the Hemorrhoids;* yet daily was I constrained to go to several places to Patients. By riding, a hardness being contracted, the Flux was stayed for fourteen days. After I fell into a most cruel torture of my teeth, and then into a deadly burning Fever, which then raged very much, killing almost all that it did infect, for which I used the following method, which, by the help of God, succeeded: First I purged thus, ℞ *Rhubarb infused* ʒi., (*surely it was infused in some proper water, I suppose* ʒiii..) *Syrup Diaserios* ʒi., *Elect. è Succ. Ras.* ʒiii. This gave four stools. After I had used the Decoction of *Hearts-horn*, and so the disease was almost cast out by Urine; it flowed very much for four days space; so that I was not only much maciated, but also weakened, so that I could not move myself in my Bed without help. I also had *Convulsion of the Mouth and Eyes.* Then was a Pigeon cut open alive, and applied to my feet, to draw down the Vapours; for I was often afflicted with a slight Delirium. Then my wife sent for two Physicians. I had used a Clyster with *Emolient Herbs and Electu, Diacath. and Leniti.* By the Physicians, my friends, was prescribed the following Electuary, of which I swallowed the quantity of a Nutmeg twice a day: ℞ *Elect. de Gem, cal* ʒii., *Spec. Plerisarch.* ʒi., (from fear of the Scurvy), *Manus Christi perlat;* ʒi. *Conserv. Buglos. et Violar.* ā ʒii. *Syr. Luju.* ʒi., *Syr Viol.* ʒss. *Limon* ʒi. *Ol. Vitrol gut.* vi. f. *Elect.* The 27th of Septemb. I was thus purged: ℞ *Elect. Lenit.* ʒiss, *Aq. Absynth* ʒiv. *Misc.* It gave three stools. At the hour of sleep, I took *Diacodium, Syrup of Red Poppies, with Diascordium.* For the heat of the Back: ℞ *Refrig. Gal.* ʒiss. *Cerat Santal.* ʒss. *Succ. Sed. Acet. Vini alb.* ā *coch.* i. f. *Unguent. mol.* An Emplaster for the Region of the Heart: ℞ *Labd.* ʒvj. *Styrac. Calam.* ʒss. *Spec, Aromat Ros.* Ƿiv., *Mosc. gr.* iv., *Misc.* I again was purged thus: ℞ *Syr. Diaserios* ʒiss, *Elect. e Succ. Ros.* ʒiii., *Aq. Cichor* q. s. It is to be observed, before the Physicians came, there were drawn ʒvii. of Blood from the Liver Vein, and three days after that were the Leeches applied to the Hemorrhoids, and thence removed ʒx. after the Decoction of Hartshorn. Thus, I was pretty well able to take Meat. After, I used *Chalybiat Wine*, with *Juyce of Scurvy-grass*, and *Syr. Sceletyrh. Foresti*, and purged once a week with *Pul. sanct. Syr. Diaserios, et infus. Rhab.* For the pain of the teeth, I used *Ol. Lig. Heraclei.* After, I was troubled with Itch in the *Scrotum*, which was cured with our Decoction of *Sarsa.* with *Anti-scorbutic Herbs.* And so I became perfectly well, praised be God."

"OBSERVATION XXXVI. Elizabeth Hall, my only daughter, [Shakespeare's granddaughter,] was vexed with *Tortura Oris*, or the convulsion of the mouth, and was happily cured as followeth : First, I exhibited these Pills : ℞ *Pil. Coch. et Aurear. ana* ʒi. f. *Pil.* 10. She took five the first day, which gave her seven stools ; the next day with the other five, she had five stools. I fomented the part with *Theriac. Andromac. et Aq. Vitæ.* To the Neck was used this : ℞ *Unguent Martiat., Martiat. Magn.* ʒi. *Ol. Laurin. Petrolei, Castor. et Terebinth. ana* ʒss. *de lateribus* ʒss. *Misc.* By this she had great advantage, her Courses being obstructed. Thus I purged her : ℞ *Pil. fœtid* ʒi. *Castor.* ʒi. *de Succin. Rhab. agaric. ana* ℈ss. f. *Mass.* She took of this five pills in the morning of the bigness of Pease ; they gave eight stools. The next day she took *Aq. Opthalm.* see *Ostor.* 3, as ℞ *Tutiæ, &c.* Her courses flowed. For an opthalmia, of which she laboured, I used our *Opthalmick Water*, dropping two or three drops into her Eye. Her Courses staying again, I gave the following *Sudorific Decoct.*, ℞ *Lign. Vitæ.* ʒii., *Sassafras* ʒss., *Sassap.* ʒi. *Chin.* ʒvi. *macerat. per* 24 *hor.* in *Aq. fontan.* ℔viii. After, boyl them to ℔iv. After the use of these, the former form of her Mouth and Face was restored (there was not omitted *Ol. Sarsap.*, which was above all to anoint the Neck), Jan. 5, 1624. In the beginning of April she went to London, and returning homewards, the 22 of the said month, she took cold, and fell into the said distemper on the contrary side of the face ; before it was on the left side, now on the right ; and although she was grievously afflicted with it, yet, by the blessing of God, she was cured in sixteen days, as followeth : ℞ *Pil. de Succin.* ʒss. *Aurear.* ℈i. f. *Pil.* v. She took them when the same night her Neck was anointed with *Oil of Sassafr.* In the morning I gave ʒss. *of Pil. Russi*, and again used the said *Oil* with *Aqua Vitæ*, and dropped into her eye the *Opthalmick Water.* The aforesaid *Oil* being wanting, I used the following : ℞ *Pul. Castor. Myrrh Nuc. Mosch. Croci. ā* ℈i. *Ol. Rutæ, Laurin. Petrol. Tereb. ā* ʒii., *Ungu. Martiat.* ʒss., *Ol. Costin de Peper. ā* ʒi., *Misc.* But first the Neck was fomented with *Aqua Vitæ*, in which was infused Nutmegs, Cinnamon, Cloves, Pepper. She eat Nutmegs often. To the Nostrils and top of the Head was used the *Oil of Amber.* She chewed on the sound side, *Pellitory of Spain*, and was often purged with the following Pills : ℞ *Pill. fœtid.* ℈i. *Castor pul.* ℈ss., *Pil. Russi. et de Succin ā* ℈i. f. *Pil. No.* v. And thus she was restored.

" In the same year, May 24, she was afflicted with an Erratick Feaver; sometimes she was hot, and by and by sweating, again cold, all in the space of half an hour, and thus she was vexed oft in a day. Thus I purged her : ℞ *The Roots of Parsley, Fennel, each* Mss., *Elder Bark* Mii., *Roots of the Vulgar Oris, of Madder, each* Mss., *Roots of Sparagus* Mii. Boyl them in sufficient quantity of Water, to six pints. To the straining, add *Rhubarb, Agarick, each* ʒss., *Sena* ʒvi., *Mechoacan* ʒii., *Calamus Aromaticus* ʒi., *Aniseeds* ʒi., *Cinamon* ʒss. Infuse them in a vessel well stopt acording to art, strain it again, and to the straining add Sugar sufficient to make a Syrup. Of this, take ʒiv., *Rhubarb infused in* ʒv. *of Chicory Water* ʒii. Mix them, and give seven spoonfulls every day fasting. It gave seven or eight stools without pain. ℞ *Sarsap.* ʒi., *Sassafr.* ʒii., *Guaiac.* ʒi., *Liquoris* ʒss. *Herb of Succory, Sage, Rosemary, each* Mss. Boyl them in ten pints of Water, till half be wasted. Of which she took a draught hot, in the morning. The following was used to anoint the spine : ℞ *Gum, Galban. Bdel. dissol. in Aq. Vit. ā* ʒss. *Benzoin* ʒi., *Styrac. liquid* ʒi., *Fol. Rut. Chamæpith. Flor. Stæchad. Lavendula, ā* ʒii., *Rad. costi.* ʒss, *Castorei* Ði., *infund. Misc. et pulverisat in Aq. Vitae.* It is to be infused in some hot place for some days. Before it was used, the spine was rubb'd. An hour after it was used, all the symptoms remitted daily till she was well. Thus was she delivered from death and deadly diseases, and was well for many years. To God be praise."

" OBSERVATION XIX. Mrs. Hall, of Stratford, my wife, [Shakespeare's daughter] being miserably tormented with Cholick, was cured as followeth : ℞ *Diaphxn. Diacatholic. ana* ʒi., *Pul. Holland* ʒii., *Ol. Rutæ.* ʒi., *Lact.* q. s. f. *Chyst.* This injected gave her two stools, yet the Pain continued, being but little mitigated; therefore, I appointed to inject a pint of sack, made hot. This presently brought forth a great deal of wind, and freed her from all pain. To her Stomach was applied a *Plaister de Labd. Crat. cum Caran. et Spec. Aromat. rosat. et Ol. Macis.* With one of these Clysters, I delivered the Earl of Northampton from a grievous Cholick."

" OBSERVATION XXXIII. Wife was troubled with the Scurvy, accompanied with Pain of the Loins, Corruption of the Gums, Stinking Breath, Melancholy, Wind, Cardiac Passion, Laziness, difficulty of Breathing, fear of the Mother, binding of the Belly, and torment there, and all of a long continuance, with restlessness and weakness. There was given this Bole : ℞ *Electuary of Tamarinds* ʒss., *Cream of Tartar* ʒi., *mix them.* To the Back was applied, *Emplast. Oxycroceum,* which freed her from pain of the Loins and Belly, Feb. 9, 1630. The tenth day, taking cold, she had again miserable pain in her joints, so that she could not lye in her Bed, insomuch as when any helped her, she cried out miserably; for which I used this Ointment: ℞ *Capon's Grease, Oil of Sweet Almonds, of Dil. et Roses, Macilage of the Roots of Althæa, drawn with Mallow Water*, each ʒi. *mix them*. After anointing, the foresaid Plaster was applied with good success, for she was quieter all night; but yet in the morning she was troubled with wind. Then I gave of *Sennurtus's Electuary*, which is thus framed: ℞ *The Conserve of the tops and leaves of Scurvy Grass* ʒiii., *The flowers of Bugloss, Clove Gilly-flowers, and Damask Roses*, each ʒss. *The flesh of Candid Nutmegs, Citron Pills, candid and cut*, each ʒi. *Honey of Juniper Berries* ʒiii., *Confectio Alkermes* ʒss., *Syrup of Cinamon* ʒvi. *Syrup of Scurvy Grass*, or that of *Forestus, sufficient to make an Electuary, to which was added Oil of Sulphur, sufficient to sharpen it*. For the constipation of the Belly was used this Suppository: ℞ *Honey* ʒi. *Spec. Hier. Pic.* ℈ii., *Troch Alband* ℈ss., *Cummin Seed* ʒss., *make a long Suppository*. For the Cardaic Passion was used *Elect. Pleresarchon*. Dose, ʒss., fasting, yea, at any hour it was used, drinking the following Stilled Wine after it: ℞ *Fumatory, Brook-lime, Water Cresses, Scurvy-grass, Betony, Agrimony, Harts-tongue*, each Mss., *Bark of Capparis, Ash, Tamaris*, each ʒss, *Roots of Elicampana, Polipody*, each ʒiii. *Madder Liquoris, Calamus Aromaticus, Eringoes*, each ʒss,, *Yellow Sanders, Red Coral, Shavings of Ivory*, each ʒvi., *Cloves, Mace, Cinamon, Ginger*, each ʒiii., *Ceterach, Flowers of Broom, Rosemary, Marygolds, Epithymum*, each p. i., *Juniper Berries*, ʒi., *Steel prepared according to Crato* ʒiv., *White Wine* ℔viii., infuse them together at the Fire in *Bal. Mar.*, for eight days at least, stirring them twice a day; after strain it three or four times, and to the straining add *Saffron* ʒss., first drawn out of *Scurvy-grass water confect. Alkermes* ℈ii., *Sugar sufficient to sweeten it*. Dose is two or three spoonfulls in the beginning, which may be increased if there be need. And by these she was cured."

Notwithstanding the amusing credulity indicated in the two first quoted cases, and in many others, measured by the knowledge of his day Hall may well have deserved the title of being "a most skilful physician," yet his statements must not be accepted as the trustworthy exponents of the nature of disease. An example of this is afforded in the record of the cases of what he calls "the new feaver," which Mr. Collier thinks it probable was the cause of the poet's own death, The "new feaver" of the Lady Beaufou appears to have been neither more nor less than a case of small-pox, with typhoid symptoms; and the "new feaver" as it affected the doctor himself, to have been an affection of the brain, proceeding from the suppression of an habitual hœmorrhoidal flux. In the olden times, when a disease was merely recognized as an aggregate of symptoms, and not as a variable condition of one or more organs of the body, recognizable by varying symptoms, it was a common thing for the physician to designate an old form of disease, modified in its appearance by epidemic or other influence, as "the new feaver," or the like. Gideon Harvey hits this weakness of his contemporaries in the following terms: "It was named by his men of physick, *the new disease*, a name of ignorance, or their accustomed *asylum ignorantiæ*, to which they take their refuge, when they know not what the disease is, or what to call it. One time they shall tell you it is an ague; another, it is a feaver; a third, it is an ague and feaver; a fourth, it's a feaver and ague; a fifth, *it's the new disease;* a denomination so idle, that every novice in physick might well suspect they had never read Hippocrates or Galen, especially, upon observing, that every autumnal or epidemick distemper is by them termed *new*, whereas the gentle pox excepted, there is not any among all those they have nominated *new diseases*, but what is amply described in many ancient authors." The very next case to the Lady Beaufou's is recognised as one of small pox; it occurred in the same house and was treated in the same manner. Her Ladyship's case is thus detailed.

"OBSERVATION LXXVII. The Lady Beaufou, godly, honest, being of a noble extract, continuing healthful till the age of 28, which was 1617, July 1, fell into a burning malign continual Feaver, with great Pain of the Head, most vehement Heat, Pain in the Stomach; the Body all over, especially the Arms, was full of Spots;

the Urine was red and little. It was then called the New Feaver; it invaded many; I was called the third day of its invasion. The Stomach being stuffed and burdened with ill humours, as I perceived, I advised the following vomit: ℞ *Emetick Infusion* ʒix. This gave twelve vomits without any great trouble. The day before she had (unknown to me) drunk much milk to quench her thirst, by reason whereof the vomit at first drew forth a wonderful quantity of curdled milk, so that she was almost choaked, after came Choler mixed with phlegm, afterward burnt Melancholy. She had also six Stools Phlegmy, mixed with green Choler and much Serosities. Her vomiting ending in three hours, I gave her a Pill of *Laudan. Paraselsi* gr. vii. (sure he mistook her, for four is a good dose), after which she slept four hours, the Pain of her head ceasing. Then to me unknown, her servant gave her a draught of Whey, which being drunk, she presently had three vomits of black stuff without any trouble, and two such like Stools, and was cruelly afflicted with the Hiccough, to allay which I gave Claret wine burnt with Aromatick, which succeeded; she was quieter the rest of the Night, but did not sleep well. In the morning I gave Chicken-broth, made with appropriate Herbs, and so for four hours she rested. At the end of that time I gave a draught of the *Decoction of Heartshorn* hot. On Munday morning, having some evacuation, I appointed the same decoct. should be given cold. She was miserably afflicted with Pustles, with great heat of the Tongue and Throat that she could not drink without great difficulty, for which she used the following Gargarism: ℞ *Diamoron simp.* ʒiv., *Honey of Roses* ʒii., *Rosewater* ℔j., *Oil of Sulphur, so much as made it sharpish*. After the use of the *Heartshorn Decoction*, the seventh day, the Pox appeared, yet the foresaid Gargarism was used for the throat, and she drunk of the *Decoction of Heartshorn* cold four times a day, and so she was cured. I ordered that the Pox after the eighth day should be anointed with this: ℞ *Common Oil and Carduus Water well shaken together*, and so there were left no scars."

The surgeons in Shakespeare's time formed a very distinct class from the physicians. They were incorporated, it is true, but they had no statutory powers corresponding to those of the physicians. The latter restricted them from giving any internal medicines, even to promote the cure of external injuries. The physicians had, by law, the power of practising surgery as a part of their art, but not the slightest reciprocal liberty was accorded to the surgeons.

Fuller notes this abrupt limitation of the art, while, with his usual sound sense, he hits upon the true reason of its absurdity. " The healing of diseases and wounds were anciently one calling (as still great the sympathy betwixt them ; many diseases causing wounds, as ulcers ; as wounds occasioning diseases, as feavers) till in process of time they were separated, and chirurgeons only consigned to the *manual operation.*" The professional custom of the present day affords a curious reverse of this state of things in the olden time, since now surgeons frequently practise physic, to a greater extent than their own art, while physicians are restricted by custom and their own laws, from the practice of surgery. Referring to the rules made by Harvey at St. Bartholomew's Hospital, for the government of the house and officers, Dr. Wells says : " The doctors' treatment of the poor chirurgeons in these rules is sufficiently despotic, it must be admitted ; but the chirurgeons in their acquiesence showed that they merited no better handling. The only point on which they proved restive, indeed, was the revelation of their *secrets* to the physician ; a great outrage, when every man had his secrets, and felt fully justified in keeping them to himself. But surgery, in the year 1633, had not shewn any good title to an independent existence. The surgeon of those days was but the hand, or instrument of the physician ; the dignitary mostly applied to his famulus when he required a wen removed, or a limb lopped, or a broken head plaistered ; though Harvey, it seems, did not feel himself degraded by taking up the knife or practising midwifery."—*Life of Harvey.*

A reference, however, to the works of Clowes and Woodall, will convince the reader that, in spite of Acts of Parliament, charters of colleges, or rules of hospitals, the treatment of some important constitutional diseases fell to the lot of the chirurgeons. Clowes writes a separate work on the treatment of lues venerea, and Woodall has a chapter on the treatment of scurvy, and another on that of plague and its pestilential feaver. Although in contradistinction to the physicians, these old surgeons wrote in the vernacular, their works bear evidence that they were learned men. John Banester, Maister in Chirurgie, translated Wecker, in 1585, adding notes of his own, and thus affording one of the best early works on surgery in our language. William Clowes makes frequent reference to the works of Galen and Celsus, and to those of continental authors, written in Latin and French; he also mentions conversations he had with French surgeons. Most of his references are to professional authors, among whom no doubt his reading principally lay. The penultimate chapter in his work is actually a justification for publishing it in English, to which many persons "envying the light of knowledge in others, and the good of our country and commonwealth" had objected. "It embaseth the art, they say; it maketh it common, whereby every bad man, and lewd woman, is become a surgeon: and thus it is a hindrance to a number of good and honest artists." Clowes however refers in his justification to Hippocrates, Galen, Avicenna, Pliny, and the many French and German authors who wrote in their own native tongue: and he especially cites the custom of Ambrose Paré, then recently deceased to the following effect. "Now they say he was a man unfurnished of the sacred gifts of Grammar and Rhetorick, neither had he ever tasted of the sweet fountain and well-spring of Philosophie, and therefore could not be a good surgeon; he answereth such like cavillers and telleth them plainly that it is possible for a man to be a good surgeon although he had never a tounge in his head: he never went about to teach the tounges, but to write and teach the art of surgery in the French tounge to all young practisers, for the better relief and comfort of many sick and diseased persons."

As a counterpart to Dr. Hall's medical cases, and a fair example of the surgery of those days, the following account from Clowes, of the method of amputation may serve. It will be observed that the application of cauterising irons for the arrest of hermorrhage is spoken of as a necessity of common occurrence, a practice referred to by the poet. The system of tying arteries, for the invention of which Ambrose Paré bears the honour, is here attributed by one of his own contemporaries, to a forgotten name, *one Gulemew;* as often happens, the real inventor may have been obscured in the bright glory of some fortunate and prominent sponsor.

" *The manner and order of the taking or cutting off a mortified and corrupt leg or arme, which commeth oftentimes, by reason of wounds made with gunshot, &c. Cap.* 24.

" Sith as I haue said, that oftentimes it happeneth, by reason of the euill accidents which follow wounds made with gunshot, &c. That the whole member commeth to gangrena, sideratio, or sphacelus, so that we are many times constrained forthwith to make a speedy dispatch, to cut off the member, which shall be don as Gale and others, very skilfully haue pointed in the whole and sound parts. And if it so fall out that the leg is to be cut off beneath the knee, then let it be distant from the joint fower inches, and three inches aboue the knee; and so likewise in the arme, as occasion is offered. These things being obserued, then through the assistance of Almightie God, you shall luckily accomplish this worke by your good industrie and diligence. But you must be very circumspect and carefull of all things, which concerne the methodicall perfection of this worke; that is, you shall have a great regard to the state of his body for evacuation and dieting: And after that his body is well prepared and purged, then the same morning you do attempt to cut off the member, be it leg or arme, let him have some two houres before, some good comfortable caudell, or other broths, according to the discretion of the Physition or Chirurgeon, onely to corroberate and strengthen his stomacke, and in any wise omit not, but that he, or shee, have ministered unto them some good exhortation concerning patience in adversitie, to be made by the minister or preacher. And you shall likewise aduertise the friends of the patient, that the worke which you go about is great, and not without danger of death, for that many accidents, and euill symptoms do happen, which in such cases many times do admit no cure; all which being well considered, then ordaine the night before, some good defensatiue, and let it be applied two or three times about the member. [The defensative appears to have been a kind of ointment, for what purpose applied is not very clear. The prescription for Gale's defensative, given by the author, is Armenian boll, barley flour, dragon's blood, sealed earth, and olibanum, mixed up with vinegar and whites of eggs.]

"All which being considered, you shall haue in readiness a good strong and steady fourme, and set the patient at the very end of it; then shall there bestride the fourme behind him, a man that is able to holde him, or hir fast, by both the armes; which done, if the leg must be taken off beneath the knee, let there be also appointed another strong man to bestride the leg, that is to be cut off, and he must hold the member very fast aboue the place where the incision is to be made, and very steadily, without shaking, drawing up the skin and muscles, and he that doth so hold, should haue a large strong hand, and a good fast gripe, whereby he may the better stay the bleeding, in the place and steede of a straight band or ligature, which hand indeed is also very necessarie, for by reason of the hard and close binding, it doth so benum that part, that the paine of the binding doth greatly obscure the sence and feeling of the incision; and the foresaid hand is also a good direction for him that doth cut off the member; but yet in some bodies, it will not be amisse to admit bleeding according to discretion, specially in such bodies as are of hot complexions, and do abound in blood, and I haue often seene, by the skilfulnes of the holder, there hath not been lost at a time fower ounces of blood : for in weake bodies it is not good to loose much blood : for blood is said to be the treasure of life, and for that cause chiefly, a good holder is not to be spared. In like manner, there must be chosen another skilfull man, that hath good experience in holding the leg below, for the member must not be held too high, for feare of staying or choking of the same, neither must he beare down his hand too low, for feare of breaking or fracturing of the bones in the time it is a sawing or cutting off: And he that is the master or Surgeon, which doth cut off the member, must be sure he have a sharpe sawe, also a very good catlin, and an incision knife, and then boldly, with a steddy and quicke hand, cut the flesh round about to the bones, without staying, being sure the periosteum, or panicle that covereth and compasseth the bones be also incised and cut, and likewise a certain muscle or sinew, that runneth betweene the bones of the leg which shall be done with your incision knife: All this being orderly performed, then set your sawe as neere unto the sound flesh, as well you may, and so cut asunder the bones, which done, *Ambrose Pare*, a man of great knowledge, and experience in Chirurgie, willeth, presently after the bones are cut asunder, that yee then draw the sides of the wound together, with fower stitches, that are deepe in the flesh, and made crosswise over the member, like unto the letter X, for saith he, you may easily draw the portions of the skin and their divided muscles, which before the section were drawne upward, over the bones, and cover them close on every side, that they may take the less aire, and the wound sooner conglutinate, &c. I must confesse I have cured many, and yet never so stitched them: notwithstanding, I wish all men to follow in the best way, for the good of their patient. But I say, having prepared in a readiness, this restrictive, to staie the flux of blood, I proceeded then as followeth. ℞ *Boli Armeniaci* ʒiii., *Sanquinis Draconis, Aloes*, ana ʒi., *Olibani* ʒiss., *Terræ sigillatæ, Mastichis* ana ʒi., *Lapidis Hæmatitis* ʒss., *Calcis ex Testis ovorum, Mumiæ,* ana ʒi., *Gypsi* ʒvj., *Farinæ Volatilis* ʒiv., *Misce*. Take of this Powder as much as will serve your turne, and mixe with the said Powder, *Pilorum leporis, et ovorum albuminum ana. quod satis est,* let your Hare haires be the whitest and the softest that is taken from under the belly of the Hare, and cut so fine as possible may be, and with the said powder let all be mixed togither, and so brought to a reasonable thicknesse. And note that before yee cut off the member, let there be in like manner made for the purpose, three or fower small bolsters or buttons, fashioned in the top or upper part like a Dove's egge, or as a sugar lofe button, flat in the bottom to the compasse of a French crown, and round upwards as aforesaid: and these you shall make of very fine towe, according to Art, wrought up in water and vinegar, whereupon you shall apply some part of the restrictive, being mixed as I have before declared. But yee shall heere further note that one *Gulemew*, a famous Chirurgeon in Fraunce, with other very learned and skilful men, counselleth us to drawe out the veins and arteries with an instrument called a Raven's bill, and then they tie those vessels with a double strong ligature or threed, and so safely stay the bleeding, but for that I never practised this order by stiching the veins and arteries, I will leave it as aforesaid, and procede with mine owne approved practise: and, therefore, I say when the holder of the member

E

above the knee doth partly release the fast holding of his hand, by little and little, whereby you may the better perceive and see the mouths of the veins, that are incised and cut, and upon those veins you shall place the round endes of the small buttons, and upon them presently lay on a round thicke bed of towe made up in water and vinegar, so that it be fit as neere as you can guess it, to the compasse of the stumpe or member that is taken off, and thereon spread the restrictive; and upon that againe you shall lay another broder bed of towe made up as you have heard, so large that it may compasse over the member, and that it may be safely tied to keepe on the rest: whereupon yee shall in like manner spread of the restrictive reasonable thick, afore yee place it to the rest, and yee shall cut it in fower places, one cut right over against another, an inch in length and somewhat more: and yee shall tie or fasten the said large bed to with a ligature, which they call a choke band doubled two or three times, being flat, and fully an inch brode and a yard long: in the middle of the said ligature or band, you shall spread some of the restrictive, so that it may take the better hold unto the large bed of tow, being very fast tied, then you shall place thereon a double large bed of soft linnen cloth, and then with a strong rowler of fower inches brode, and three or fower yards long, let it be artificially rowled, and where the blood beginneth to shew, in that place speedily lay on a good compressor or thicke bolster made of tow brought up in water and vinegar, the thickness in the middle to a man's hand, and the thinner towards the edges, in compasse of a Philip's dolor, more or lesse, as you suppose the greatness of the flux to be, and couch them close to, in as many places as the blood doth shew itselfe, and thus with two or three rowlers, and as many soft linnen beds, some single, and some double, with a sufficient number of bolsters, some great and some small, you may safely stay the flux of blood: which order and way did never faile me, nor any other that have used the same according unto the order here prescribed: also sometimes we do use to draw over the great bed of tow being surely tied with the foresaid chokeband, a wet Oxe bladder, and so do pull it close up over the same, the which is tied fast also with a ligature or chokeband, and upon the same a double or single bed of soft linnen cloth, and thus with a few brode bolsters and rowlers very orderly is staied the flux of blood. All which being artificially done, then you shall as easily as possible may be, carie the patient to his bed, having a pillow made ready to rest the member on: Thus let him lie with as much quietness as you can, keeping a convenient diet: then the third or fourth day if nothing do let, you shall have in a readiness steuphs of white wine, with decent rowlers and bolsters, and other necessaries meete for the second dressing. To conclude, yee shall here observe, that if at any time you have not of my restrictive power in a readiness, you may use either *Vigoes* order, to cauterize the place, with a bright canterizing iron, or else with *M. Gales* powder, which is a most worthy invention, and better pleaseth the patients, than the hot glowing irons, which are very offensive unto the eie. But yet the powder wrought with extreme paine, and made a very great eschar, and by that meanes the bone hath been afterwards new cut againe, and so did make a very long worke in some, ere ever they were cured. The powder which I have here published, is of my own invention, and it never causeth paine, but often bringeth with it a perfect white digestive matter, which powder I did keepe secret to mine own private use, and I did first put it in practise in the Hospitall of Saint Bartholomewes, as it is well knowne at this day unto some of the Surgeons that then served with me there, who were present with me at that time, when there was taken off in one morning, seaven legs and armes, where, by the assistance and helpe of Almightie God, we staied all their fluxes of blood, without any paine unto them, but onely in the compression and close rowling, and tenderness of the wound excepted. After that time, it was given out, and made knowne to divers Surgeons, that were very desirous to have it. Amongst the rest, *Master Crowe*, a man of great experience and knowledge in Chirurgerie, he was very earnest with me for it, which for divers speciall occasions, I was the more willing to impart it unto him, but not at his first request, untill he had seene with his own eies, the experience and profe of it. Not many daies after, the masters of the said Hospitall requested me, with the rest of the Surgeons, to go to High-gate, some three or fower miles from London, to cut off a maids leg, which they had seene in the visitation of those poore spittle houses: the said leg was so grievously corrupted, that we were driven upon necessitie, to cut it off above the knee, which we did performe by the order before prescribed, and he did see, we staied the flux, and lost not much above fower ounces of blood, and so cured hir within a short time after. Then I gave him the true maner and order of the making of the said powder. Onely this I am to let you to understand, that since my first collection, I have added other simples, as *Crocis martis*, which though it be here left out in this booke upon purpose, the powder will be profitable notwithstanding. And after the publishing abroad of the said restrictive powder, I did give and impart the same unto many good Chirurgeons, which have been thankfull for it. But I must needes say againe, other some have rewarded me most unkindly, notwithstanding, I have knowne they have used it, unto the profit of their patient, and so credit unto themselves: neverthelesse, these could finde in their harts behinde my backe, to reward evill for good: instead of thanks, I have been back-bitten, and thus I reape for my labour chaffe for corne, ill will and private grudge for curtesies and friendship offered. Therefore I wish all good Artists, considerately to beware and take heede unto whom they impart heereafter their secrets, least they also enter with me into the gap of ingratitude, or the unsavorie dunghill of despitefull toongs, &c."

In the pharmacologia of Dr. Paris, late president of the College of Physicians, is the following passage, on a contemporary of Shakespeare, illustrative of the dirtiness of old medicine. "Amongst the remedies of Sir Theodore Mayerne, known to commentators as the Doctor Caius of Shakespeare, who was physician to three English Sovereigns, and who by his personal authority put an end to the distinctions of chemical and galenical practitioners in England, we shall find the bowels of a mole cut open alive; mummy made of the lungs of a man who had died a violent death; with a variety of remedies, equally absurd and alike disgusting:" p. 17. The learned author would have been more correct if he had stated that Mayerne was among those who introduced the distinction between the chemical and galenical physicians, rather than that he terminated them. Mayerne having defended his friend Quercetan for his chemical opinions, in a work which brought upon him the wrath of the College of Physicians of Paris, was expelled by the College from their body. Dr. Nedham's translation of the document recording this expulsion is an interesting example of the high handed manner in which the "Galenick Dons" avenged any dissent from their professional creed.

"The Colledg of Physicians in the University of Paris being lawfully congegrated, having heard the Report made by the Censors, to whom the business of examining the Apology, published under the name of Turquet de Mayern, was committed, do with unanimous consent condemn the same as an infamous libel, stuffed with lying reproaches, and impudent calumnies, which could not have proceeded from any but an unlearned, impudent, drunken, mad fellow : And do judg the said Turquet unworthy to practise physick in any place, because of his rashness, impudence, and ignorance of true physick: But do exhort all Physicians which practise physick in any nations or places whatsoever, that they will drive the said Turquet, and such like monsters of men and opinions, out of their company and coasts; and that they will constantly continue in the doctrine of Hippocrates and Galen. Moreover, they forbid all men that are of the Society of the Physicians of Paris, that they do not admit a consultation with Turquet, or such like persons. Whoever shall presume to act contrary, shall be deprived of all honours, emoluments and priviledges of the University, and be expunged out of the Register of Regent Physitians. Given at Paris, in the Upper Schools, the Fifth day of December, Anno Salutis, 1603. E. HERON, Dean of the Colledg."

After this expulsion, Mayerne came to England, and attained from the first such high repute and success, that it is difficult, notwithstanding the opinions of the commentators, to reconcile with his position, the character of Dr. Caius, in the Merry Wives, the only character in which Shakespeare represents a physician in a mean and ridiculous light. His contemporary, Dr. Nedham, says, that Mayerne "became physician to two kings of France, and two of England, and left a name of great honour and wealth behind him."

Another of his contemporaries, Dr. Harris, writes, "Mayerne is still flourishing in our own memory, and his eminency was sufficiently proved by an argument that will easily persuade, I mean, by the greatest estate that perhaps ever was got by physick. His favour with the great Henry the fourth of France, and his royal reception here, do all speak loudly his great name."—*Pharmacologia Anti-Empirica*, 1683.

Mayerne's christian name, Turquet, which means a little dog, had been made the peg for ridicule, by his angry countrymen : hence perhaps the change to the more euphonious prefix which he assumed in this country. He was, says Nedham, "a different guess sort of chemical, than Paracelsus, or Van Helmont, dogmatical or rational, as well as chemical, and did not despise reason, though it came from the mouth of a Galenist;" and although in the exercise of this temperance of judgment he may have contributed to reconcile the differences of the two factions, he certainly did not put an end to them, as Dr. Paris supposes, since we find the controversy at its height in the very works we have cited, published many years after his decease in 1655, at the age of 82. According to Fuller, the first person who introduced chemical doctrines among the methodical physicians of England was Dr. Butler, whose Abernethian eccentricities are thus noted in the quaint pages of the biographer.

"William Butler, born at Ipswich, was bred Fellow of Clare Hall, in Cambridge, where he became the Esculapius of our age. *He was the first Englishman who quickened Galenical Physick with a touch of Paracelsus, trading in Chemical Receits with great successe.* His eye was excellent at the instant discovery of a *cadaverous face*, on which he would not lavish any art. This made him at the first sight of sick Prince Henry, to get himself out of sight. Knowing himself to be the Prince of Physicians, he would be observed accordingly. Compliments would prevail nothing with him, entreaties but little, surly threatnings would do much; and a witty jeere do any thing. He was better pleased with presents than money, loved what was pretty rather than what was costly, and prefered rarities before riches. Neatness he neglected into slovingliness; and, accounting cuffs to be manacles, he may be said not to have made himself ready for some seven years together. He made his humoursomnesse to become him, wherein some of his profession have rather aped than imitated him, who had *morositatem æquabilem*, and kept the tenor of the same surliness to all persons. He was a good Benefactor to Clare Hall; and, dying 1621, he was buried in the Chancel of St. Marie's, under a fair Monument. Mr. John Crane, that expert Apothecary, and his Executour, is since buried by him; and, if some eminent Surgeon was interred on his other side, I would say, that Physick lay here in state, with his two pages attending it."

Mayerne did not come to England until after the death of his patron, Henri Quatre, in 1610, so that Butler might well have preceded him in promulgating the new opinions of the chemical school, but the priority of the Englishman could only have been that of a few years.

Although we may doubt whether Shakespeare intended to represent the learned and wealthy Sir Theodore Mayerne, Baron d' Aubonne, &c., under the ridiculous character of Dr. Caius, there can be no mistake as to the physician named in Henry VIII.

"*Enter* Dr. Butts.
Butts. This is a piece of malice : I am glad
    I came this way so happily. The King
    Shall understand it presently.   [*Exit.*]
Cranmer [*aside*].   'Tis Butts,
    The King's physician ; as he passed along,
    How earnestly he cast his eyes upon me !
    Pray Heaven he sound not my disgrace !—
    Enter at a Window above, the King *and* Butts.
Butts. I'll shew your Grace the strangest sight—
K. Henry.   What's that Butts ?—
Butts. I think your Highness saw this many a day.
K. Henry. Body o'me where is it ?
Butts.   There, my Lord :
    The high promotion of his Grace of Canterbury ;
    Who holds his state at door, 'mongst pursuivants,
    Pages and footboys.
K. Henry.   Ha ! 'tis he indeed,
    Is this the honour they do one another ?

    .   .   .   .   .

    By Holy Mary, Butts, there's knavery :
    Let them alone, and draw the curtain close ;
    We shall hear more anon."   *Act* v. *Scene* 2.

The man, who is here represented defeating for a time the machinations of the detestable Gardiner, was Dr. William Butte, who is noticed in the following terms by Goodall, in the *Epistle Dedicatory.*

"Dr. William Butte, Fellow of Gonville Hall, in Cambridge, and Physician to King Henry VIII., was, Anno Domini 1529, admitted into the College of Physicians. Upon which he was required to subscribe to the due observation of the Statutes of the College, and to give his promise to use his best endeavours for advancing the honour and perpetuity thereof. He is mentioned by Bishops Parkhurst and Fox with honour; Ascham, in his *Epistle Commendatory* to Dr. Wende, extols him highly, and the learned Dr. Caius hath dedicated most of his books to him. His esteem was such in the College of Physicians, that he is entered in the Annals with the following character: 'Vir gravis; eximiâ literarum cognitione, singulari judicio, summâ experientiâ, et prudenti consilio Dr.' He died in the reign of King Henry VIII., and lies buried in Fulham Church, with this Inscription: 'Guil. Buttius, Eg. Aur., et Medicus Regis Henry VIII., &c. Obit Novemb. 17, 1545,' &c."

THE TEMPEST.

The passages having reference to medical subjects in this play are mainly those which would be suggested by an aguish district, but they certainly indicate no precise knowledge of aguish disease; moreover the pinches and cramps so frequently referred to as inflicted by Prospero's imps upon his enemies, appear to be rather a part of the phantasmagoria of the piece, than intended to represent natural phenomenon. Caliban's first curse breathes the poison of miasma, but in form it must be owned more poetical than scientific.

> "*Cal.* As wicked dew as e'er my mother brushed
> With raven's feather from unwholesome fen,
> Drop on you both! a southwest blow on ye,
> And blister you all o'er." *Act* i., *Scene* 2.

Again he says,

> "All the infections that the sun sucks up
> From bogs, fens, flats, on Prosper fall, and make him
> By inch-meal a disease." *Act* ii., *Scene* 2.

The foul breath of the fen indeed pervades the country.

> "*Adrian.* The air breathes upon us here most sweetly.
> *Seb.* As if it had lungs, and rotten ones!
> *Ant.* Or, as 'twere perfumed by a fen." *Act* i., *Scene* 1.

Stephano refers the trembling of Caliban, really produced by fear, to ague.

"He's in a fit now; and does not talk after the wisest; he shall taste of my bottle. If he have never drunk wine afore, it will go near to remove his fit."

"How now, moon-calf, how does thine ague?" *Act* ii., *Scene* 2.

The conspirators against Prospero are actually led into the rotten fen, the emanations from which "overstink their feet;" they emerge with the "nose in great indignation" at their own unsavoury plight, and as a climax to their distress, with their bottles lost in the pool.

The punishments inflicted by Prospero upon his half-human slave are half-medical, half-magical, and certainly do not represent a scientific description of aguish disease.

"*Pros.* For this be sure to-night thou shalt have cramps, Side-stitches that shall pen thy breath up."

"Ill rack thee with old cramps, Fill all thy bones with aches."

"Go, charge my goblins that they grind their joints With dry convulsions; shorten up their sinews With aged cramps; and more pinch-spotted make them, Than pard or cat o' the mountain."

"*Cal.* The dropsy drown this fool—let's alone, And do the murder first. If he awake, From toe to crown he'll fill our skin with pinches; Make us strange stuff."

"O, touch me not; I am not Stephano, but a cramp!"

Another train of medical thought in this drama has reference to insanity. The disease of the brain in this instance is brought on by the magic art of Prospero, and therefore affords no example of that natural development of mental alienation of which such wondrous examples are represented in so many other plays. It is remarkable that even here mania should be described under two forms. Prospero, referring to the destruction produced by the storm, says,

"Who so firm, so constant, that this coil Would not infect his reason?
Ariel. Not a soul But felt a fever of the mind, and played Some tricks of desperation." *Act* i., *Scene* 2.

At Prospero's command Ariel charms Alonzo, Sebastian, and Antonio into madness.

> "*Ariel.*   I have made you mad
> And even with such-like valour, men hang and drown
> Their proper selves."   *Act* iii., *Scene* 3.

The intention of suicide is expressed by Alonzo, that of desperate fight by the other two. The phrensy of Alonzo is also distinguished by the fixed idea of his own guilt, and a state resembling hallucination founded upon it.

> "*Alon.* O, it is monstrous! monstrous!
> Methought the billows spoke, and told me of it;
> The winds did sing it to me; and the thunder,
> That deep and dreadful organ-pipe, pronounc'd
> The name of Prosper; it did bass my trespass.
> Therefore my son i' the ooze is bedded; and
> I'll seek him deeper than e'er plummet sounded,
> And with him there lie mudded."   *Act* iii. *Scene* 3.

This affords a beautiful example of the transition of absorbing emotion into perverted sensation through the influence of excited fancy, representing the lunatic of "imagination all compact." It is the very opposite of matter of fact reason, like the rebuke of the heroine's fancy in Sheridan's "*Rehearsal.*"

> "The Spanish fleet thou canst not see, because
> It is not yet in sight."

Gonzalo has a remarkable observation on the madness of the three princes.

> "All three of them are desperate; their great guilt,
> *Like poison given to work a great time after,*
> Now 'gins to bite the spirits:—I do beseech you,
> That are of suppler joints, follow them swiftly,
> And hinder them from what this ecstacy
> May now provoke them to."   *Act* iii. *Scene* 3.

This distraction is removed from the brains of the three princes by the charm of music, which Prospero calls, for the purpose of chasing "the ignorant fumes that mantle their clearer reason."

The invocation to this music is couched in the following pathological language.

"A solemn air and the best comforter
To an unsettled fancy, *cure thy brains
Now useless, boiled within thy skull!*"

When Alonzo recovers from the magic madness, and the tide of understanding once more "fills the reasonable shores that lay foul and muddy," he cannot at first make out whether Prospero is not some "enchanted trifle," but he determines on his reality on medical grounds, "thy pulse beats as of flesh and blood." There are two or three passages of physiological significance, independent of the leading train of thought on ague and madness. Ferdinand replies to Prospero's caution, that "strongest oaths are straw to the fire o' the blood,"

"The white, cold, virgin snow upon my heart
Abates the ardour of my liver." *Act* iv., *Scene* 1.

Gonzalo, referring to Sebastian's unfeeling speech to the king on the supposed loss of his son, says

"The truth you speak doth lack some gentleness
And time to speak it in; you rub the sore
When you should bring the plaster.
Ant. And most chirurgeonly." *Act* ii., *Scene* 1.

The same cool-headed old lord comments upon the strange appearance of the imps that had brought the magic banquet, by reference to the real monstrosities of human nature.

"*Gon.* Faith, Sir, you need not fear: When we were boys,
Who would believe that *there were mountaineers
Dew-lapp'd like bulls, whose throats had hanging at them
Wallets of flesh?* Or that there were such men
Whose heads stood in their breasts? which now we find,
Each puttter-out of five for one will bring us
Good warrant of." *Act* iii., *Scene* 3.

Shakespeare had, perhaps, the authority of some legend for the assertion, that there were men whose "heads stood in their breasts." (See *Othello, Act* i. *Scene* **3**.) Ambrose Paré describes and depicts infant monsters of this kind, but Shakespeare may only refer to the effect produced by forward curvature of the spine, in which the head appears to be set below the shoulders. The mountaineers with wallets of flesh at their throats were, without doubt, subjects of goître, who abound in mountainous districts.

TWO GENTLEMEN OF VERONA.

After Speed has given to Valentine his ludicrous description of a lover, in which, among other signs, are "to walk alone like one that had the pestilence," and "to fast like one that takes diet," the following quibble takes place upon the within and the without of the symptoms.

"*Val.* Are all these things perceived in me?
Speed. They are all perceived without ye.
Val. Without me they cannot.
Speed. Without you? Nay, that's certain, for without you were so simple, none else would; but you are so without these follies, that these follies are within you, and *shine through you like the water in an urinal, that not an eye that sees you but is a physician to comment on your malady.*" *Act* ii., *Scene* 1.

The singular pretence, to which these passages refer, of recognizing diseases by the mere inspection of the urine, is alleged to have arisen, like the barber surgery, from the ecclesiastical interdicts upon the medical vocations of the clergy; priests and monks being unable to visit their former patients are said first to have resorted to the expedient of divining the malady, and directing the treatment, upon simple inspection of the urine. However this may be, the practice is of very ancient date. Richardus Anglicus, the earliest of English Physicians, who flourished about the year 1230, left two works on the subject, *A Tractate of Urines*, and a work *On the Rules of Urines*. The uncertain and pretentious nature of medical opinions founded upon this basis was also recognized in early times. Thus Fuller speaking of Robert Recorde, a physician of Oxford 1550, whose "soul did not live in the lane of a single science, but traversed the latitude of learning," says that he wrote "*Of the Judgments of Urines;* and though it be commonly said *urina meretrix*, yet his judicious rules have reduced that harlot to honesty, and in a great measure fixed the uncertainty thereof."

We learn from Dr. Harris' *Pharmacologia Anti-Empirica*, 1683, that the illustrious founder of the College of Physicians set his face against this quackery then so much in vogue.

"Nor have mountebanks on stages been the only physical impostors; there have been as bad a race of deluders, both men and women, who will, or have, undertaken to tell all things from the urine, and the poor people who hardly know them, *quid distant æra lupinis*, are throughly convinced of their skill, by some cunning stratagem or other.

"Linacer, a famous physician who lived in the time of Henry the Eighth, was even then so concerned at the ridiculous humour of nurses and other women, who upon every ailment, both great and small, were too ready to carry about the patient's urine, expecting they should be told all things from the mere speculation of it, would often advise them in ridicule, to bring the patient's shoe instead of the urine, and he would prophesie full as well over that. Nay, further, there were a sort of knaves in his days, who, considering how well the vulgar would relish anything of novelty, though never so absurd, would undertake to make discoveries of diseases from the smell of the patient's shoe, as solemnly and seriously as others from the urine."

The same author refers to an old statute of the College itself, in which water-casting was denounced as belonging to tricksters and impostors, and any member of the College was forbidden to give advice upon the mere inspection of the urine without he also saw the patient. The statute of the College runs thus,

"*Statuimus, et ordinamus, ut nemo, sive socius, sive candidatus, sive permissus consilii quidquam impertiat veteratoriis, et impostoribus, super urinarum nuda inspectione, nisi simul ad ægrum vocetur, ut ibidem, pro re natû, idonea medicamenta ab honesto aliquo Pharmacopola componenda præscribat.*"

The same rule is practically laid down in the excellent work on *Medical Politics* by Forestus, who, in his chapter "*De Uromantia sive Inspectione Urinarum* ; *plures agyrtarum fraudes, et vulgi errores deteguntur,*" insists that the signs of the urine must be studied in conjunction with those of the pulse, "Urinæ fraudes aperit *discretio pulsus,*" which, as the pulse cannot be felt without the presence of the patient, comes to much the same thing as the rule of the College. Forestus condemns the practice of water-casting, as, in his opinion, altogether evil, and expresses an earnest desire that medical men would combine to repress it; but recognizing the difficulty of persuading men to act in concert uprightly, he adopts the middle course of advising them to act prudently, and so to deal with this *fallax nuncius* as to derive either from revelations ingeniously extorted from the persons who brought it, or from the appearance of the excretion itself, some indications of the disease which may exist. The custom which he ridicules had, he acknowledges, become so rooted, and practised even by learned physicians, that it appeared necessary to yield to the errors and prejudices of the public. *Quia mundus decipi, gaudet decipiatur,* is his maxim ; and his cautions and directions, as might be expected, contain more craft than science. But it is very evident from his pages that the old physicians, while pretending to knowledge they did not possess, had need of all their cunning to prevent themselves from becoming the dupes of their dupes. Thus Forestus, having told his readers what were the probable ailments of " mulierculæ subridentes, aut pudore quodammodo suffusæ," proceeds to explain how various attempted frauds are to be detected, how wine or any other liquor, or the urine of cattle is to be recognized when used to deceive the water-caster. The need of the latter diagnosis may be illustrated, by what Primrose calls, "a merry story." "A certain maid did carry her mistress's urine to a physician, and having by chance spilled it, not knowing what to doe, she catched the urine of a cow, which at that time by good hap staled, and carried it to the physician: he gave answer that the patient did eat too many salletts."

Forestus also gives some stories on this subject which were thought droll in those days. The following shews one use of botany. A noble lady wishing to deceive a physician, celebrated for his skill in water-casting, took to him the urine of a sick farmer; the physician, suspecting deceit from the lady's arch look, and observing that the jug was stoppered with a herb which grew in a certain spot, said, while he poured the urine from the poculum to the matula, This belongs to some rustic not of this town, but of the country through such a gate; and thus astonishing his visitor, he easily got from her an account of the disease, and obtained her great admiration of his skill.

The glass *matula*, or male urinal, as distinguished from the *scaphum*, was the vessel in which the fluid was examined. It is to this that Dr. Gideon Harvey so quaintly describes the physician as "giving the round toss" to make the sediment subside; it is this which, in the painting of the old Dutch master, is held against the light by the grave-looking charlatan, whose fair client, with form expressing her real ailment, stands bashfully by; and this is the urinal through which Speed supposes that all Valentine's symptoms are so transparently visible.

"*Val.* O, flatter me; for love delights in praises."
Pro. When I was sick you gave me bitter pills;
And I must minister the like to you." *Act* ii., *Scene* 4.

"*Pro.* Even as one heat another heat expels, or as one nail by strength drives out another." *Ibid.*

This notion of one heat driving out another has a parallel in a passage in *King John*.

"And falsehood, falsehood cures, as fire cures fire
Within the scorch'd veins of one new burned."
Act iii., *Scene* 1.

The idea appears to be formed upon an old-fashioned custom of approaching a burnt part to the fire, to drive out the fire, as it is said; a practice certainly not without benefit, acting on the same principle as the application of turpentine and other stimulants to *recent* burns.

"The private wound is deepest; O time most accurs'd!
' Mongst all foes, that a friend should be the worst."
Act v., *Scene* 4.

Probably a reference to the well-known surgical fact that such stabbing wounds as would be given by assassins are of the deepest and most dangerous kind.

F

MERRY WIVES OF WINDSOR.

The character in this play of "Master Caius, that calls himself doctor of physic," has been supposed to have been intended to represent Sir Theodore Mayerne; but upon what grounds the opinion has been formed that the learned, noble, and wealthy Frenchman sat for this caricature does not appear, beyond the fact that both possessed a common calling and country. Dr. Caius, whom Dame Quickly designates a combination "of fool and physician," plays no medical rôle. The mischievous host does, indeed, refer to him as practising his profession.

"Shall I lose my doctor? no; he gives me the potions, and the motions."
Act iii., *Scene* 1.

But in truth he is merely a comic counterpart to the Welsh parson, the two being made to murder the Queen's English in different jargons.

Falstaff, in his coarse love-making to Mistress Ford, makes a reference not only to the herbalism of those days, but to the place where the herbs were sold, as he might now refer to Covent Garden.

" Come, I cannot cog, and say thou art this and that, like many of these lisping hawthorn buds, that come like women in men's apparel, and smell like Bucklersbury in simple-time."
Act iii., *Scene* 3.

After Falstaff has been packed in the bucking basket, Mrs. Page plots more tricks upon him, expressing her opinion that

" His dissolute disease will scarce obey this medicine."
Act iii., *Scene* 3.

Sir John, however, who has been cooled with his bucking and his ducking, calls for the appropriate antidote.

"*Fal.* Come let me pour some sack to the Thames water; for my belly's as cold as if I had swallowed snow-balls for pills to cool the reins." *Act* iii., *Scene* 5.

Falstaff in the forest with the two merry wives invokes the virtues of aphrodisiacs.

"Let the sky rain potatoes; let it thunder to the tune of *greensleeves*; hail kissing-comfits and snow eringoes; let there be a tempest of provocation, I will shelter me here." *Act* v., *Scene* 5.

This potatoe must not be supposed to mean the now common esculent. Dr. Paris, in the work before quoted, comments upon this speech of Falstaff's with the remark, that "our potatoe *(solanum tuberosum)* when it was first imported into England by the colonists in the reign of Queen Elizabeth, gained its appellation from its supposed resemblance to an esculent vegetable at that time in common use, under the name of the sweet potatoe *(convolvulus battatus)*, and which like eringo root had the reputation to be able to restore decayed vigour." Gerard in his *Herbal*, 1597, denominates it (our potatoe) by way of distinction, from the potatoe of Virginia, and recommends it to be eaten as a delicate dish, not as common food. The eringo, or sea holly, according to Salmon, "is very white, and is commonly made into confects and candies." It is enumerated among the remedies given by Dr. Hall to his wife.

"*Nym.* I will incense Ford to deal with poison: I will possess him with yellowness, for the revolt of mien is dangerous."
Act i., *Scene* 3.

Reference here appears to be made to jaundice as the effect of splenetic humour, an idea more definitely expressed in the *Merchant of Venice.*

When the sham duel between Dr. Caius and Evans is the jest of the moment, the host says to the latter,

"What says my Esculapius? My Galen? My heart of elder? Ah, is he dead, bully Stale? Is he dead?"
"Thou art a Castilian, king Urinal."
"Ah, Monsieur Mock-water." *Act* ii, *Scene* 3.
"*Evans.* I will knog his urinals about his knave's costard, when I have good opportunities for the work." *Act* iii., *Scene* 1.

The urinal is thus made the frequent subject of coarse jest, probably because the poet saw through the shallow pretension of its medical use. Does Stale here mean urine, as in *Anthony and Cleopatra,* "Didst drink the stale of horses?"

Chaucer mentions the urinals as something medical, in mine host's comments upon the tale of the Doctour of Physick.

> "I pray to God to save thy gentle corce,
> And thy urinalles, and thy jordanis,
> Thine ypocras, and eke thy galianis,
> And every boxe of letuarie.
> God blesse 'hem and our Lady Saint Marie."

―

MEASURE FOR MEASURE.

In writing this play, the mental bias of the medical profession to indifference respecting death had certainly no hold upon the poet; for the various points of view in which death may be contemplated, form the philosophy of the piece. The brutal indifference of Barnardine is exactly like that of a character delineated with great analytic power in "Barnaby Rudge," and in which the able author appears to direct all his force to prove the immense difference of the same punishment acting on different organizations, and the consequent injustice of inflicting, for the same crime, that which to one man is no punishment whatever, and to another is the most fearful torture. Barnardine, like Barnaby, is

> "A man that apprehends death no more dreadfully, but as a drunken sleep; careless, reckless, and fearless of what's past, present, or to come; insensible of mortality, and desperately mortal." *Act* iv., *Scene* 2.

To Claudio, on the other hand, the apprehension of death is fearful torture. The active fancy, which might have made him brave in the battle-field, lacerates him with horrible thoughts in the condemned cell; and it is to no purpose that his self-centred sister encourages him to believe that,

> "The sense of death is most in apprehension;
> And the poor beetle, that we tread upon
> In corporal sufferance finds a pang as great
> As when a giant dies." *Act* iii., *Scene* 1.

This physiological opinion would scarcely be supported by modern science, which teaches that the corporeal sufferings of death must be great or small in proportion to the development of the sentient centre of the system, this development being great or small in proportion to the rank of the animal. Size has little to do with pain, compared with the influence of a high degree of cerebral organization.

Claudio's agony, however, arises, not from fear of the pain of death, but from that of the conditions of the future existence; seizing upon the thought that he may be among those "that lawless and uncertain thoughts imagine howling," fear debases him into abject meanness. He would readily sacrifice his sister's honour to avoid this terror and it is, therefore, not surprising that he derives little comfort from the Duke's picture of the miseries of life. It is not the present life which he clings to, but the unknown horrors of the future which he dreads. The Duke's description of life is, perhaps, the most sombre picture in all the Plays; deeper in its shades than those of 'Hamlet' or 'Jaques,' more general than those of 'Lear;' it indicates moreover a peculiar medical and physiological tendency of thought, and as such we shall quote it.

"*Duke.*   So, then you hope of pardon from lord Angelo?
Claud.   The miserable have no other medicine,
But only hope:
I have hope to live, and am prepar'd to die.
   Duke.   Be absolute for death; either death, or life,
Shall thereby be the sweeter.   Reason thus with life:—
If I do lose thee, I do lose a thing
That none but fools would keep: a breath thou art,
(Servile to all the skiey influences,)
That dost this habitation, where thou keep'st,
Hourly afflict: merely, thou art death's fool;
For him thou labour'st by thy flight to shun,
And yet runn'st toward him still: Thou art not noble;
For all the accommodations that thou bear'st,
Are nurs'd by baseness: thou art by no means valiant;
For thou dost fear the soft and tender fork
Of a poor worm: Thy best of rest is sleep,
And that thou oft provok'st; yet grossly fear'st
Thy death, which is no more.   Thou art not thyself;
For thou exist'st on many a thousand grains
That issue out of dust: Happy thou art not;
For what thou hast not still thou striv'st to get;
And what thou hast, forget'st: Thou art not certain;
For thy complexion shifts to strange effects,
After the moon: if thou art rich, thou art poor;
For, like an ass, whose back with ingots bows,
Thou bear'st thy heavy riches but a journey,
And death unloads thee: Friend hast thou none:
For thine own bowels, which do call thee sire,
The mere effusion of thy proper loins,
Do curse the gout, serpigo, and the rheum,
For ending thee no sooner: Thou hast no youth, nor age;
But, as it were, an after-dinner's sleep,
Dreaming on both; for all thy blessed youth
Becomes as aged, and doth beg the alms
Of palsied eld; and when thou art old, and rich,

> Thou hast neither heat, affection, limb, nor beauty,
> To make thy riches pleasant. What's yet in this,
> That bears the name of life? Yet in this life
> Lie hid more thousand deaths; yet death we fear,
> That makes these odds all even."   *Act* iii., *Scene* 1.

The afflictions of the body produced by the influences of the weather and climate—the baseness of the functions of animal life—the contemptible means by which it is often destroyed—the similitude of death to sleep—the dependence of life upon food issuing from the dust—the uncertainty of temperament—the desires of indigent youth—and the apathy of palsied eld when riches are abundant—indicate a turn of thought to which the physiological infirmities of man were a familiar subject.

"The gout, serpigo, and the rheum," form a singular trio, as diseases peculiarly fatal to age. The three words fall well into the cadence of the line, which is, perhaps, all that Shakespeare thought of when he strung them together. It must, however, be remarked that neither one of them represents a form of disease generally supposed to be fatal. The serpigo, a skin disease, is indeed never fatal. The rheum, in Shakespeare's time, sometimes meant mere humours from the nose and eyes; sometimes the more serious symptoms of watery expectoration, common enough from the emphasematous lungs of old men, and therefore often a fatal symptom. Gout is not usually supposed to be a fatal disorder. "Gout in the spring, is physick for a king," says the old proverb. Insurance societies, however, tell a different tale. Still Shakespeare's learned contemporary 'Montaigne,' whose works he is known to have availed himself of, thus refers to gout as a disease not mortal. "All ills that carry no other danger along with them, but simply the evils themselves, we despise as things of no danger." "The tooth-ache or the gout, painful as they are, yet being not reputed mortal, who reckons them in the catalogue of diseases?"

In the early part of the play, *Act* i. *Scene* 2, is a conversation between some licentious young men, in which allusion is made, either to piles (hœmorrhoids), or to baldness produced by lues venerea; also to a venereal disease of the bones, and to a French crown, which from the context is evidently a quibbling reference to some form of disease. In the fine quarto edition of the plays, Oxford, 1744, I find two notes on this passage, 1st, that the 3000 dollars is a quibble upon the word *dolours*, and 2nd, that a French crown "alludes to the venereal scab upon the head, called *corona veneris*."

"1*st Gent*. And thou the velvet: thou art good velvet: thou art a three-piled piece, I warrant thee: I had as lief be a list of an English kersey, as be piled, as thou art piled, for a French velvet. Do I speak feelingly now?

Lucio. I think thou dost; and, indeed, with most painful feeling of thy speech: I will, out of thine own confession, learn to begin thy health; but, whilst I live, forget to drink after thee.

1*st Gent*. I think I have done myself wrong, have I not?

2*nd Gent*. Yes, that thou hast; whether thou art tainted, or free.

Lucio. Behold, behold, where Madam Mitigation comes! I have purchased as many diseases under her roof, as come to—

2*nd Gent*. To what, I pray?

1*st Gent*. Judge.

2*nd Gent*. To three thousand dollars a year.

1*st Gent*. Ay, and more.

Lucio. A French crown more.

1*st Gent*. Thou art always figuring diseases in me: But thou art full of error; I am sound.

Lucio. Nay, not as one would say, healthy; but so sound as things that are hollow: thy bones are hollow; impiety has made a feast of thee.

[*Enter* BAWD.

1*st Gent*. How now? Which of your hips has the most profound sciatica?" *Act* i., *Scene* 2.

The treatment of the venereal disease by *diet* is referred to further on in this play, and also in *Timon of Athens*, under the name of "the tub diet."

> "*Clown.* Why very well: I telling you then, if you be remembered, that such an one, and such an one, were past cure of the thing you wot of, unless they kept very good diet, as I told you."
> *Act* ii., *Scene* 1.

A surgeon would make the following distinction—

> "Let us be keen, and rather cut a little,
> Than fall, and bruise to death." *Act* ii., *Scene* 1.

When Isabel applies to the hypocrite Angelo for pardon, she argues that the fault which appears so great in her brother might be overlooked in those yielding authority to punish; an opinion she illustrates by a medical simile, like that which Hamlet uses to his mother when he warns her against excuses, which would but "skin and film the ulcerous place" of her soul.

> "*Ang.* Why do you put these sayings upon me?
> *Isa.* Because authority, though it err like others,
> Hath yet a kind of medicine in itself,
> That skins the vice o' the top." *Act* ii., *Scene* 2.

The *flow* of the blood is very distinctly recognized in the following:

> "Lord Angelo is precise;
> Stands at a guard with envy; scarce confesses
> That his blood flows, or that his appetite
> Is more to bread than stone —" *Act* i., *Scene* 4.

In the next scene this supposed absence of all desire is not only referred to coldness of the blood and to torpidity of sense, but the best means by which it may be acquired, are stated with more than scientific brevity.

> "A man whose blood
> Is very snow-broth; one who never feels
> The wanton stings and motions of the sense;
> But doth rebate and blunt his natural edge
> With profits of the mind, study and fast." *Act* i., *Scene* 5.

Angelo's soliloquy, when he contemplates the seduction of Isabel, or rather the base sale of his mercy for her honour, contains a wonderful example of physiological insight.

> "*Ang.*   O heavens!
> Why does my blood thus muster to my heart,
> Making both it unable for itself,
> And dispossessing all my other parts
> Of necessary fitness?
> So play the foolish throngs with one that swoons;
> Come all to help him, and so stop the air
> By which he should revive: and even so
> The general, subject to a well-wish'd king,
> Quit their own part, and in obsequious fondness
> Crowd to his presence, where their untaught love
> Must needs appear offence."   *Act* ii., *Scene* 4.

This mustering of the blood to the heart is referred to by Warwick, in describing the death of John of Gaunt; it is perfectly in accordance with modern physiological science, and when it is remembered that in Shakespeare's time the circulation of the blood, and even the relation of the heart to the blood, was yet undiscovered, the passage is in every way remarkable. The first simile of the oppressed heart to one that swoons, surrounded by an anxious crowd, excluding the vivifying air, is one which, however true to nature and to fact, would scarcely suggest itself, except to a mind imbued with medical thought. The second simile, likening the heart to a king, and the blood to his subjects, is somewhat more strained, yet fairly consistent with fact.

COMEDY OF ERRORS.

One can only surmise whether, in the following passage, Ægeon refers to the faintness which attends the period of quickening, or to the exhaustion of parturition. If to the former, it is remarkable that the time mentioned, 'not six months', is made to correspond with the proper time for the physiological event.

> " Drew me from kind embracements of my spouse:
> From whom my absence was not six months old,
> Before herself (almost at fainting under
> The pleasing punishment that women bear,)
> Had made provision for her following me,
> And soon, and safe, arrived where I was.
> There she had not been long, but she became
> A joyful mother of two goodly sons." *Act* i., *Scene* 1.

Are the articles mentioned by Dromio of Syracuse part of the medical stores of the ship which is "in her trim," and ready to sail?

> " Our fraughtage, Sir,
> I have convey'd aboard; and I have bought
> The oil, the balsamum, and aqua-vitæ." *Act* iv., *Scene* 1.

The following use of the word 'illusion,' as applied to a deception of the senses, in which one thing is mistaken for another, is strictly in accordance with its modern scientific use. Shakespeare, however, does not use the words 'delusion' and 'hallucination' by which the narrow sense of 'illusion' is now complemented.

> "*Antipholus S.* The fellow is distract, and so am I;
> And here we wander in illusions." *Act* iv., *Scene* 3.

The facial expression of mania, sharp-featured, fiery-eyed,

pale and haggard, is correctly touched on, even by the conjuror and the courtezan.

> "*Luciana.* Alas, how fiery and how sharp he looks!
> *Cour.* Mark, how he trembles in his extasy!
> *Pinch.* Give me your hand, and let me feel your pulse."
>
> "*Pinch.* Mistress, both man and master is possess'd;
> I know it by their pale and deadly looks:
> They must be bound, and laid in some dark room."
> *Act* iv., *Scene* 4.

The excellent account of the causation of melancholia by domestic trouble, given by the Abbess, could scarcely be improved upon even by the science of the present day. Discomfort, disturbed meals, indigestion, loss of recreation, loss of sleep followed by active disease, present a picture of medical etiology drawn with more knowledge than most members even of the profession of medicine could themselves display, and indicating that which is sufficiently apparent from many other passages in his works, that Shakespeare had paid especial attention to the physiology of mental diseases.

> "*Abbess.* And therefore came it, that the man was mad:
> The venom clamours of a jealous woman
> Poison more deadly than a mad dog's tooth.
> It seems, his sleeps were hinder'd by thy railing:
> And thereof comes it, that his head is light.
> Thou say'st, his meat was sauc'd with thy upbraidings:
> Unquiet meals make ill digestions,
> Thereof the raging fire of fever bred;
> And what's a fever but a fit of madness?
> Thou say'st, his sports were hinder'd by thy brawls:
> Sweet recreation barr'd, what doth ensue
> But moody and dull melancholy,
> Kinsman to grim and comfortless despair,
> And, at her heels, a huge infectious troop
> Of pale distemperatures, and foes to life?
> In food, in sport, in life-preserving rest
> To be disturb'd, would mad or man or beast:
> The consequence is then, thy jealous fits
> Have scar'd thy husband from the use of wits." *Act* v., *Sc.* 1.

This medical and most commendable Abbess not only traces

the causation of disease, but undertakes its cure. Adriana demands permission to nurse her husband and "diet his sickness;" but the dear old Abbess keeps the jealous wife where she ought to be, out of tongue shot, and promises more active measures than diet. She promises prayers also; but in the spirit of the injunction to "trust in the Lord and keep your powder dry," she prefaces their use with that of syrups and drugs. The monkish physic of the middle ages was practised by religious orders of both sexes: indeed, it seems primarily to have belonged to the women, in the times when every educated lady was a leech.

> "*Abb.* Be patient; for I will not let him stir,
> Till I have us'd the approv'd means I have,
> With wholesome syrups, drugs, and holy prayers
> To make of him a formal man again:
> It is a branch and parcel of mine oath,
> A charitable duty of my order:
> Therefore depart, and leave him here with me."
> *Act* v., *Scene* 1.

Ægeon's account of the infirmities of feebleness—age a second time cracking the tone of voice, the hair grey from the want of sap, the ears deaf from the dullness of sense—contains yet another reference to the flow of the blood. The "conduits of the blood froze up," is a kind of physiological poetry which we may look in vain for elsewhere.

> "*Ægeon.* Not know my voice! O, time's extremity!
> Hast thou so crack'd and splitted my poor tongue,
> In seven short years, that here my only son
> Knows not my feeble key of untun'd cares?
> Though now this grained face of mine be hid
> In sap-consuming winter's drizzled snow,
> And all the conduits of my blood froze up;
> Yet hath my night of life some memory,
> My wasting lamps some fading glimmer left,
> My dull deaf ears a little use to hear:
> All these old witnesses (I cannot err,)
> Tell me, thou art my son Antipholus." *Act* v., *Scene* 1.

LOVE'S LABOUR LOST.

The first medical passage in this play is a prescription of phlebotomy.

"*Rosaline.* Is the fool sick?
Biron. Sick at the heart.
Ros. Alack, let it blood.
Biron. Would that do it good?
Ros. My physic says, ay.
Biron. Will you prick't with your eye?
Ros. No *poynt*, with my knife. *Act* ii., Scene 1.

A quibble on the French negative. The next quotation also which belongs to our subject is a quibble on another French word not quite so intelligible. The prescription of a plantain for a broken shin is also given in *Romeo and Juliet*, in which "your plantain leaf" is pronounced excellent "for your broken shin." Plantain water was a remedy in common use with the old surgeons. [*Woodall's Surgeon's Mate*, p. 42, 184.]

" *Moth.* A wonder, master; here's a Costard broken in a shin.
Armado. Some enigma, some riddle: come, thy *l'envoy*; begin.
Cost. No egma, no riddle, no *l'envoy*; no salve in them all, Sir: O Sir, plantain, a plain plantain; no *l'envoy*, no *l'envoy*, no salve, Sir, but a plantain!
Arm. By virtue, thou enforcest laughter; thy silly thought, my spleen; the heaving of my lungs provokes me to ridiculous smiling: O pardon me, my stars! Doth the inconsiderate take salve for *l'envoy*, and the word *l'envoy* for a salve?" Act iii., Sc. 1.

The following quotation is anatomical, referring mental operations not merely to the brain, but to special parts of it which are indicated by technical terms. Rabelais frequently refers thought not to the brain at large, but to the ventricles

of the brain. Here is the old opinion definitely expressed. "It was believed that the three principal faculties of the mind, the understanding, the imagination, and the memory, resided in the different ventricles of the brain; the imagination having its seat in the fore part, the memory in the hinder cell, and the judgment or understanding in the middle."
—*Hakewill.*

Shakespeare, in at least two other passages, places the pia mater for the whole brain; a part for the whole, as one would speak of a ship as 'a sail.'

The pia mater is no part of the brain substance, but the vascular membrane by which the brain proper is closely invested, and from which it is mainly nourished. That part of the brain especially, which modern science indicates as the organ of thought, namely, the grey substance of the cerebral convolutions, is in immediate contact with the pia mater, and derives all its nourishment therefrom.

The pia mater, therefore, is in very much the same anatomical relation to that portion of the brain in which thought is located, as the womb is to the embryo, and Shakespeare's assertion that the pia mater is the womb which nourishes thought is therefore in strict accordance with modern physiology. It is only, however, within a quite recent date that these views, localising thought in the grey substance of the convolutions, have been established or indeed suggested, and therefore the full truth of this remarkable expression must be accepted only as a happy accident.

"*Holofernes.* This is a gift that I have, simple, simple; a foolish extravagant spirit, full of forms, figures, shapes, objects, ideas, apprehensions, motions, revolutions: these are begot in the *ventricle* of memory nourished in the womb of *pia mater*, and delivered upon the mellowing of occasion."   *Act* iv., *Scene* 2.

The foldings of the brain are used in the same general sense for the brain itself even by modern poets; thus Shelley says of conscience

"They say that sleep, most healing dew of Heaven,
Steeps not in balm the *foldings of the brain*
Which thinks thee an impostor."

In the same scene, Holofernes makes use of a technical term of pharmacy,

"Twice sod simplicity, *bis coctus*."

If thought is generated within the foldings of the pia mater, one, at least, of the passions also, is in the following passage, supposed to make its way through the brain to the other organs of the body. Some looseness of expression in the use of the word 'power,' is here observable, as if there were a function of a power. In other passages Shakespeare uses the proper word 'organ,' which he has missed here, with scientific strictness.

"But love, first learned in a lady's eyes,
Lives not alone immured in the brain;
But with the motion of all elements,
Courses as swift as thought in every power;
And gives to every power a double power,
Above their functions and their offices." *Act* iv., *Scene* 3.

When Biron and Boyet are making ridiculous comparisons on the countenance of Holofernes, which he asserts he will not be put out of; the one suggests that it should be put in "a brooch of lead." Biron adds, "Aye, and worn in the cap of a tooth-drawer." This appears to refer to some old dentist practice of which we now have not the key.

The mind of the dramatist seems rather to have run upon blood-letting in this play; for in the following quotation he expresses, not only the humoral pathology of fever, and prescribes its antiphlogistic treatment, but alludes to a custom of the phlebotomists of the old time.

"*Dumain.* I would forget her; but a fever she
Reigns in my blood, and will remember'd be.
Biron. A fever in your blood! why, then incision
Would let her out in saucers: Sweet misprision!" *Act* iv., *Sc.* 3.

Here is a passage from the works of a surgeon contemporary with the poet, fully illustrating the custom and its *rationale* of letting out blood in saucers, or, as they are here called, porringers.

"*Of the Blood Porringers.* Blood Porringers are necessary at sea, to be more certaine of the quantity of blood which is let; for since the blood of man is so precious, it is to be well weighed what quantitie is taken. The German surgeons do always let blood in a bason, yet I hold it not good for the Surgeon's mate to imitate at first, except he be of good judgment indeed, to judge of the quantity. The Blood Porringers which are made for that purpose being full, hold just three ounces, and somewhat more. For my owne practise I hold this course; if one chance to come to me of himselfe, or by advice of a Physician to be let blood, though he have a strong body I never take from him more than two porringers and a halfe, but often lesse. If the partie be not strong, except in the case of a pleurisie or some like urgent cause, I take lesse. For in that work except my reason give me good satisfaction to doe the the contrary, I will rather offend in too little, than in too much taking of blood away; for I have seen much hurt to have ensued by great quantity of blood taken away at one time: 7 or 8 ounces, I hold, a strong body may beare to lose, having good nourishment to recover it againe, and that without harme: but if you grow to 10 ounces you may many waies doe harm in the body, except your warrant be good. I speake this not to discourage young Surgeons from a worke so behovefull, but admonish them to warinesse in a point so dangerous."—*Woodall's Surgeon's Mate,* p. 23.

In numerous passages, Shakespeare refers the cause of disease to surfeiting, but in the following he attributes it to abstinence, and to the less power of enduring abstinence which is possessed by the young.

"Say, can you fast? your stomachs are too young;
And abstinence engenders maladies." *Act* iv., *Scene* 3.

Here is black letter authority quoting still older authority for this opinion.

"Hipocrates saythe, old menne maye susteyne fastynge easyly, nexte unto theym, menne of myddeil age, yonge menne maye wars beare it, chylderne warst of all, specially they that be lustye, not withstandynge here Galene corrected Hipocrates, sayenge, that he shulde have excepted menne very olde, who, as experyence declareth, muste eate often and lyttelle."—*Castell of Helthe*, p. 55.

In the same speech of Biron's the following remarkable passage occurs, which leaves no doubt that, although Shakespeare may, with the intuition of genius, have guessed very near the truth respecting the circulation of the blood, he was also well acquainted with the old false theory. "The nimble spirits in the arteries" expresses, with an exactness which cannot be questioned, the medical theory which prevailed before Harvey's time, and which maintained that the arteries were not the conduits of the blood, but of the vital spirits; and hence the name 'artery' from $αηρ$, 'air,' and $τηρειν$, 'to preserve,' a receptacle of air. These vessels were supposed to contain air, because they were found empty of blood after death. The windpipe was called *arteria aspera*, from the roughness of its rings.

> "Why, universal plodding prisons up
> The nimble spirits in the arteries;
> As motion, and long-during action, tires
> The sinewy vigour of the traveller." *Act* iv., *Scene* 3.

When Hamlet breaks away from Horatio to follow the ghost, he exclaims,

> "My fate cries out,
> And makes each petty artery in this body
> As hardy as the Nemean lion's nerve."

Here the function attributed to the arteries, though not so fully expressed as in the former quotation, is, no doubt, that of the old theory, that they contain the vital spirits, and are inflated in a state of excitement. See also Falstaff's reflections on Prince John in the second part of *Henry IV.* *Act* iv., *Scene* 3.

The concluding quotation from this comedy must be a pleasing one to medical men, for it gives them the poet's express authority to be merry, even in their most anxious duties. As a class, doctors certainly are jocose—men of a cheerful countenance, oftentimes "with the skin of their bellies a long way from their kidneys," as Rabelais says; and some of the ablest and most humane of them have been notorious as punsters and jesters; and when Rosaline sentences her lover to a twelve months' service in a hospital, it is not to break his spirit, but to render his jesting temper more humane in its exercise, and to teach him to do that which a cheery physician constantly attempts to do, " enforce the pained impotent to smile."

" *Ros.* To weed this wormwood from your fruitful brain,
And, therewithal, to win me, if you please,
(Without the which I am not to be won,)
You shall this twelvemonth term from day to day
Visit the speechless sick, and still converse
With groaning wretches; and your task shall be,
With all the fierce endeavour of your wit,
To enforce the pained impotent to smile.
Biron. To move wild laughter in the throat of death?
It cannot be; it is impossible:
Mirth cannot move a soul in agony.
Ros. Why, that's the way to choke a gibing spirit,
Whose influence is begot of that loose grace
Which shallow laughing hearers give to fools:
A jest's prosperity lies in the ear
Of him that hears it, never in the tongue
Of him that makes it: then, if sickly ears,
Deaf'd with the clamours of their own dear groans,
Will hear your idle scorns, continue then,
And I will have you, and that fault withal;
But, if they will not, throw away that spirit,

> And I shall find you empty of that fault,
> Right joyful of your reformation.
> *Biron.* A twelvemonth ? well, befal what will befal,
> I'll jest a twelvemonth in a hospital."   *Act* v., *Scene* 2.

It is to be hoped that Biron was cured of his wounding flouts, but not of that bright and merry temper, which is good for both subject and object of jest. The Dr. Merryman, quoted at page 27, must have his brassplate in the heart of the patient, but a kindly jest from the actual doctor will sometimes do more good than physic. There is a tale, I think in Dr. John Brown's clever book, *Horæ Subsecivæ*, of a poor lady who was at the point of death from an inaccessible abscess in the throat, which entirely prevented her from swallowing; all remedies had been tried in vain, and her Scotch doctor, standing at the bedside in hopeless anxiety, at last cried "Try her wi' a compliment!" with a grimace of comical despair, as if it were his conviction that a compliment was the very last thing a lady could refuse to swallow. The idea tickled the humorous faculty of the patient, and the involuntary convulsion of laughter broke the abscess and she was cured.

TAMING OF THE SHREW.

The separation *a toro*, between the mock Duke and his mock wife, is urged on medical reasons.

> " For your physicians have expressly charg'd,
> In peril to incur your former malady,
> That I should yet absent me from your bed."   *Induction.*

The excuse for the play is also medico-psychological, and soundly reasoned, though on false premises.

"For so your doctors hold it very meet:
Seeing too much sadness hath congeal'd your blood,
And melancholy is the nurse of frenzy:
Therefore, they thought it good you hear a play,
And frame your mind to mirth and merriment,
Which bars a thousand harms, and lengthens life." *Ibid.*

The description of the infirmities and diseases of Petruchio's horse affords an amusing insight into Shakespeare's knowledge of 'veterinary.' Eminent medical men have frequently been ardent veterinarians; Sir Astley Cooper for instance. The alliance, therefore, between human and veterinary medicine is sufficiently intimate to justify the inclusion of this passage as part of our subject.

Petruchio is described coming to his wedding fantastically apparelled, and mounted upon a steed which is

"Possessed with the glanders, and like to mourn in the chine,; troubled with the lampass, infected with the fashions, full of windgalls, sped with spavins, raied with the yellows, past cure of the fives, stark spoiled with the staggers, begnawn with the bots; swayed in the back, and shoulder-shotten; near-legg'd before."
Act iii., *Scene* .2

The terms of this description are singularly preserved in the veterinary art to the present day. "Possessed with the glanders" is a term still appropriate to that infectious and fatal disease. Farsin, or farcy, and glanders, are, according to Mr. Youatt, different types or stages of the same disease; they are both infectious, and therefore the horse is rightly described as "infected with the farcin." "Lampas" or "lumpas" is still a term of veterinary art, indicating a swelling of the upper palate which interferes with mastication; a comparatively slight affection, which is properly designated as merely troublesome. "Full of wind galls" is also appropriate, since these enlargements are apt to occur in numbers on the legs of a hard-worked hack. "Sped with spavins" indicates ruin from a well-known cause of unsoundness. "Raied" or dirtied "with the yellows" describes the prominent symptom of jaundice, a discoloration of eye or skin; Mr. Youatt says, that jaundice is 'commonly called the yellows.' The word 'staggers' is used to designate apoplexy in the horse, a fatal disease which would prevent him from being mounted; but there are also what are called 'half attacks of staggers,' and 'sleepy staggers,' the indications of slight cerebral congestion, which would not prevent Petruchio from making use of his bundle of equine imperfections, although the animal would indeed be 'stark spoiled,' and perhaps rendered blind by them. To be "be-gnawn with the bots," or the magot of the horse gadfly, may have been thought a more serious affair in the olden time than it is now, for Youatt says, that the horse may enjoy perfect health, while his stomach (to the lining membrane of which they adhere) is filled with their larvæ. The carrier, in the first part of *Henry IV.*, complains that

"Pease and beans are as dank here as a dog, and this is the next way to give the poor jades the bots."   *Act* ii., *Scene* 1.

"Shoulder shotten" appears an old term for shoulder lameness. "Near legged before" is merely a mode of designating an awkward canter.

In the *New Farrier's Guide*, by W. Gibson, (A.D. 1727,) that symptom of glanders which is called 'Mourning in the Chine,' is discussed at some length. Quoting from Snape, the author says: "From this alteration of the colour (of the discharges of the glandered horse) I do believe they give the disease this proper and distinguishing name of 'mourning of the chine,' whereas it is only a greater degree of one and the same disease" (Glanders).—p. 100. The origin of the term 'mourning of the chine,' he explains to have been an old false notion that the glanders proceeded from a wasting of the brain, and that at last this wasting reached the spinal marrow or chine. The phrase in the drama, " possessed with the glanders, and like to mourn in the chine," exactly corresponds with this explanation. The horse was decidedly possessed with the disease, and 'like to' have its last and worst form, but it could not have been described as actually suffering from this, or it would not have been rideable. The 'fives,' we learn from the same authority, are " a swelling of the parotid glands, which has a near affinity to the strangles," but differs in this, that the strangles happen to young horses at grass, while "the fives will happen to a horse at any time, and is more particularly seated in the glands or kernels under the ears."—p. 115.

On another point mentioned in this passage, this author says : " A swayed back is a pain and weakness of the reins caused by a fall. By 'a swaying of the back' is properly to be understood a stretching and relaxation of the muscles and ligaments of those parts."—p. 225.

Gibson does not use the word " shoulder-shotten," but he has a chapter on different forms of injury to the shoulder by blows or sprains, under the terms " of a shoulder-wrench, shoulder-pight, shoulder-splait."

Petruchio's objection to the burnt meat is founded on the notions which prevailed among the old physicians, that certain meats and the modes of cooking them were choleric or phlegmatic.

"*Pet.* I tell thee, Kate, 'twas burnt and dried away;
And I expressly am forbid to touch it,
For it engenders choler, planteth anger,
And better 'twere that both of us did fast,
Since, of ourselves, ourselves are choleric,
Than feed it with such over-roasted flesh." *Act* iv., *Scene* 1

The statements of Petruchio in the following act, that neat's-foot is "too phlegmatic a meat," and that "fat tripe finely boiled is choleric," are founded upon the same old medical notion, respecting the hot or cold tendency of diets, and their adaptation to the supposed choleric or phlegmatic temperaments of the sick.

Sir Thomas Elyot's *Castell of Helthe,* (A.D. 1541,) is mainly occupied with precepts on the choleric and phlegmatic, or hot and cold, moist and dry qualities of diet. Here are his opinions on one of the articles of diet rejected by Petruchio.

" Galene commendeth the feete of Swyne, but I have proved that the feete of a yonge Bullocke, tenderly sodden, and laid in sowse two days or thre, and eaten colde in the evenynge, have brought a cholerycke stomake into a good digestion and sleape, and therewith also expelled salt fleume and choler."—p. 32.

The sixteenth and seventeenth chapters of his "thyrde boke" are " on the diete of colerike persons," and " on the diete of fleumatic persons."

MIDSUMMER NIGHT'S DREAM.

The general contagiousness of disease was a prevalent opinion in the old time.

" Sickness is catching ; O, were favour so." *Act* i., *Scene* 1.

The passage quoted from *Measure for Measure,* giving a *double entendre* to the ' French crown,' has been supposed to refer to a venereal scab, probably *rupia ;* but in the retort which Quince makes upon Bottom's catalogue of beards, the loss of hair from the crown of the head, also a symptom of the *morbus Gallicus,* appears to be referred to.

" *Quince.* Some of your French crowns have no hair at all, and then you will play bare-faced." *Act* i., *Scene* 2.

Titania varies her description of floods from the rainfall of " contagious fogs," as they affect the face of the country, with a touch of their influence upon the health of men.

" Therefore, the moon, the governess of floods,
Pale in her anger, washes all the air,
That rheumatic diseases do abound." *Act* ii., *Scene* 2.

The constant references to the effects of surfeit scattered throughout the plays, would indicate that this form of indisposition had come peculiarly under the poet's notice, and that Abernethey's quaint remedy of a muzzle might have been frequently adopted with great advantage.

" For, as a surfeit of the sweetest things
The deepest loathing to the stomach brings." *Act* ii., *Sc.* 3,

Here is a reference to domestic surgery, good of its kind, like the "flax and whites of eggs" prescribed for Gloster's bleeding orbits in *King Lear*. Cobwebs are still used to staunch the bleeding from small wounds.

"*Bottom.* I shall desire you of more acquaintance, good master Cobweb : If I cut my finger, I shall make bold with you."
Act iii., *Scene* 1.

The increased intensity of one sense compensating for inactivity of another is expounded thus.

" Dark night, that from the eye his function takes,
The ear more quick of apprehension makes ;
Wherein it doth impair the seeing sense,
It pays the hearing double recompense." *Act* iii., *Scene* 2.

"'Tis a physic that's bitter to sweet end," in *Measure for Measure*, qualifies the nauseousness of the dose ; but here the repulsiveness of medicine is stated without reserve.

" Out, loathed medicine ! hated poison, hence ! "
Act iii., *Scene* 2.

Here is reference to one of the most constant symptoms of sickness.

" But, like in sickness, did I loath this food ;
But, as in health, come to my natural taste,
Now do I wish it, love it, long for it,
And will for evermore be true to it." *Act* iv., *Scene* 1.

Here is another singular reference to the physiology of vision. By an effort of will, the axes of the two eyes can be parted, or held from converging, so as to produce the effect described.

" Methinks I see these things with parted eye,
When everything seems double." *Act* iv., *Scene* 1.

The exposition of the pranks of fantasy contained in the

very remarkable speech of Theseus is more psychological than physiological.

> "Lovers and madmen have such seething brains,
> Such shaping fantasies, that apprehend
> More than cool reason ever comprehends.
> The lunatic, the lover, and the poet,
> Are of imagination all compact;
> One sees more devils than vast hell can hold—
> That is the madman:" &c. *Act* v., *Scene* 1.

Here imagination is referred to "seething brains," but in the song in the *Merchant of Venice* the question of its cerebral source is involved.

> " Tell me where is fancy bred,
> Or in the heart, or in the head?
> How begot, how nourished?" *Act* iii., *Scene* 2.

Every one of course knows on which side the heart beats, but here is authority:

> "The pap of Pyramus:
> Ay, that left pap
> Where heart doth hop." *Act* v., *Scene* 1.

Mother's marks and congenital deformities are deprecated by Oberon from the issue of the happy lovers.

> " And the blots of nature's hand
> Shall not in their issue stand;
> Never mole, hare-lip, nor scar,
> Nor mark prodigious, such as are
> Despised in nativity,
> Shall upon their children be." *Act* v., *Scene* 2.

MERCHANT OF VENICE.

In the following passage the intimate connexion between mind and body is sketched with exact physiological truth. Perhaps the most curious and undoubted instance of the mind's influence in the production of bodily disease, is jaundice caused by depressing emotion. It is not always 'crept' into, since bad news has frequently been known to cause jaundice in a few hours. In Dr. Copland's great and learned *Dictionary of Medicine*, it is stated, that "The most common exciting causes of jaundice are the more violent mental emotions," and in the list of these emotions, which he adds, he specially includes "peevishness." In Dr. Watson's *Lectures on Physic*, that able physician states, that among the causes of jaundice " the *pathemata mentis* play their assigned part; fits of anger and fear and alarm have been presently followed by jaundice." He mentions the instance of a friend of his who became jaundiced from needless anxiety about an approaching examination, and adds, "there are scores of instances on record to the same effect." This curious medical fact is sketched with exact fidelity in the following passage. The effect of wine on the temperature of the liver, and despondency on that of the heart, are also unquestionably medical thoughts.

> " With mirth and laughter let old wrinkles come;
> And let my liver rather heat with wine,
> Than my heart cool with mortifying groans.
> Why should a man whose blood is warm within
> Sit like his grandsire cut in alabaster?
> Sleep when he wakes? and creep into the jaundice
> By being peevish? *Act* i., *Scene* 1.

The very same medical idea is more tersely expressed in *Troilus and Cressida.*

"What grief hath set the jaundice on your cheeks?"
Act i., *Scene* 3.

The bad effect on the health of the two extremes of diet, abstinence and excess, are here marked.

"*Nerissa.* For aught I see, they are as sick that surfeit with too much, as they that starve with nothing: It is no small happiness, therefore, to be seated in the mean; superfluity comes sooner by white hairs, but competency lives longer." *Act* i., *Scene* 2.

The tyranny of desire over reason is here stated physiologically: the blood in this sense being always used poetically for the promptings of animal passion. A better knowledge has indeed exploded the theory, and attributed both reason and passion to the brain, though to different parts of it.

"*Portia.* The brain may devise laws for the blood; but a hot temper leaps o'er a cold decree: such a hare is madness the youth, to skip o'er the meshes of good counsel the cripple." *Act* i., *Sc.* 2.

I have not met with an explanation of the term sand-blind, Sand may be a cause of blindness, as in Egypt, but this guess will scarcely help. The term was probably one in vulgar use.

"*Launcelot.* O heavens, this is my true-begotten father! who, being more than sand-blind, high-gravel blind, knows me not."

"*Gobbo.* Alack, sir, I am sand-blind, I know you not."
Act ii., *Scene* 2.

The common nature of man is argued medically and physiologically in Shylock's speech; the use of the word 'organs,' being almost technical.

"Hath not a Jew eyes? hath not a Jew hands, organs, dimensions, senses, affections, passions? fed with the same food, hurt with the same weapons, subject to the same diseases, healed by the same means, warmed and cooled by the same winter and summer, as a Christian is? If you prick us, do we not bleed? if you tickle us, do we not laugh? if you poison us, do we not die? and if you wrong us, shall we not revenge?" *Act* iii., *Scene* 1.

A flesh wound across the muscle fibre bleeding a man to death is here in the thought:

> "*Bassanio.* Here is a letter, lady;
> The paper as the body of my friend,
> And every word in it a gaping wound,
> Issuing life-blood." *Act* iii., *Scene* 2.

Shylock's exposition of antipathies might possibly have found its examples from Shakespeare's own observation of these curious phenomena. The only one of the three which is common is that to a cat.

> " Some men there are love not a gaping pig;
> Some, that are mad if they behold a cat;
> And others, when the bagpipe sings i' the nose,
> Cannot contain their urine; for affection,
> Master of passion, sways it to the mood
> Of what it likes, or loaths." *Act* iv., *Scene* 1.

The following has reference to the practices of the old herbalists, who attributed peculiar virtues to plants gathered during particular phases of the moon and hours of the night.

> "*Jessica.* In such a night,
> Medea gather'd the enchanted herbs
> That did renew old Æson." *Act* v., *Scene* 1.

ALL'S WELL THAT ENDS WELL.

The very plot of this drama may be said to be medical. The orphan daughter of a physician cures the king of a fistula by means of a secret remedy left to her as a great treasure by her father. The royal reward is the choice of a husband among the nobles of the court, and "thereby hangs the tale." The story is copied from *Boccaccio*. Giletta (Helena) had heard news that the King of France had a fistula, which had been left by a tumour in the chest, for which he had been badly treated; and that, among all those who had tried, he had not been able to find a physician who could effect a cure, all of them, indeed, having made him worse; on which account, the King despaired of himself, and would have no further advice or assistance. This greatly pleased the young lady, who thought that it would afford her a legitimate excuse for making a journey to Paris, and that if she could readily cure this disease, as she believed she could, she might procure Bertram for her husband. Wherefore having made a powder of a certain herb useful in this disease, in the manner which she had been taught by her father, she mounted her horse and went to Paris. She obtained an audience of the king, and asked permission to see the diseased part, which the king, charmed with her youth and beauty, could not deny. When she had seen the part affected, she said, Monseigneur, I trust in God to be able to cure you of this disease within eight days, without subjecting you to any pain or fatigue. The king laughed at the proposition, and said he was resolved to take no more remedies; she persisted, and argued—You despise my skill because I am young and a woman, but bear in mind that I do not assume the rôle of a physician on account of any knowledge of my own, but by the aid of God, and the science of Master Gerard of Narbon, who was my father, and who in his life-time enjoyed a great reputation as a physician. She offered to be burnt alive if she did not effect a cure, on condition that, if she succeeded, the king promised to give her the husband whom she should demand, his sons and the princes of the blood excepted. The king having acquiesced in this proposition, Helena commenced her treatment, and his majesty was entirely cured before the term prescribed, to the great astonishment of his physicians.

It is to be observed that Shakespeare only refers to the king having a fistula, whereas Boccaccio refers to the cause and nature of it. The passage, which in the original Italian describes the disease, runs as follows,

"Al Re di Francia *per una nascienza che avuta avea nel petto, et era male stata curata, gli era rimasa una fistola*, la quale di grandissima noja, e di grandissima angoscia gli era, nè s'era ancor potuto trovar Medico, come che molti se ne fossero esperimentati, che di ciò l'avesse potuto guerire, ma tutti l'avean peggiorato: per la qual cosa il Re disperatosene, piu d'alcun non voleva nè consiglio, nè ajuto.

A fistula at the present day means an abscess external to the rectum, but in Shakespeare's day it was used in the more general signification for a burrowing abscess in any situation.

The following passages will shew how Shakespeare developes Boccaccio's sketch.

"*Countess.* What hope is there of his majesty's amendment?

Lafeu. He hath abandoned his physicians, madam; under whose practices he hath persecuted time with hope, and finds no other advantage in the process but only the losing of hope and time.

Count. This young gentlewoman had a father, (O, that *had!* how sad a passage 'tis) whose skill was almost as great as his honesty; had it stretched so far, would have made nature immortal, and death should have play for lack of work. 'Would, for the king's sake, he were living! I think it would be the death of the king's disease.

Lafeu. How called you the man you speak of, madam?

Count. He was famous, sir, in his profession, and it was his great right to be so: Gerard de Narbon.

Lafeu. He was excellent, indeed, madam; the king very lately spoke of him admiringly and mourningly; he was skilful enough to have lived still, if knowledge could be set up against mortality.

Bertram. What is it, my good lord, the king languishes of?

Lafeu. A fistula, my lord.

Bertram. I heard not of it before.

Lafeu. I would it were not notorious.—Was this gentlewoman the daughter of Gerard de Narbon?" *Act* i., *Scene* 1.

In *The Secretes of the Reverend Maister Alexis, of Piemont,* imprinted at London for John Wight, (A.D. 1580,) the old signification of the term fistula is denoted in a receipt which he gives "To make oyle of Brimstone, to heale all manner of cankers, diseases, or sores, whiche come of a putrified humour, and runne continually, commonly called Fistules."—p. 11.

In the dialogue in which Lafeu prefaces his introduction of Helena to the King, the epithets given to her, and the playful misuse of the pronouns, "I have seen a medicine," "What her is this?" "Why doctor she," seem intended as quizzical allusions to the sex of the fair practitioner. This feeling, as we have seen, did not always exist, but Shakespeare fixes the incidents of this story as having occurred at a time when there was a "congregated college" of physicians, and when

H

the art of healing was considered the monopoly of "learned and authentic fellows."

"*Lafeu.* But, my good lord, 'tis thus;
Will you be cur'd of your infirmity?
King. No.
Laf. O, will you eat no grapes, my royal fox?
Yes, but you will my noble grapes, an if
My royal fox could reach them: I have seen a medicine
That's able to breathe life into a stone." *Act* ii., *Scene* 1.

Helena's commendation of her secret remedy, and the king's reason for rejecting it, give an excellent idea of the state of opinion with regard to the practice of physic in Shakespeare's time. "Our most learned doctors" of "the congregated college" would, no doubt, be most unanimously of opinion that the king had stained his judgment by submitting a disease, which they had pronounced incurable, to the treatment of any one not of their body, and therefore an empiric. It would not so much be the nature of the remedy, as the irregularity of its source and application, which would constitute the offence against law and decency. Helena, in fact, would find herself in much the same position as poor Margaret Kennix, whose "curing of diseases and wounds by means of certain simples," neither Walsingham nor his despotic mistress could effectually defend against "the congregated college." (*See* page 32.) Secret remedies, as we have seen, were held with tenacity in Shakespeare's time by the surgeons as a rule, and by some physicians against rule: they are now justly regarded as the attribute of quacks; and singularly enough they are most in vogue for the relief of "past-cure maladies."

"*King.* Now, fair one, does your business follow us?
Helena. Ay, my good lord. Gerard de Narbon was
My father: in what he did profess, well found.

King. I knew him.
Hel. The rather will I spare my praises towards him;
Knowing him is enough. On his bed of death,
Many receipts he gave me; chiefly one,
Which, as the dearest issue of his practice,
And of his old experience the only darling,
He bad me store up, as a triple eye,
Safer than mine own two, more dear; I have so :
And, hearing your high majesty is touch'd
With that malignant cause wherein the honour
Of my dear father's gift stands chief in power
I come to tender it, and my appliance,
With all bound humbleness.
    King.   We thank you, maiden :
But may not be so credulous of cure,—
When *our most learned doctors* leave us; and
The *congregated college* have concluded
That labouring art can never ransom nature
From her inaidable estate,—I say we must not
So stain our judgment, or corrupt our hope,
To prostitute our past-cure malady
To empirics; or to dissever so
Our great self and our credit, to esteem
A senseless help, when help past sense we deem." *Act* ii., *Sc.* 1.

Before the fair " she medicine" arrives at court, the king asks Bertram,

  " *King.*   How long is't, count,
    Since the physician at your father's died?
    He was much fam'd.
      Bertram.   Some six months, my lord.
      King. If he were living I would try him yet;—
    Lend me an arm;—the rest have worn me out
    With several applications :—nature and sickness
    Debate it at their leisure."   *Act* i., *Scene* 2."

In the following passage Helena explains to the countess, the widow of her father's patron, and her own protectress, her intention to visit Paris to offer her aid to the king.

  " *Helena.* You know my father left me some prescriptions
    Of rare and prov'd effects, such as his reading
    And manifest experience had collected
    For general sovereignty; and that he will'd me
    In heedfullest reservation to bestow them,

H²

As notes, whose faculties inclusive were,
More than they were in note: amongst the rest,
There is a remedy, approv'd, set down,
To cure the desperate languishings whereof
The king is render'd lost.
* * * * *
Countess. But think you, Helen,
If you should tender your supposed aid,
He would receive it? He and his physicians
Are of a mind; he, that they cannot help him,
They, that they cannot help: How shall they credit
A poor unlearned virgin, when *the schools,
Embowell'd of their doctrine,* have left off
The danger to itself?" *Act* i., *Scene* 3.

For once, our sympathies are enlisted against the doctrine of the schools, and in favour of the selfish quackery of secret specific remedies. The following are the quaint but sound reasons assigned by Don Alexis of Piemont, for disclosing his Secrets.

"Now it chanced these fewe daies past, beyng in Milan in the fowerscore and twoo yere and seven monethes of myne age, that a poore artificer was marveilous tormented with the stone and had beene twoo daies without making his urine. The Chirurgeon that dressed him knowying well that I had many secretes and singularly for the stone, came to me, and requested me, that I would teach him the receite redie, or at least give hym the medicine composed and made for the healthe of the Pacient. But I perceivyng that he would use other mennes thinges, for his owne profite and honoure, refused to give it him, but willed hym to bryng me unto the sicke manne, and that I myself would minister the Medicine unto hym *gratis*. The Physician, either fearing blame if it should be knowne that he had recourse to the aide of an other manne, havyng boasted that he had the secret himself, or els in the meane tyme, still to make his profite in dissemblyng the matter, and deferryng it yet twoo daies more with diverse excuses and colours, until he brought me to the Pacient, who at my commyng I founde so nigh his ende, that after he had a little lifted up his eyes, castyng them piteouslie towards me, passed from this into a better life. Not having any neede, neither of my Secrete, nor any other Receipt to recover his healthe.

"With this case I was moved to suche a compassion and sorowe, that not onely I wished myself evil, but also I desired to dye, seeing my ambition and vainglorie, to have been the cause that this poore man was not succoured, with the remedie and gift that God the

Father, and Lorde of us had given me. Wherefore, so greate was the remorse of conscience in me, that desiryng to sequestrate myself from the worlde, and not finding myself of suche a disposition of minde that I could live in a Monasterie among Religious men better edified than I, I was at the laste fullie resolved with myself, to chuse a place separate from any Towne, where I have a little Lande, some Bookes, and a studie, for to avoide idlenesse. Here I live a life which I call a Monkes life, with one servante, which goeth to the towne, not to begge, but to buie my provision, and other thynges necessarie, for to sustain his poore life and myne, as long as it shall please God.

"But not yet havyng the power to put out of my fantasie, but that I was verie homicide and murderer, for refusing to the Phisition, the receite and remedie for the healyng of this poore man, I have determined to communicate and publishe to the worlde all that I haue, beyng assured that few other men have so many as I. And mindyng to set forth none, but suche as bee moste true and proved."

The king at length submits himself to Helena's treatment, who promises him a cure in a much shorter time than Boccaccio thought needful, namely, in two days instead of eight; in that time she promises,

"What is infirm from your sound parts shall fly,
Health shall live free, and sickness freely die."
Act ii., *Scene* 1.

The cure is effected in a manner which appears miraculous; the account of it is amusingly given in the following dialogue.

"*Lafeu.* They say, miracles are past; and we have our philosophical persons, to make modern and familiar things supernatural and causeless. Hence it is, that we make trifles of terrors; ensconcing ourselves into seeming knowledge, when we should submit ourselves to an unknown fear.
Parolles. Why, 'tis the rarest argument of wonder that hath shot out in our latter times.
Bertram. And so 'tis.
Laf. To be relinquish'd of the artists,——
Par. So say I; *both of Galen and Paracelsus.*
Laf. Of all the *learned and authentic fellows,*——
Par. Right, so say I.
Laf. That gave him out incurable,——
Par. Why, there 'tis; so say I too.

Laf. Not to be helped,——
Par. Right: as 'twere a man assured of an——
Laf. Uncertain life, and sure death.
Par. Just, you say well ; so would I have said.
Laf. I may truly say, it is a novelty to the world."
Act ii., *Scene* 3.

To be "relinquished of the artists," "both of *Galen* and *Paracelsus*," means to be relinquished of the physicians who practised their art according to the doctrines of Galen *or* of Paracelsus. This passage is very remarkable when considered in relation to the history of medicine; we have seen, page 52, that Turquet de Mayerne was ignominiously expelled by the College of Physicians of Paris, 'lawfully *congregated*,' in 1603, for maintaining the doctrines of Paracelsus; and that William Butler, who died in 1621, "was the first Englishman who quickened Galenical physic with a touch of Paracelsus;" and in Shakespeare's time, whether in France or in England, those physicians who would be spoken of as "our most learned doctors" of "the congregated college," or still more pointedly designated "the learned and authentic fellows," would not be the disciples "both of Galen and Paracelsus," but of the former only. This appears to be quite consistent with the manner in which the two names are mentioned, which, indeed, can only be taken to indicate that Shakespeare was acquainted with the existence of the two rival schools. The appropriate, and indeed, technical use of the term "congregated college" is worthy of note. The term "artists," as applied to medical men, was also consistent with the custom of the time; thus Clowes appeals to his professional brethren as "all good artists."

The restored and grateful king reappears before his court with the following speech, which indicates that his disease had in some way affected the nervous sensibility; but how this happened is not more clear than how the miraculous cure was effected.

"*King.* Go, call before me all the lords in court.—
Sit, my preserver, by thy patient's side;
And with this healthful hand, whose banish'd sense
Thou hast repeal'd, a second time receive
The confirmation of my promis'd gift,
Which but attends thy naming." *Act* ii., *Scene* 3.

Helena chooses for her fee, the hand of Count Bertram with whom she is in love, who disdainfully rejects the proffered felicity because she is "a poor physician's daughter," and thus brings the king to her rescue, who asserts the all-worthiness of merit, and that worldly position without virtue "is a dropsical honour." Enforced by the king, Bertram marries the poor she-doctor, who finds the barren union no remedy for her own love sickness, since her husband immediately deserts her for the wars, to which she follows him, and thus developes the plot of the comedy.

The two first items in the clown's comic list of things fit for each other have a legal and a medical reference.

"*Countess.* Will your answer serve fit to all questions?
Clown. As fit as ten groats is for the hand of an attorney, as your French crown for your taffata punk." *Act* ii., *Scene* 2.

The French crown has already been explained as the cant term for venereal scab; taffeta punk is a prostitute in coarse clothing, and the fitness of one to the other is obvious.

Here is the quibble on apothecaries' weight, which occurs in Shakespeare again and again.

"*Parolles.* I have not, my lord, deserved it.
Lafeu. Yes, good faith, every dram of it; and I will not bate thee a scruple." *Act* ii., *Scene* 3.

The French lord, speaking of the war in Italy, refers to the idea so repeatedly expressed of disease from surfeit.

> " I am sure the younger of our nation,
> That surfeit on their ease, will day by day
> Come here for physick." *Act* iii., *Scene·*1.

In the conversation between Lafeu and the clown, Shakespeare's herbalist knowledge appears, though here it is not medicinal, as he merely distinguishes between nose-herbs and salad-herbs.

> "*Lafeu*. 'Twas a good lady, 'twas a good lady; we may pick a thousand salads, ere we light on such another herb.
> *Clown*. Indeed, sir, she was the sweet-marjoram of the salad, or rather, the herb of grace.
> *Laf*. They are not salad-herbs, you knave, they are nose-herbs." *Act* iv. *Scene* 5.

When the cowardice and treachery of Parolles are discovered, Bertram refers to that antipathy to cats which Shylock remarks, and which is one of the most unquestionable and curious of these emotions of repulsion. There are persons who feel sick and faint when there is a cat near to them, though they have no knowledge of the fact except from the peculiar sensation. Ambrose Paré quotes such cases from Mathiolus, and maintains that cats "send forth pestiferous airs and exhalations."

> " I could endure any thing before but a cat, and now he's a cat to me."
> " He's more and more a cat."   " He's a cat still."
> *Act* iv., *Scene* 3.

The following has reference to the old belief that gold is one of the most efficacious of medicines.

> "*King*.   Plutus himself,
> That knows the tinct and multiplying medicine,
> Hath not in nature's mystery more science,
> Than I have in this ring."   *Act* v., *Scene* 3.

A more distinct reference to the medicinal use of gold is found in the *Second Part of Henry IV*.

> " Other, less fine in carat, is more precious ;
> Preserving life in medicine potable." *Act* iv., *Scene* 4.

Chaucer refers to this medicinal property of gold in his sarcastic excuse for the doctour's avarice.

> " And yet he was but esy of despence :
> He kept that he wan in the pestilence.
> For gold in physic is a cordial ;
> Therefore he loved it in special."

It was assumed by all the old writers that gold must be a medicine of wonderful efficacy, but the difficulty was how to give it, as they do not appear to have possessed the knowledge of its solubility in the mixed acids.

In John Wight's translation of the *Secretes of Alexis*, is a receipt " To dissolve and reducte golde into a potable licour, whiche conserveth the youth and healthe of a man, and will heale every disease that is thought incurable, in the space of seven daies at the furthest." The receipt is a complicated one, the gold being acted upon by juice of lemons, honey, common salt, and *aqua vitæ*, and distillation frequently repeated from " an urinall of glasse." " For the oftener it is distilled, the better it is. Thus doyng, ye shall have a right naturall, and perfecte *potable golde*, whereof somewhat taken alone every monthe once or twice, or at least with the said licour, whereof we have spoken in the second chapter of this boke, is verie excellent to preserve a man's youthe and healthe, and to heale in fewe daies any disease rooted in a man, and thought incurable. The said gold will be also good and profitable for diverse other operations and effectes : as good wittes and diligent searchers of the secreetes of nature may easily judge."—p. 7.

In Sir Kenelm Digby's *Receipts*, (A.D. 1674,) is a complicated one for "an excellent tincture of gold;" the gold is to be calcined with three salts, ground with flowers of sulphur, and burnt in a reverbatory furnace with sulphur twelve times, then digested with spirit of wine "which will be tincted very yellow, of which, few drops for a dose in a fit vehicle hath wrought great effects." Great is the power of faith. In the olden times there were remedies especially appropriated for rich people, and for middling people, and for poor people. There was even a separate *Pharmacopœia Pauperum;* while Sir Kenelm's tincture of gold might have suited Miss Killmansegg. Maister Alexis has "remedies to purge the ayre, that are of the smallest pryce, for men of small habilitie"; and "a sovereigne pouder against the venyme of the plague for ryche men and princes."—p. 46.

AS YOU LIKE IT.

Old Adam gives the following good medical reason for the haleness of his years,—he had been temperate and chaste in youth.

> "Though I look old, yet I am strong and lusty:
> For in my youth I never did apply
> Hot and rebellious liquors in my blood;
> Nor did I with unbashful forehead woo
> The means of weakness and debility;
> Therefore my age is as a lusty winter,
> Frosty, but kindly. Let me go with you."
> Act ii., Scene 3.

When Adam is suffering from starvation in the forest, Orlando leaves him to seek for food, with an exhortation, proving that Shakespeare well knew the power of the mind to sustain for a while the failing functions of life.

> "*Orlando.* Why, how now, Adam! no greater heart in thee? Live a little; comfort a little; cheer thyself a little: If this uncouth forest yield any thing savage, I will either be food for it, or bring it for food to thee. Thy conceit is nearer death than thy powers. For my sake, be comfortable; hold death awhile at the arm's end: I will be here with thee presently; and if I bring thee not something to eat, I'll give thee leave to die; but if thou diest before I come, thou art a mocker of my labour. Well said! thou look'st cheerily." *Act* ii., *Scene* 6.

Touchstone's moralizing upon life repeated by Jaques, expresses the gradual maturing of the body, and its gradual decay after the point of perfect growth and organization has been turned.

> "And so, from hour to hour, we ripe and ripe,
> And then, from hour to hour, we rot and rot,
> And thereby hangs a tale." *Act* ii. *Scene* 7.

When Jaques expresses in medical form of thought and phrase his desire to reform the moral evils of the world, the class of disease to which the half-technical phrase of 'cleansing the foul body' appears to refer to, is that which by its novelty and prevalence engrossed so much attention at that time. The reply of the duke makes this certain, "the embossed sores and headed evils" of the libertine referring without doubt to venereal rupia, a sore which is embossed by its dried secretions until the scab assumes the form of limpet shells adherent to the skin. The moral meaning is no doubt a denunciation of coarsemindedness and pruriency disseminated under the specious disguise of advice and warning; a mischievous foul sin which impure minds, acting as confessors and conscience directors, are certain to commit.

"*Jaques.* Invest me in my motley; give me leave
To speak my mind, and I will through and through
Cleanse the foul body of the infected world,
If they will patiently receive my medicine.
   Duke Senior. Fie on thee! I can tell what thou wouldst do.
   Jaques. What, for a counter, would I do but good?
   Duke S. Most mischievous foul sin, in chiding sin:
For thou thyself hast been a libertine,
As sensual as the brutish sting itself;
And all the embossed sores and headed evils,
That thou with license of free foot hast caught,
Wouldst thou disgorge into the general world."   *Act* ii., *Scene* 7.

In Jaques' description of the seven stages of life, the second change of the voice in advancing age is noted.

"And his big manly voice,
Turning again towards childish treble, pipes
And whistles in his sound."   *Ibid.*

The first physiological change of the voice is noted by Portia, when she and Nerissa propose to assume the manners and habits of young men.

> "And speak between the change of man and boy
> With a reed voice." *Merchant of Venice.*

For the second change of voice, see also Ægeon's speech in *The Comedy of Errors.*

The contention, respecting court and country manners between Corin and Touchstone, shews Shakespeare's knowledge of the disgusting source of a favourite medicine in those times, used also as a perfume. The point in debate is, the cleanliness of kissing hands.

> "*Corin.* And they [the shepherd's hands] are often tarred over with the surgery of our sheep; and would you have us kiss tar? The courtier's hands are perfumed with civet.
> *Touchstone.* Most shallow man! Thou worms'-meat, in respect of a good piece of flesh: Indeed!—Learn of the wise, and perpend: Civet is of a baser birth than tar; the very uncleanly flux of a cat." *Act* iii., *Scene* 2.

Rosalind describing those "whom time ambles withal," indicates persons who enjoy quiet of mind and repose of body, and indirectly refers gout to the luxury of wealth.

> "With a priest that lacks Latin, and a rich man that hath not the gout; for the one sleeps easily, because he cannot study; and the other lives merrily, because he feels no pain." *Act* iii., *Scene* 2.

Orlando, seeking a remedy for his love-sickness, obtains from Rosalind the reply,

> "No; I will not cast away my physic, but on those that are sick. There is a man haunts the forest, that abuses our young plants with carving Rosalind on their barks; hangs odes upon hawthorns, and elegies on brambles; all, forsooth, deifying the name of Rosalind: if I could meet with that fancy-monger, I would give him some good counsel, for he seems to have the *quotidian* of love upon him.
> *Orlando.* I am he that is so love-shaked; I pray you, tell me your remedy." *Act* iii., *Scene* 2.

Rosalind's theory of the nature and treatment of this amatory quotidian is, that

"Love is merely a madness: and, I tell you, deserves as well a dark house and a whip as madmen do: and the reason why they are not so punished and cured is, that the lunacy is so ordinary that the whippers are in love too: Yet I profess curing it by counsel."

"I drave my suitor from his mad humour of love, to a living humour of madness; which was, to forswear the full stream of the world, and to live in a nook merely monastic: And thus I cured him; and this way will I take upon me to *wash your liver as clean as a sound sheep's heart, that there shall not be one spot of love in't.*"
Act iii., Scene 2.

In this last passage, surely the words heart and liver should be transposed, since the text is evidently an inversion of the true meaning. Love is generally said to dwell in the heart; while, on the other hand, unsound sheep are not known by the condition of this organ, but by that of the liver; the well-known peculiarity of sheep disease being flukes or hydatids of the liver, which give that organ the spotted appearance to which Rosalind refers. Every one who has had to deal with printers knows that there is no error so common, or so easily overlooked, as transposition of words having nearly the same sense.

'To reek,' means, to smoke or cast forth vapour or stench or mist. Juliet speaks of "dead men's reeky shanks." In the following passage, 'a great reeking' probably means the smoke and vapour of fire in a room without outlet, which is well-known to be noisome and even fatal.

"*Touchstone.* When a man's verses cannot be understood, nor a man's good wit seconded with the forward child, understanding, it strikes a man more dead than a great reeking in a little room."
Act iii., Scene 3.

Phœbe tells her lover

"That eyes,—that are the frail'st and softest things,
Who shut their coward gates on atomies,"

cannot inflict wounds, and thus pettishly challenges him to prove his injuries.

> "Now show the wound mine eye hath made in thee.
> Scratch thee with but a pin, and there remains
> Some scar of it; lean upon a rush,
> The cicatrice and capable impressure,
> Thy palm some moment keeps." *Act* iii., *Scene* 5.

Oliver describes his rescue from the lioness by Orlando,

> "Who led me instantly unto his cave,
> There stripp'd himself, and here upon his arm
> The lioness had torn some flesh away,
> Which all this while had bled; and now he fainted,
> And cried, in fainting, upon Rosalind.
> Brief, I recover'd him; bound up his wound:
> And, after some small space, being strong at heart,
> He sent me hither," &c. *Act* iv., *Scene* 3.

Oliver shews the napkin dyed in his brother's blood, whereupon Rosalind faints, and elicits the remark.

> "Many will swoon when they do look on blood." *Ibid*.

A man does recover from fainting by becoming once more "strong of heart," but in this place it seems probable that the most appropriate term of common parlance only accidentally concurs with physiological truth..

MUCH ADO ABOUT NOTHING.

The contagiousness of pestilence, and one of its symptoms, are thus alluded to by Beatrice.

"*Beatrice.* O Lord! he will hang upon him like a disease: he is sooner caught than the pestilence, and the taker runs presently mad. God help the noble Claudio! if he have caught the Benedick, it will cost him a thousand pound ere he be cured."
Act i., *Scene* 1.

To recognize love's grief or wound by the complexion, and to salve it or apply remedies, seems the thought in Claudio's speech, though it must be owned that the meaning is a little obscure—

"How sweetly do you minister to love,
That know love's grief by his complexion!
But lest my liking might too sudden seem,
I would have salv'd it with a longer treatise."
Act i., *Scene* 1.

Sadness dependent upon disposition is truly stated to be more radical and less curable than that which can be referred to a definite outward cause. The would-be physician recommends reason as an anodyne, but the patient repudiates the moral treatment.

"*Conrade.* What the goujere, my lord! why are you thus out of measure sad?
D. John. There is no measure in the occasion that breeds it, therefore the sadness is without limit.
Con. You should hear reason.
D. John. And when I have heard it, what blessing bringeth it?
Con. If not a present remedy, yet a patient sufferance.
D. John. I wonder that thou, being (as thou say'st thou art) born under Saturn, goest about to apply a moral medicine to a mortifying mischief."
Act i., *Scene* 3.

The 'goujere' has been said to mean venereal disease, though I know not on what authority. Mr. Collier and Mr. Knight substitute 'good year,' meaning 'bad year,' the year of pestilence: *lucus a non*. The word recurs in *Lear*, "The goujeres shall devour them."

Heart-burn referred to acidity is good medical doctrine.

"*Beatrice.* How tartly that gentleman looks! I never can see him but I am heart-burned an hour after." *Act* ii. *Scene* 1.

The causes to which tooth-ache is attributed in the following passage appear at first sight but a gratuitous piece of nonsense; but the singular fact that John of Gatisden, one of our oldest medical authors, attributes decay of the teeth to these very causes, "a humour or a worm," should teach us that Shakespeare seldom or never threw down even the most trifling or careless opinion without grounds for it. So far as I can discover no translation into English has ever been made of John of Gatisden's works. Fuller records "that lately his works have been printed in Italy in a folio, no small honour, seeing that in physick the Italians account all tramontain doctours but apothecaries in comparison of themselves;" so that although "this John flourished in the year of our Lord 1320," it would appear from this recent edition of his works, that even in Fuller's time, 1650, his works were by no means out of date. The edition from which I quote was published in the midst of Shakespeare's working years.

" *Benedick.* I have the tooth-ache.
D. Pedro. Draw it.
Bene. Hang it!
Claud. You must hang it first, and draw it afterwards.
D. Pedro. What? sigh for the tooth-ache?
Leon. Where is but a humour, or a worm?
Bene. Well, every one can master a grief, but he that has it."
Act iii., *Scene* 2.

I

The following is the remarkable passage of Gatisden's *Rosa Anglica*, which gives our poet good medical authority for the above curious pathological notion.

De Corrosione Dentium.

"Corrosio dentium causatur ab humore putrido inviscato radici dentis.

"1. Curatio consistit in tribus. Prima, est *evacuatio humiditatum* putridarum cum turpeto, agarico, foliis senæ, catholico.

"2. Secunda, est solutio ipsarum ex ipsis dentibus, cum aceto decoctionis nigellæ, aut cum aceto decoctionis capparum, zinzib aut similium: aut nigella trita cum cinamomo, linita super dentem.

"3. Tertia, est prohibitio corrosionis cum iis, quibus dens corrosus impletur, aut linitur, ut est galla, cyperus ; Galla sola prohibet dentis corrosionem, et mastix, cyperus, et collutio oris cum aceto. Item repletio dentis cum camphora, est ultimum remedium in prohibitione corrosionis dentis. Replere dentem cum zinzibere, decocto in melle vel aceto, optimum est. Item, asafœtida quæ cum cera bullierit, vehemens est: Similiter castoreum et lusquiamus, simul mixta valent: Replere dentem corrosum cum corallis tritis, prohibet corrosionem: Myrrha optima est, et castoreum, et opium, piper torrefactum, assafœtida, storax calamita, zinziber, semen lusquiami : quodlibet istorum valet per se, cum melle, aut pice, radice dentis fricata. Si vermes sint in dentibus, ℞ semen porri, seu lusquiami contere et misce cum cera, pone super carbones, et fumus recipiatur per embotum, quoniam sanat. Solum etiam semen lusquiami valet coctum in aqua calida, supra quam aquam patiens palatum apertum si tenuerit, cadent vermes evidenter vel in illam aquam, vel in aliam quæ ibi fuerit posita. De myrrha et aloë ponantur in dentem, ubi est vermis : semen caulis, et absinthium, per se vermes interficit."—*Rosa Anglica*, Liber secundus, "De Febribus," p. 923. Edit. 1595.

Si vermes in dentibus

It is curious to observe that our old quackeries are still new, in that remarkable country where folly and wisdom are alike stereotyped. In *Pictures of the Chinese, drawn by themselves*, by the Rev. R. H. Cobbold,

"The first portrait is that of the quack doctress, who pretends to cure tooth-ache by extracting a maggot—the cause of the disorder. This is done—or rather pretended to be done—by simply placing a bright steel pin on the part affected, and tapping the pin with a piece of wood. Mr. Cobbold compares the operation to procuring worms for fishing, by working a spade backwards and forwards in the ground. He and a friend submitted to the process, but in a very short time compelled the doctress to desist, by the excessive precautions they took against imposition."—*Athenæum*, Jan. 28th, 1860.

The following passage is one of the few in which Shakespeare mentions a drug by name. It is done here by way of quibble on the name of the sick lady's lover Benedick.

"*Beatrice.* I am stuffed, cousin, I cannot smell.
Margaret. A maid, and stuffed! there's goodly catching of cold.
Beat. O, God help me! God help me! How long have you profess'd apprehension?
Marg. Ever since you left it: doth not my wit become me rarely?
Beat. It is not seen enough, you should wear it in your cap.—By my troth I am sick.
Marg. Get you some of this distilled Carduus Benedictus, and lay it to your heart: it is the only thing for a qualm.
Hero. There thou prick'st her with a thistle.
Beat. Benedictus! Why Benedictus? You have some moral in this Benedictus.
Marg. Moral? No, by my troth, I have no moral meaning; I meant, plain holy-thistle."   *Act* iii., *Scene* 5.

Woodall, (A.D. 1639,) in his chapter on *Medicines and their Uses*, says, "*Carduus benedictus* water doth ease the paine of the head, conformeth the memory, cureth a quartane, provoketh sweat, and comforteth the vitall spirits." —p. 40.

The Garden of Health, by William Langham, practitioner of physicke, (2nd Edition, A.D. 1633) enumerates the medical virtues of the blessed thistle under sixty-six heads.

Salmon, (A.D. 1693,) in his *Seplasium, or Druggist Shop opened*, p. 1095, records fifteen preparations of the carduus benedictus, or holy thistle, in use among medical men; and reports that "it is excellent against pleurisie, obstructions,

I²

malign humours, vertigo, worms, agues, plague, cures green wounds, and is good against the biting of mad dogs or any other venomous creatures." In truth it was a medicine in great repute in Shakespeare's time and long afterwards.

The friar's advice to Leonato contains a thought which must often present itself to the reflecting mind of a physician facing any great new difficulty.

"*Leon.* Being that I flow in grief,
The smallest twine may lead me.
Friar. 'Tis well consented : presently away ;
For to strange sores strangely they strain the cure."
Act iv., Scene 1.

The passage is evidently copied from the sixth aphorism of Hippocrates, sec. 2. " For extreme diseases, extreme methods of cure as to restriction are most suitable." Galen and other commentators, says Dr. Adams, understood these extreme methods to apply to regimen only, but Heurnius understands them to mean, that in any dangerous diseases the physician is warranted in using " diæta quam tenuissima, pharmacia exquisita, et crudeli chirurgia." Cicero adopts the maxim, though without referring to the authority. "In adeundis periculis consuetudo imitanda medicorum est, qui leviter ægrotantes leniter curant : gravioribus autem morbis periculosas curationes et ancipites adhibere coguntur."—*De Officiis,* i., 24.

Dr. Adams remarks that our earlier modern authorities in surgery also adopted this interpretation. (*Hippocrates, of Sydenham Society.*) I have not, however, met with the doctrine in the works of Shakespeare's contemporaries, and therefore am inclined to think that he derived it from some work on the original.

Leonato, however, is not so easily led as he thinks, for he resists "moral medicine" against anger, as thoroughly as

Don John refuses its aid against sadness. The two passages are remarkable in these days when the moral treatment of mental affections is supposed to be a great novelty; days, however, in which we are proud to have succeeded in that which would have appeared impossible and absurd to our forefathers; for, although " preceptial medicine" may still be as inefficient as ever to influence frenzy, we do not now use even silken threads to restrain strong madness, any more than we use " a dark house and a whip" according to Rosalind's recipe for the treatment of lunatics.

> " Their counsel turns to passion, which before
> Would give preceptial medicine to rage,
> Fetter strong madness in a silken thread,
> Charm ache with air, and agony with words."
>
> " I pray thee, peace; I will be flesh and blood;
> For there was never yet philosopher
> That could endure the tooth-ache patiently." *Act* v., *Sc.* 1.

The merry taunt of Beatrice, that she takes pity on her lover because she heard he was " in a consumption," is the only place where Shakespeare uses this word apparently in its modern sense. Timon's use of it, " Consumptions sow in hollow bones of men," is less appropriate, and Lear's " Consumption catch thee!" is less definite. Beatrice, it appears, thought 'consumption curable.' Falstaff, however, speaks of a consumption of the purse as an incurable, though lingering, disease:—*Henry IV.*, 2*nd Part; Act* i., *Scene* 2.

> " *Beat.* I would not deny you; but, by this good day, I yield upon great persuasion; and, partly, to save your life, for I was told you were in a consumption." *Act* v., *Scene* 4.

TWELFTH NIGHT.

The opinion, that the poison of pestilence dwells in the air, is again expressed here.

> " Oh, when mine eyes did see Olivia first,
> Methought she purg'd the air of pestilence."
> *Act* i., *Scene* 1.

The "liver, brain, and heart" are described as the "three sovereign thrones" of the body—the centres of organic vitality. Cymbeline uses the thought as a simile to the men who had gained victory for him—" to you the liver, heart, and brain of Britain."

> " How will she love, when the rich golden shaft
> Hath kill'd the flock of all affections else
> That live in her! when liver, brain, and heart,
> Three sovereign thrones, are all supplied, and fill'd,
> (Her sweet perfections,) with one self king." *Act* i., *Scene* 1.

The word 'passage' is a term often used by medical men, as when they speak of the 'digestive passages.' Shakespeare also has "the hollow passage of my voice."—*Henry VI.*

> "I'll drink to her as long as there is a passage in my throat, and drink in Illyria." *Act* i., *Scene* 3.

Disordered digestion affects the sense of taste.

> "You are sick of self-love, Malvolio, and taste with a distempered appetite." *Act* i., *Scene* 5.

The *pia mater* is again mentioned here. It is used for the brain at large, as one might speak of 'a petticoat' in place of 'a woman,' an old form of periphrasis, but now-a-days more appropriate than ever. *Pia mater* is used in the same sense in *Troilus and Cressida*.

"*Clown.* Thou hast spoke for us, madonna, as if thy eldest son should be a fool: whose skull Jove cram with brains! for here comes, one of thy kin, has a most weak *pia mater*."
Act i., *Scene* 5.

Lunar influences, it appears, affect women as well as lunatics; and surely the time of the moon when Olivia was playful must have been when it was "a gracious moon."

"'Tis not that time of moon with me, to make one in so skipping a dialogue." *Act* i., *Scene* 5.

The "invisible and subtle stealth," of Viola's perfections is almost a technical term, transferred from the idea which precedes, the infection of the plague.

"How now?
Even so quickly may one catch the plague?
Methinks, I feel this youth's perfections,
With an invisible and subtle stealth,
To creep in at mine eyes." *Act* i., *Scene* 5.

The idea of infection has now become unpopular, at least in this country, partly because it has been exaggerated, partly because it often leads to inhumanity, but mostly perhaps, because in the operation of the quarantine laws it has been anti-commercial. A voice, which deserves to be listened to like that of a ministering spirit of life, has recently said: "Does not the popular idea of "infection" involve that people should take greater care of themselves than of the patient? that, for instance, it is safer not to be too much with the patient, not to attend too much to his wants? Perhaps the best illustration of the utter absurdity of this view of attending on "infectious" diseases is afforded by what

was very recently the practice, if it is not so even now, in some of the European lazarets—in which the plague-patient used to be condemned to the horrors of filth, over-crowding, and want of ventilation, while the medical attendant was ordered to examine the patient's tongue through an opera-glass, and to toss him a lancet to open his abscesses with!"
Notes on Nursing, by Florence Nightingale, p. 20.

Whether Sir Toby Belch's '*diluculo surgere*' was, or was not, derived from a medical prescription, there can be no doubt that his theory of the composition of our lives of the four elements, was adopted from the medical opinions of Shakespeare's day.

"*Sir Toby.* Approach, Sir Andrew; not to be a-bed after midnight—is to be up betimes; and *diluculo surgere*, thou know'st.

Sir Andrew. Nay, by my troth, I know not: but I know, to be up late is to be up late.

Sir To. A false conclusion: I hate it as an unfilled can: to be up after midnight, and to go to bed then, is early; so that, to go to bed after midnight, is to go to bed betimes. Do not our lives consist of the four elements?

Sir And. 'Faith, so they say; but, I think, it rather consists of eating and drinking.

Sir To. Thou art a scholar; let us therefore eat and drink.—Marian, I say!—a stoop of wine!" *Act* ii. *Scene* 3.

That our bodies consist of the four elements—fire, air, earth, and water, and that all diseases arise from derangement in the due proportion of these elements, was the pathological hypothesis of Plato. He maintained that if the element of fire was in excess, continual fever was the result; if air, predominated, quotidians; if water, tertians; and if earth, quartans were the result.—Le Clerc's *History of Medicine.*

The opinion of Hippocrates on this subject was somewhat more elaborated. He "expressed them not by the names of substances, but by proper qualities, saying hot, cold, moist, and drie, because some one of these qualities is inherent in every element—thus fire, hot and drie; aire, moist and hot; water, cold and moist; earth, cold and drie."—Ambrose Paré.

These curious opinions were substantially adopted by Galen, and embraced, on his authority, by the middle age physicians, by whom his teaching was as implicitly received as that of Aristotle by the schoolmen.

The opinion is set forth at large, in its connection with physic, in *The Arcadia* of Sir Philip Sydney.

> " O elements, by whose (men say) contention,
> Our bodies be in living power maintained,
> Was this man's death the fruit of your dissension?
> O physic's power, which (some say) hath restrained
> Approach of death, alas, thou helpest meagerly,
> When once one is for *Atropos* distrained.
> Great be physicians' brags, but aide is beggarly,
> When rooted moisture failes, or groweth drie,
> They leave off all, and say, death comes too eagerly.
> They are but words therefore that men doe buy
> Of any, since god Esculapius ceased."

The following twisted thought involves the idea that contagion is bound up with something appealing to the sense of smell; a mellifluous voice being miscalled contagious; unless one could apply one organ to the functions of another, and thus admit contagion, not through its usual portal, the nose.

" *Sir Andrew.* A mellifluous voice, as I am true knight.
Sir Toby. A contagious breath.
Sir And. Very sweet and contagious, i'faith.
Sir Toby. To hear by the nose, it is dulcet in contagion."
Act ii., Scene 3.

Maria's mischief is to be the physic of Malvolio's pride.

" I know my physic will work with him." Act ii., Scene 3.

The liver is referred to as the seat of animal desire and of passion founded upon it, the heart as that of affection, and the brain of intellect. While in this sense the Duke maintains that the liver, heart, and brain are the three sovereign thrones of love; rightly or wrongly, he locates the love of man in the liver, and that of woman in the palate, as a matter of mere taste. The word appetite seems here rather loosely used for inclination depending upon taste.

> "*Duke.* There is no woman's sides,
> Can bide the beating of so strong a passion
> As love doth give my heart: no woman's heart
> So big, to hold so much; they lack retention.
> Alas, their love may be called appetite,—
> No motion of the liver, but the palate,—
> That suffer surfeit, cloyment, and revolt;
> But mine is all as hungry as the sea,
> And can digest as much." *Act* ii., *Scene* 4.

The cause and main symptoms of chlorosis or green-sickness, the *febris amatoria*, as it has been called by medical authors, are here quaintly and touchingly described. Chlorosis under its vulgar name of green-sickness is referred to in several places. "Troubled with the green-sickness."—*Anthony and Cleopatra.* "Pox upon her green-sickness for me."—*Pericles.* "You green-sickness carrion."—*Romeo and Juliet.* In *Henry IV.*, (2nd Part,) the word is used in a manner which shewed Shakespeare's knowledge that it was a disease of women, since he distinguishes a particular instance as being the contrary. "A kind of *male* green-sickness."

> "She never told her love,
> But let concealment, like a worm i' the bud,
> Feed on her damask cheek: she pin'd in thought:
> And, with a green and yellow melancholy,
> She sat, like patience on a monument,
> Smiling at grief." *Act* ii., *Scene* 4.

Sir Toby speaking of Maria, "that wittiest piece of Eve's flesh in all Illyria," who is procuring mad excitement for him and his boon companions, says,

"Here comes the little villain; How now, *my nettle of India?*" *Act* ii., *Scene* 5.

The nettle of India is the *Cannabis Indica,* or Indian hemp, from which the natives of that country, from time immemorial, have prepared bang and various other stimulating narcotics, which produce in them a state of excitement more wild than that of the opium eater. Its use is frequently referred to in that old collection of Eastern tales, the *Arabian Nights.* The cannabis appears to have been freely used as a medicine, when Salmon wrote his *Seplasium* in 1693, in which the medicinal uses of the various parts of the plant are described. In Goodman's *Fall of Man,* exception is taken to the use of Indian drugs. "In fetching this physick, these Indian drugs, thousands do yearly endanger their lives; * * * * * * instead of natural, we make ourselves artificial stomachs, when our English bodies must prove the storehouses of Indian drugs." There was, therefore, an extensive use of Indian drugs at this time. I must, however, admit that such an interpretation of this passage would seem overstrained, and that the reading of the folio edition, "metal of India," which is gold—although less appropriate, is also more probable.

The absence of blood in the liver was the supposed property of a coward. "The liver white and pale" is Falstaff's pathological "badge of pusillanimity and cowardice." The old theory of the circulation of the blood gave rise to this opinion, which explains Sir Toby's remark on his dupe.

"*Sir Toby.* For Andrew, if he were opened, and you find so much blood in his liver as will clog the foot of a flea, I'll eat the rest of the anatomy." *Act* iii. *Scene* 2.

Obstruction to the flow of blood by pressure on the veins is thus referred at.

"This does make some obstruction in the blood, this cross-gartering." *Act* iii., *Scene* 4.

When Malvolio is definitely pronounced to be mad, Fabian says, "Carry his water to the wise woman;" and when he argues with the clown that he is not mad, the latter replies with pathological point,

"Nay, I'll ne'er believe a madman, till I see his brains."
Act iv., *Scene* 2.

When Sebastian has broken Sir Toby's head, he cannot get it plaistered, for a reason not very complimentary to one branch of the profession. The olden times were truly early times, unless, indeed, Dick Surgeon had debauched the night through, and was thus enabled to be up early, *diluculo surgere*, in Sir Toby's fashion.

"*Sir Toby.* That's all one; he has hurt me, and there's the end on't.—Sot, did'st see Dick surgeon, sot?
"*Clown.* Oh! he's drunk, Sir Toby, an hour agone; his eyes were set at eight i' the morning." *Act* v. *Scene* 1.

WINTER'S TALE.

The effect of narcotics on the judgment, by obscuring the senses, and thus closing the inlets of knowledge, is here stated.

"*Archidamus.* We will give you sleepy drinks, that your senses, unintelligent of our insufficience, may, though they cannot praise us, as little accuse us." *Act* i., *Scene* 1.

Leontes, exclaiming against what he takes to be the certain signs of his wife's unfaithfulness, makes use of a Latin term of medicine.

"Too hot, too hot:
To mingle friendship far, is mingling bloods.
I have *tremor cordis* on me;—my heart dances;
But not for joy—not joy."   *Act* i., *Scene* 2.

He speaks of his jealousy as "the infection of my brains," and refers the cause of his wife's supposed faithlessness to disease produced by the predominance of a planet, thus giving a passing allusion to astronomical medicine, once so widely received.

"Physic for't there's none;
It is a bawdy planet, that will strike
Where 'tis predominant:
* * * * *
Many thousand of us
Have the disease, and feel't not.
Have not you seen, Camillo,
(But that's past doubt: you have; or your eye-glass
Is thicker than a cuckold's horn)."   *Act.* i., *Scene* 2.

Is not the eye-glass referred to as opaque, like horn, the cornea, which in disease becomes so?

Leontes, describing his wife's desire for opportunities of indulging her supposed wickedness, makes her wish that possible witnesses may be blind, and blind of a certain disease, the name for which is now quite obsolete. In the statute of the 34 & 35 of Henry VIII., quoted at page 20, 'a pin and web in the eye' is recited among the "customable diseases" which honest persons, not being surgeons, might treat with 'herbs, roots, and waters,' with the knowledge of whose nature God had endowed them. In *King Lear, Act* iii. *Scene* 4, Edgar says of "the foul fiend Flibbertigibbet," "he gives *the web and the pin*, squints the eye, and makes the hare-lip." Mr. Knight has the following note on this passage. "Florio, in his *New World of Words*, thus interprets the Italian *catarátta*—a dimness of sight occasioned by humours hardened in the eyes, called a cataract, or *a pin and a web*."

> "*All eyes blind*
> With *the pin and web*, but theirs, theirs only,
> That would unseen be wicked?"   *Act* i., *Scene* 2.

The jealous king thinks the very life of his queen a disease, which in a bodily organ would be fatal.

> " Were my wife's liver
> Infected as her life, she would not live
> The running of one glass."   *Act* i., *Scene* 2.

His invitation to Camillo to poison his hated rival, is answered by an allusion to the use of slow and secret poison.

> " *King.*   Might'st bespice a cup,
> To give mine enemy a lasting wink;
> Which draught to me were cordial.
>   *Camillo.*   Sir, my lord,
> I could do this; and that with no rash potion,
> But with a ling'ring dram, that should not work
> Maliciously, like poison."   *Act* i., *Scene* 2.

Polixenes, surprised and wounded by the threatening aspect of his jealous friend, asks the reason of the change, which Camillo, in medical periphrasis, indicates to be jealousy.

> "There is a sickness
> Which puts some of us in distemper: but
> I cannot name the disease; and it is caught
> Of you that yet are well." *Act* i., *Scene* 2.

Polixenes, on learning that his friend accuses him of having "touched his queen forbiddenly," imprecates upon himself, if he is guilty, a pathological punishment. The connection between infection and bad smells is here more distinctly stated than in *Twelfth Night.*

> "O, then my best blood turn
> To an infected jelly: and my name
> Be yok'd with his that did betray the Best!
> Turn, then, my freshest reputation to
> A savour that may strike the dullest nostril
> Where I arrive; and my approach be shunn'd,—
> Nay, hated too, worse than the great'st infection
> That e'er was heard or read!" *Act* i., *Scene* 2.

By the old medical writers, spiders, like toads, were supposed to be poisonous. Ambrose Paré says, "The ancients have thought the bitings of spiders to be venomous. Now their poison is, therefore, thought to be cold, because the symptoms thence arising are winde in the belly, refrigerations of the extreme parts of the body, numbnesse in the bitten part, with sense of cold and shaking." The following passage would seem to call in question the truth of the old opinion; or at least to express the power of the fancy in the production of such phenomena.

> "There may be in the cup
> A spider steep'd, and one may drink; depart,

And yet partake no venom : for his knowledge
Is not infected ; but if one present
The abhorr'd ingredient to his eye, make known
How he hath drunk, he cracks his gorge, his sides,
With violent hefts :—I have drunk, and seen the spider."
Act ii., *Scene* 1.

The following is half medical, half legal, and beautifully expresses the merciful theory of the English law, that an unborn child is innocent of the guilt of its mother; a theory carried out to the reprieve of a person condemned to death if she be found pregnant, until parturition, "the law and process of great nature," has separated the innocent from the guilty life. The accused queen has been brought to be bed in prison, and Paulina claims the infant from the gaoler, who demurs to let it pass.

"*Paulina.*   You need not fear it, sir ;
The child was prisoner to the womb; and is,
By law and process of great nature, thence
Free'd and enfranchis'd :—not a party to
The anger of the king, nor guilty of,
If any be, the trespass of the queen."   *Act* ii., *Scene* 2.

When Joan of Arc is condemned to the stake as a sorceress, she claims the privilege of reprieve on this ground.

"*Pucelle.*   Will nothing turn your unrelenting hearts ?—
Then, Joan, discover thine infirmity ;
That warranteth by law to be thy privilege.—
I am with child, ye bloody homicides :
Murder not, then, the fruit within my womb,
Although ye hale me to a violent death."
First Part of Henry VI., *Act* v., *Scene* 4.

Leontes' description of the sickness of the young prince, occasioned by grief at the shame of his mother, gives exactly the symptoms to be expected in such a case of nervous disturbance in a child, arising from grief and shame.

> "*Leontes.* How does the boy?
> *Attendant.* He took good rest to night;
> 'Tis hop'd his sickness is discharg'd.
> *Leon.* To see, his nobleness!
> Conceiving the dishonour of his mother,
> He straight declin'd, droop'd, took it deeply;
> Fasten'd and fix'd the shame on't in himself;
> Threw off his spirit, his appetite, his sleep,
> And downright languish'd." *Act* ii., *Scene* 3.

Miss Nightingale, in her *Notes on Nursing*, shews how those slight noises which excite attention, are far more destructive to the repose of the patient than much louder noises which are decided and undisguised.

"I have often been surprised at the thoughtlessness, (resulting in cruelty, quite unintentionally) of friends or of doctors who will hold a long conversation just in the room or passage adjoining to the room of the patient, who is either every moment expecting them to come in, or who has just seen them, and knows they are talking about him. If he is an amiable patient, he will try to occupy his attention elsewhere, and not to listen—and this makes matters worse—for the strain upon his attention and the effort he makes are so great, that it is well if he is not worse for hours after. If it is a whispered conversation in the same room, then it is absolutely cruel, for it is impossible that the patient's attention should not be involuntarily strained to hear. Walking on tip-toe, doing anything in the room very slowly, are injurious for exactly the same reasons."—p. 26.

These remarks, which would appear as novel as they are excellent, have, however, been anticipated by Shakespeare in a passage which shews that he was keenly alive to the disturbance which these muffled sounds occasion to a restless patient. The scene is in the sick chamber of Leontes.

K

"*Attendant.*   Madam, he hath not slept to night; commanded None should come at him.
   Paulina.   Not so hot, good Sir;
I come to bring him sleep. 'Tis such as you,—
That creep like shadows by him, and do sigh
At each his needless heavings,—such as you
Nourish the cause of his awaking: I
Do come with words as med'cinal as true;
Honest as either: to purge him of that humour
That presses him from sleep."   *Act* ii., *Scene* 3.

Hermione complains at her trial of the bitter ill-usage she has received. From her child she says "I am barred like one infectious," and

"Myself, on every post,
Proclaim'd a strumpet! with immodest hatred,
The child-bed privilege denied, which 'longs
To women of all fashion, *hastily* hurried
Here to this place, i' the open air, before
I have got strength of limit."   *Act* iii., *Scene* 2.

The word 'hastily' is a reading which I venture to suggest in the place of "lastly hurried," which breaks the construction and sense of the passage, it being evident that the denial of child-bed privilege is one and the same offence against decency and humanity, as the poor woman's exposure in open court while still suffering from parturient debility.

The poor queen faints when she hears the death of her son announced, and the king, who believes "she will recover" because "her heart is but overcharged," calls for the use of restoratives.

"'Beseech you, tenderly apply to her
   Some remedies for life."   *Ibid.*

Paulina returns to the court with an exclamation which shews that Shakespeare knew the effects of tight lacing.

"*Paulina.*   Woe the while!
O, cut my lace; lest my heart, cracking it,
Break too!"   *Ibid.*

She maintains that the queen is dead, and gives four signs of death, which, if they existed, would go a long way to enforce her opinion, although it is confessedly a difficult medical problem to fix upon certain signs of the recent cessation of life. The signs she gives are the pallor, the lustreless eye, the cessation of breath, and the loss of animal heat.

"*Paulina.* I say, she's dead; I'll swear't; if word, nor oath,
Prevail not, go and see: if you can bring
Tincture, or lustre, in her lip, her eye,
Heat outwardly, or breath within." *Act* iii., *Scene* 2.

The refusal of Polixenes to grant the request of Camillo to return to Sicilia is thus expressed, "'Tis a sickness to deny thee anything, a death to grant this."

The clown describing the death of Antigonus, says "to see how the bear tore out his shoulder bone." When Autolycus feigns to have been injured by thieves, he says to the clown, "O good sir, softly good sir, I fear my shoulder-blade is out." The shoulder-blade, however, cannot be dislocated.

The malady referred to in the following passage is, no doubt, consumption, a malady to which persons of the age and sex indicated are peculiarly liable. The lines are in Perdita's beautiful description of flowers.

" Pale primroses,
That die unmarried, ere they can behold
Bright Phœbus in his strength—a malady
Most incident to maids." *Act* iv., *Scene* 3.

The enquiry of the disguised Polixenes, respecting his own condition to judge of and be present at the nuptials of his son, embraces most of the points of mental capacity which an alienist physician would raise.

K²

> "Is not your father grown incapable
> Of reasonable affairs? Is he not stupid
> With age, and altering rheums?—Can he speak? hear?
> Know man from man? dispute his own estate?
> Lies he not bed-rid? And again does nothing,
> But what he did being childish?"
> *Act* iv., *Scene* 3.

When Autolycus attempts to frighten the clown by a description of the tortures he is to endure, he confounds *aqua vitæ* with hot infusions; a form of speech in accordance with a character who spake no more truth than what was needful to pass deception current, and was only honest by accident.

> "He has a son, who shall be flayed alive; then, 'nointed over with honey, set on the head of a wasp's nest; then stand, till he be three quarters and a dram dead: then recovered again with aqua-vitæ, or some other hot infusion." *Act* iv., *Scene* 3.

KING JOHN.

The pulsation of the blood in the temporal arteries and the life of the blood are referred to as follows:

> "How comes it then, that thou art called a king,
> When living blood doth in these temples beat,
> Which owe the crown that thou o'ermasterest?"
> *Act* ii. *Scene* 1.

Pandulph also speaks of the life of the blood in the veins.

> "That whiles warm life plays in that infant's veins."
> *Act* iii. *Scene* 4.

The idea of life residing in the blood is again and still more pointedly referred to by Prince Henry, when describing the effects of poison on the wretched king.

> " The life of all his blood
> Is touch'd corruptibly."   *Act* v. *Scene* 7.

The theory of 'the life of the blood' is older than Hippocrates, for it is found in the writings of Moses: "the life of the flesh is in the blood."—*Levit.* xvii. 11.

The notion that the blood may be thickened, turned to jelly, by emotional influences, is stated by Polixenes. The expression, that the blood runs trickling up and down the veins, seems to point to the thought that there is a flux and reflux of the current. It is in John's temptation of Hubert to murder Arthur.

> " Or if that surly spirit, melancholy,
> Had bak'd thy blood, and made it heavy, thick,
> (Which, else, runs trickling up and down the veins,
> Making that idiot, laughter, keep men's eyes,
> And strain their cheeks to idle merriment,
> A passion hateful to my purposes.) "   *Act* iii. *Scene* 3.

Congenital defects are catalogued by Constance, as idiocy, deformity, and as the marks prodigious despised in nativity, which are named by Oberon.

> " *Constance.* If thou, that bid'st me be content, wert grim,
> Ugly, and sland'rous to thy mother's womb,
> Full of unpleasing blots, and sightless stains,
> Lame, foolish, crooked, swart, prodigious,
> Patch'd with foul moles and eye-offending marks,
> I would not care, I then would be content;
> For then I should not love thee; no, nor thou
> Become thy great birth, nor deserve a crown."
>   *Act* iii. *Scene* 1.

The transition in Constance of passionate excitement

into acute mania has been traced in the *Psychology of Shakespeare*, and the only remarks needful in this place are, that this tempest of passion prevailed in a sickly body,

"For I am sick, and capable of fears." *Act* iii. *Scene* 1.

And that the acute mania which succeeded is represented to have been fatal.

"The Lady Constance in a frenzy died." *Act* iv. *Scene* 2.

This passage unquestionably refers to the medical doctrine of crises which was universally prevalent in Shakespeare's time.

"*Pandulph.* Before the curing of a strong disease,
Even in the instant of repair and health,
The fit is strongest; evils, that take leave,
On their departure most of all shew evil." *Act* iii. *Scene* 4.

When Hubert communicates to Arthur his horrible commission to burn out both his eyes, Arthur pleads the exquisite sensitiveness of the organ :

"Have you the heart? When your head did but ache,
I knit my hand-kercher about your brows.
* * * * *
Is there no remedy?
Hubert.   None, but to lose your eyes.
Arthur. O Heaven! that there were but a mote in yours,
A grain, a dust, a gnat, a wandering hair,—
Any annoyance in that precious sense !
Then, feeling what small things are boist'rous there,
Your vile intent must needs seem horrible." *Act* iv. *Scene* 1.

When the peers accuse King John of the Prince's death, he says,

"Why do you bend such solemn brows on me?
Think you, I bear the solemn shears of destiny?
Have I commandment of the pulse of life?"
Act iv. *Scene* 2.

The maturation and discharge of an abscess appear to be the basis of the simile here employed.

> "*Salisbury.* His passion is so ripe it needs must break.
> *Pembroke.* And when it breaks, I fear, will issue thence
> The foul corruption of a sweet child's death."
> Act iv. Scene 2.

The confusion of the brain-functions, in the first moments of drowning, seems referred to by John.

> "Bear with me, cousin; for I was amaz'd
> Under the tide: but now I breathe again
> Aloft the flood." Act iv. Scene 2.

John thus appeals to Pandulph for aid when his discontented Barons league themselves against him with the enemy.

> "This inundation of mistemper'd humour
> Rests by you only to be qualified.
> Then pause not; for the present time's so sick,
> That present medicine must be minister'd,
> Or overthrow incurable ensues." Act v. Scene 1.

The same medical form of illustration is adopted by Salisbury, one of the revolted peers.

> "I am not glad that such a sore of time
> Should seek a plaster by contemn'd revolt,
> And heal the inveterate canker of one wound
> By making many.   *   *   *
> But such is the infection of the time,
> That, for the health and physic of our right,
> We cannot deal but with the very hand
> Of stern injustice and confused wrong." Act v. Scene 2.

King John is driven from the field of battle by illness, possibly by the accession of a fit of ague superinduced only by the breath of the Lincolnshire fens; since the fever, a common term for ague, has troubled him long.

> "*K. John.* This fever, that hath troubled me so long,
> Lies heavy on me; O, my heart is sick! * *

> Ah, me! this tyrant fever burns me up,
> And will not let me welcome this good news.—
> Set on toward Swinstead: to my litter straight;
> Weakness possesseth me, and I am faint." *Act* v. *Scene* 3.

The description of death from hœmorrhage is quaintly given by the wounded Melun.

> " Have I not hideous death within my view,
> Retaining but a quantity of life,
> Which bleeds away, even as a form of wax
> Resolveth from his figure 'gainst the fire ? "
> *Act* v. *Scene* 4.

He did not, however, die thus, if Salisbury's observation were correct. The eye would become dim under the exhaustion of hœmorrhage, while it would be bright under "cruel pangs."

> " For I do see the cruel pangs of death
> Bright in thine eye." *Act* v. *Scene* 4.

The whole of the poison scene is very remarkable. The Bastard exhorts Hubert to tell him the horrible news without delay or disguise.

> "Show me the very wound of this ill news;
> I am no woman, I'll not swoon at it.
>   *Hubert.* The king, I fear, is poison'd by a monk:
> I left him almost speechless.   *   *   *
>   *Bastard.* How did he take it? Who did taste to him?
>   *Hub.* A monk, I tell you; a resolved villain,
> Whose bowels suddenly burst out: the king
> Yet speaks, and peradventure may recover." *Act* v. *Scene* 6.

In the olden days, the fear of poison was so prevalent that great men had all their food tasted by persons who were supposed to have made themselves acquainted with its wholesomeness. This plan, however, could not afford security when the taster was ready to sacrifice his own life. The ideas which prevailed in Shakespeare's time on the subject of poisons, both among the ignorant and learned, were strangely chimerical; the description of this death by poison is, however, as accurate as it is fearful; the only point of error being in Hubert's description of the poison upon the monk "whose bowels suddenly burst out." No poison known to modern science would produce such an effect. It is, however, quite consistent with the old opinion, both medical and general, which attributed to poison, swelling and bursting of the body, as one of its effects.

> "*P. Henry.* It is too late; the life of all his blood
> Is touch'd corruptibly; and his pure brain
> (Which some suppose the soul's frail dwelling house,)
> Doth, by the idle comments that it makes,
> Foretell the ending of mortality.
>   *Pembroke.* His highness yet doth speak; and holds belief,
> That, being brought into the open air,
> It would allay the burning quality
> Of that fell poison which assaileth him.
>   *P. Henry.* Let him be brought into the orchard here.—
> Doth he still rage?
>   *Pem.*   He is more patient
> Than when you left him; even now he sung.
>   *P. Henry.* O, vanity of sickness! fierce extremes,
> In their continuance, will not feel themselves.
> Death, having prey'd upon the outward parts,
> Leaves them insensible: and his siege is now
> Against the mind, the which he pricks and wounds
> With many legions of strange fantasies;
> Which, in their throng and press to that last hold,
> Confound themselves. 'Tis strange, that death should sing."
>   *Act* v. *Scene* 7.

The observations and theories included in the above quotation are remarkable. The life of the blood, the cerebral localization of the mental functions, the cessation of bodily pain at a certain stage of the operation of corrosive poison, when death, "having preyed upon the outward parts, leaves them insensible," the confused throng of thoughts which characterize some forms of delirium, all these points of physiological observation are wonderfully conceived and expressed.

The supervention of delirium, upon the cessation of pain in the outward parts, was noted and expressed by Hippocrates in the sixth aphorism, section 2, " Persons who have a painful affection of any part of the body, and are in a great measure insensible of pain, are disordered in intellect."

When John is brought into the orchard, the throng and press of strange fantasies have ceased to confound themselves. He does not rage as he has done before, but expresses himself again sensible of suffering, in similes of terrible power.

It would perhaps, however, have been more consistent with the strict probability of the course of events, if the cessation of what may be called traumatic delirium, and the restoration of painful sensation, had not been represented; for when death, having preyed upon the outward parts, lays his siege against the mind, the delirium generally continues to the end.

> "*King John.* Ay, marry, now my soul hath elbow room;
> It would not out at windows, nor at doors.
> There is so hot a summer in my bosom,
> That all my bowels crumble up to dust:
> I am a scribbled form, drawn with a pen
> Upon a parchment; and against this fire
> Do I shrink up.
>   *Prince Henry.* How fares your majesty?
>   *K. John.* Poison'd,—ill-fare;—dead, forsook, cast off:
> And none of you will bid the winter come,
> To thrust his icy fingers in my maw;
> Nor let my kingdom's rivers take their course
> Through my burn'd bosom; nor entreat the north
> To make his bleak winds kiss my parched lips,
> And comfort me with cold:—I do not ask you much;
> I beg cold comfort; and you are so strait,
> And so ungrateful, you deny me that.

P. Henry.   O, that there were some virtue in my tears,
That might relieve you!
   K. John.   The salt in them is hot.—
Within me is a hell; and there the poison
Is, as a fiend, confin'd to tyrannize
On unreprievable condemned blood.
                              [*Enter the* BASTARD.
   Bast.   O, I am scalded with my violent motion,
And spleen of speed to see your majesty.
   K. John.   O cousin, thou art come to set mine eye:
The tackle of my heart is crack'd and burnt;
And all the shrouds, wherewith my life should sail,
Are turned to one thread, one little hair:
My heart hath one poor string to stay it by,
Which holds but till thy news be utter'd:
And then all this thou see'st, is but a clod,
And module of confounded royalty."   *Act* v. *Scene* 7.

Where elsewhere is to be found a description so terrible, and yet so graphic, of the agonies of death from corrosive poison!

KING RICHARD II.

In the following passage the quibble upon the two senses of the word choler, viz., anger and bile, is followed up by a reference to its medical treatment, by blood-letting, and to the too deep incision which it was possible to make in the operation. The times of the year, too, for bleeding are referred to; the old doctors thinking it sanatory to bleed in the spring and fall, but avoiding the lancet during the intermediate months.

> "*K. Richard.* Wrath-kindled gentlemen, be rul'd by me;
> Let's purge this choler without letting blood:
> This we prescribe, though no physician;
> Deep malice makes too deep incision;
> Forget, forgive; conclude, and be agreed:
> Our doctors say, this is no month to bleed." *Act* i., *Scene* 1.

The forty-seventh aphorism of Hippocrates, section 6, is that "Persons who are benefited by venesection or purging should be bled or purged in the spring."

Here also is authority for the opinion from one of Shakespeare's century, though rather before his time.

> "Concernynge lettynge of bloudde, these thynges folowynge, wolde be had in contynuall remembraunce, and be afore thought on.—The tyme of the yere must be speciallye marked. For in the begynnynge of sprynge tyme, it is beste lettynge of bloudde, as Oribasius saythe, and so doth continue, after the opinyon of Arnolde, unto the eyght calendes of June. Ætius affirmeth, that in wynter, or in a colde countrey, or where the persone is of a very colde nature, the veynes shuld not be opened."—*The Castell of Helthe*, of Syr Thomas Elyot, Knyght, A.D., 1541, page 62.

In Homer's surgery, the rust of the spear which inflicted the wound was thought its appropriate remedy. See also the more distinct statement of the opinion in *Henry VI., Second Part.*

> "I am disgrac'd, impeach'd, and baffled here;
> Pierc'd to the soul with slander's venom'd spear,
> The which no balm can cure, but his heart-blood
> Which breath'd this poison." *Act* i., *Scene* 1.

A medical truth, known to many a man with a weak stomach, is that

> "Things sweet to taste prove in digestion sour."
> *Act* i., *Scene* 3.

Gaunt's persuasion to contentment in exile, again records the atmospheric theory of pestilence, and refers to the custom, then prevalent, of persons attempting to avoid the pestilence, by forsaking infected localities. Let those who would wish to know the extent to which this desertion was carried, read the introduction to the *Decameron*, which describes a great city thus converted into a desert.

"Suppose
Devouring pestilence hangs in our air,
And thou art flying to a fresher clime." *Act* i., *Scene* 3.

Here is a surgical passage again recognizing the important difference between a clean cut wound, and one in which the tissues are bruised and lacerated.

" Fell sorrow's tooth doth never rankle more,
Than when it bites but lanceth not the sore."
Act i., *Scene* 3.

The interview between the king and aged Gaunt, "grievous sick," "suddenly taken," is scarcely medical, although Gaunt plays upon medical similes : thus he reminds the king,

" Ill in myself to see, and in thee seeing ill.
Thy death-bed is no lesser than the land,
Wherein thou liest in reputation sick ;
And thou, too careless patient as thou art,
Commit'st thy anointed body to the cure
Of those physicians that first wounded thee."
Act ii., *Scene* 1.

The petulant king scarcely accords the privilege to the dying man of permission to speak the unwelcome truth.

" *K. Richard.* And thou a lunatic lean-witted fool,
Presuming on an ague's privilege,
Dar'st with thy frozen admonition
Make pale our cheek." *Act* ii., *Scene* 1.

York, to dissuade the king from pardoning an offender, employs a simile which would scarcely have been either thought of, or understood, by a person who had not some knowledge of the science of surgery.

> "This fester'd joint cut off, the rest rests sound;
> This, let alone, will all the rest confound."
> Act v., Scene 3.

It at once suggests the thought of some joint injured by gun-shot wound, or by some accident, and undergoing those suppurative changes, which would prove fatal unless amputation were resorted to.

A transposition of lines in the following passage would reunite the different parts of each simile, and make the reading far more simple and emphatic. Surely it stands in its present confusion by the printer's error. The inheritance of blood was, of old, the universal faith; but science now points to the far more important inheritance of nerve.

> "One vial full of Edward's sacred blood,—
> One flourishing branch of his most royal root,—
> Is crack'd, and all the precious liquor spilt;
> Is hack'd down, and his summer leaves all vaded."

Read instead,—

> "One vial full of Edward's sacred blood,—
> Is crack'd, and all the precious liquor spilt;
> One flourishing branch of his most royal root,—
> Is hack'd down, and his summer leaves all vaded."
> Act i., Scene 2.

The decent habits of the table which prevail in our time afford few examples of an accident to which men, from whom the restraints of decency are removed, are greatly liable. Thus in lunatic asylums, the accident referred to is of frequent occurrence, and when its effects are aggravated by paralysis, it is not unfrequently fatal.

> "With eager feeding, food doth choke the feeder."
> Act ii., Scene 1.

The *cordon sanitaire* of the quarantine laws appears to be

referred to as one of the advantages attributed to the insular position of this country.

> "This fortress, built by nature for herself,
> Against infection from the hand of war." *Act* ii., *Scene* 1.

The mystical connection between the soul and the brain is of a kind which demands the aid of allegory, that the idea may in any way be grasped, and, perhaps, it has never been better put than in the following passage. It will be remarked, however, that the soul divides with the material organ the honour of being the source of thought, and that it is represented as something distinct from thought.

> "My brain I'll prove the female to my soul;
> My soul, the father: and these two beget
> A generation of still-breeding thoughts." *Act* v., *Scene* 5.

This passage is interesting in connexion with the employment of music to effect the restoration of Lear from his madness, and the old belief, not yet quite exploded, that the regulated succession of sweet sounds is a powerful agent in the induction of a well-regulated succession of ideas.

> "This music mads me—let it sound no more;
> For, though it have holpe madmen to their wits,
> In me it seems it will make wise men mad."
> *Act* v., *Scene* 5.

KING HENRY IV. First Part.

Hotspur's half-humourous, half-splenetic, description of the fop who demanded his Scotch prisoners, contains several points of medical interest. The description of his own state, when the fight was done, is of this nature:

> " When I was dry with rage and extreme toil,
> Breathless and faint, leaning upon my sword,
> *   *   *   *   *   *
> I then, all smarting, with my wounds being cold."
> Act i., Scene 3.

The absence of pain from wounds received in battle so long as the excitement continues, is a well known fact; but when the excitement ceases, the pain is felt, and the condition here described occurs.

The source of the material for the courtly messenger's recipe,

> " The sovereign'st thing on earth
> Was parmaceti for an inward bruise,"   Act i. Scene 3.

seems to have been rather a mystery. Dr. Salmon says of spermaceti, or parmacety, that it is found in Egypt, and in the river Nilus; " what it is, is scarcely determined; some think it a kind of bitumen made of a sulphurous earth and salt; others say it is the seed of the whale, or, at least, taken out of some part of the whale," which latter opinion he believes to be probably true, as gentlemen had told him that they had taken it out of the head of the whale; an assertion, we now know to be more than probably true. Among its effects, Salmon says, " it is said to be anodyne, and some physicians affirm that it resolves coagulated blood;" hence its supposed efficacy on an inward bruise.

Woodall, in the work before quoted, affirms this especial virtue, almost in the words of Shakespeare. "*Sperma Ceti*, or *Spuma Maris*, or the spawne of the whale, is sowre in taste, spongie and white in shew, unsavoury in smell, and weighty, having a sharp quality: It is of a cold faculty, cleanseth and digesteth, and is sometimes used of women to cleare the skin from spots and morphew [ringworm]: *It is good also against bruises inwardly*, taken with the former, namely *Mummia*, and also outwardly warme, to anoint the parts contused therewith, and a *Paracelsus emplaister*, or of *Pix Grœcum*, put thereon."

The sweet-smelling ambassador did not make so good a shot in his assertion, that saltpetre was digged "out of the bowels of the harmless earth."

This gentleman's foppish habits afford occasion for a reference to the remarkable narcotic newly introduced in Shakespeare's time.

" 'Twixt his finger and his thumb he held
A pouncet-box, which ever and anon
He gave his nose, and took't away again;
Who, therewith angry, when it next came there,
Took it in snuff."   *Act* i., *Scene* 3.

It is singular that this is the only allusion, (if indeed it be one,) made to tobacco throughout the plays. A contemporary poet calls it divine tobacco, "whether it divine tobacco were," and describes the application of its juice to a wound.—*Fairie Queen*, Book iii., Chapter 5.

A reasonable theory of earthquakes is thus illustrated by a medical simile.

L

> "Diseased nature oftentimes breaks forth
> In strange eruptions: oft the teeming earth
> Is with a kind of cholic pinch'd and vex'd
> By the imprisoning of unruly wind
> Within her womb; which, for enlargement striving,
> Shakes the old beldame earth, and topples down
> Steeples, and moss-grown towers." *Act* iii. *Scene* 1.

The healing influence of good deeds to the chronic ulcer of a dissolute life is thus invoked:

> "The which if He be pleas'd I shall perform,
> I do beseech your majesty, may salve
> The long-grown wounds of my intemperance."
> *Act* iii. *Scene* 2.

Hotspur's interruption to Vernon's praises of Prince Henry conveys a medical fact, which, in these anti-aguish days of agricultural improvement, would scarce be thought of, in opposition to the proverbial value of a peck of March dust.

> "*Hotspur.* No more, no more; worse than the sun in March, This praise doth nourish agues." *Act* iv. *Scene* 1.

The main exigencies of military surgery are referred to as the setting of bones and the removal of the pain of wounds.

> "Honour pricks me on. Yes, but how if honour prick me off when I come on? How then? Can honour set to a leg? No. Or an arm? No. Or take away the grief of a wound? No. Honour hath no skill in surgery, then? No." *Act* v. *Scene* 1.

The following passage indicates the most ready test of hallucination, namely, an appeal to the testimony of another sense. Fancy may deceive the sight, but will scarcely play pranks, at the same time, upon other senses. Banquo, seen only by Macbeth, is silent; it is an hallucination. The ghosts of Hamlet's father and of Julius Cæsar appear to eye and ear, and are recognized as the representatives of the old ghost faith, not as errors of sense.

"Art thou alive? or is it phantasy
That plays upon our eye-sight? I pr'ythee, speak;"
We will not trust our eyes without our ears:
Thou art not what thou seem'st." *Act* v. *Scene* 4.

The science of becoming lean could scarcely be embodied in a more pithy and practical resolution, than

"If I do grow great, I'll grow less; for I'll purge, and leave sack, and live cleanly, as a nobleman should do." *Act* v. *Scene* 4.

One would almost think that Shakespeare was also acquainted with the anatomy of obesity, and that he had seen the midriff pressed upwards by the fat-laden organs of the abdomen, and encroaching upon that cavity in which the heart beats, and in which old opinions located the nobler attributes of man.

"Sirrah, there's no room for faith, truth, nor honesty, in this bosom of thine; it is all filled up with guts and midriff."
Act iii., *Scene* 3.

KING HENRY IV. Second Part.

Northumberland, whom illness has prevented from taking part in Shrewsbury fight, when he hears from Mortimer the news of his son's death and the defeat of his army, commences his reply with the medical axiom, *ubi virus ibi vertus*, and describes the effect of delirium in restoring temporary strength to a fever-weakened patient.

> "In poison there is physic; and these news,
> Having been well that would have made me sick,
> Being sick, have in some measure made me well:
> And as the wretch, whose fever-weaken'd joints,
> Like strengthless hinges, buckle under life,
> Impatient of his fit, breaks like a fire
> Out of his keeper's arms; even so my limbs,
> Weaken'd with grief, being now enrag'd with grief,
> Are thrice themselves." *Act* i., *Scene* 1.

His friends exhort him to check this "stormy passion," which, if indulged, must destroy his health.

> "*Morton.* The lives of all your loving 'complices
> Lean on your health; the which, if you give o'er
> To stormy passion, must perforce decay." *Act* i., *Scene* 1.

Mortimer accounts for the defeat of the rebel army, by the want of good-will to their cause among the soldiers. Queasiness, 'a tendency to nausea,' constrained by the will, is the most fitting expression which could be found, for the sense of disgusted taste caused by medicine.

> "And they did fight with queasiness, constrain'd,
> As men drink potions." *Act* i., *Scene* 1.

Laughter-loving and laughter-moving Sir John appears to

have suffered a little in health by the Shrewsbury campaign. He enquires of that "whoreson mandrake" of a page, whom the Prince hath given him as a foil,

"*Falstaff.* Sirrah, you giant, what says the doctor to my water?
Page. He said, sir, the water itself was a good healthy water: but, for the party that owed it, he might have more diseases than he knew for." *Act* i., *Scene* 2.

A good honest opinion this, though quite at variance with the doctrines of the old water-doctors, who pretended to recognise all diseases from the aspects of this excrement. Sir John has fallen upon evil times, his tailor will not trust him and demands security, "I had as lief they put rat's-bane in my mouth, as offer to stop it with security." He is in ill health, and in ill credit, "can get no remedy against this consumption of the purse, borrowing only lingers and lingers it out, but the disease is incurable." In this frame of mind, he encounters the chief justice, who has good cause and ample power to crush him, but Gascoyne, who had the courage to imprison the Prince of Wales, was magnanimously slow to take offence. Falstaff evidently knows this well, and has taken accurate guage of his man; he pretends to sympathise with his lordship on his supposed illness: "I am glad to see your lordship abroad; I heard say your lordship was sick; I hope your lordship goes abroad by advice; I most humbly beseech your lordship to have a reverend care of your health." This put-off to the subject of the chief justice's enquiry, the night's exploit on Gadshill, not answering its purpose, Falstaff struggles hard to divert attention to the king's illness, which he describes as an apoplexy, and correctly refers to some of its causes and earlier symptoms, lethargic feelings, tingling sensations, deafness.

"*Fal.* And I hear, moreover, his highness is fallen into this whoreson apoplexy."

"This apoplexy is, as I take it, a kind of lethargy; a kind of sleeping in the blood, a whoreson tingling."

"It hath its original from much grief; from study, and perturbation of the brain: I have read the cause of his effects in Galen; it is a kind of deafness." *Act* i., *Scene* 2.

A wilful deafness on Sir John's part, for which the chief justice proposes to be his physician. The patient, however, objects:

"Your lordship may minister the potion of imprisonment to me, in respect to poverty; but how I should be your patient to follow your prescriptions, the wise may make some dram of a scruple, or indeed a scruple itself." *Act* i., *Scene* 2.

The chief justice, "loath to gall a new healed wound," lets the fat reprobate off very easily. But when he assumes the privileges of youth, and attributes to his opponent the harshness of age, "you measure the heat of our livers with the bitterness of your galls," the reverend man of law shews that he can play a good stick in the duello of controversy; and thus holds a glass up to the hoary debauchee, in which he may contemplate the physical defects of age.

"*Chief Justice.* Do you set down your name in the scroll of youth, that are written down old with all the characters of age? Have you not a moist eye, a dry hand, a yellow cheek, a white beard, a decreasing leg, an increasing belly? Is not your voice broken? your wind short? your chin double? your wit single? and every part about you blasted with antiquity? and will you yet call yourself young? Fie, fie, fie, Sir John." *Act* i., *Scene* 2.

Falstaff exclaims against fighting on a hot day, and wishes he may "never spit white again," should it so happen. The colour of the spittle was, with the medical men of olden times, an important point of diagnosis, especially of temperaments.

With admirable effrontery, Falstaff concludes the war of words by asking the great law lord to lend him a thousand pounds, and he comments on the refusal as an old physician might do.

"A man can no more separate age and covetousness, than he can part young limbs and lechery; but the gout galls the one, and the pox pinches the other; and so both the degrees prevent my curses."
Act i., *Scene* 2.

Sir John indeed speaks feelingly on this point.

"A pox of this gout! or, a gout of this pox!—for the one or the other plays the rogue with my great toe. It is no matter, if I do halt; I have the wars for my colour, and my pension shall seem the more reasonable. A good wit will make use of any thing; I will turn diseases to commodity." *Act* i., *Scene* 2.

The force of imagination in madness is referred to by Lord Bardolph, in his account of Hotspur's defeat, who

"With great imagination,
Proper to madmen, led his powers to death,
And, winking, leap'd into destruction." *Act* i., *Scene* 3.

The archbishop's bitter reproach on the fickleness of popular favour alludes to surfeit from greedy feeding, and to vomiting wilfully provoked, as by tickling the fauces, to relieve the overloaded stomach.

"The commonwealth is sick of their own choice;
Their over-greedy love hath surfeited:—
An habitation giddy and unsure
Hath he that buildeth on the vulgar heart.
O, thou fond many; with what loud applause
Didst thou beat heaven with blessing Bolingbroke,
Before he was what thou wouldst have him be!
And being now trimm'd in thine own desires,
Thou, beastly feeder, art so full of him,
That thou provok'st thyself to cast him up.
So, so, thou common dog, didst thou disgorge
Thy glutton bosom of the royal Richard;
And now thou wouldst eat thy dead vomit up."
Act i., *Scene* 3.

The fat hostess, of the immortal Boar's Head, has sundry medical opinions. When she reminds Sir John of his oath, sworn " upon a parcel gilt goblet," she endeavours to help his recollection by the association of the idea with his head at that time broken, and with gossip Quickly's dish of prawns, which "were ill for a green wound."

Further on, she 'affects to nod' even in the technical language of the profession, though she uses the terms most malapropriately. Doll Tear-sheet is suffering, probably from the effects of a debauch, when the sympathising hostess attempts to console and cheer her, feeling her pulse, and pronouncing on the symptoms.

" *Hostess.* I'faith, sweetheart, methinks now you are in an excellent good temperality: your pulsidge beats as extraordinarily as heart would desire; and your colour, I warrant you, is as red as any rose. But, you have drunk too much canaries; and that's a marvellous searching wine, and it perfumes the blood ere one can say, What's this? How do you now?
Doll Tearsheet. Better than I was. Hem!
Host. Why, that's well said; a good heart's worth gold. Look, here comes Sir John.
Fal. When Arthur first in court—Empty the jordan—*And was a worthy king.* How now, Mistress Doll?
Host. Sick of a calm; yea, good sooth." *Act* ii., *Scene* 4.

'Temperality,' no doubt, means 'temperature,' and pulsidge of course, means pulse, but how canaries 'perfumes' the blood is not quite so evident. The probable meaning is that it "inflames" the blood. The 'calm' of which Doll was sick was, evidently, a qualm, though Falstaff wilfully misunderstands it in the quieter sense. The word 'jordan,' which occurs twice in this play, reminds one that Chaucer distinguishes it from the urinal.

Prince Henry gives the best simile of Falstaff of which

medicine is capable; namely a wen, a monstrous fatty tumour.

"I do allow this wen to be as familiar with me as my dog."
Act ii., *Scene* 2.

This is far better than the one he applies to the same person in the *First part of Henry IV.*, "Thou swollen parcel of dropsies," which evidently cannot hold water as a simile, and is a mere vituperative untruth.

The distinction between rank and dangerous diseases, and slighter indispositions, is freely drawn in the dialogue between the king and Warwick. The 'good advice,' which in the mere distemperature of the body may render much medicine needless, would appear to mean what modern physicians call 'regimen.'

"*K. Henry.* Have you read o'er the letters that I sent you?
Warwick. We have, my liege.
K. Hen. Then you perceive, the body of our kingdom
How foul it is; what rank diseases grow,
And with what danger, near the heart of it.
War. It is but as a body yet distemper'd;
Which to his former strength may be restor'd,
With good advice, and little medicine:—
My lord Northumberland will soon be cool'd."
Act iii., *Scene* 1.

Is the formation of abscess referred to in Richard's prophecy?

"The time will come, that foul sin, gathering head,
Shall break into corruption." *Act* iii., *Scene* 1.

The archbishop's reasons for joining the insurrection are couched in purely medical forms of thought. The state of the times is as a burning fever brought on by surfeiting; infectious also, and to be cured only by loss of blood. This is the prescription; but the hand of the ecclesiastic is not ready to carry it into effect, even under the figurative character of national physician. *Ecclesia abhorret a sanguine,* and therefore the priest comforts himself with the idea that he joins the rebels only for the purpose of dieting the rankness and of purging the obstructions of the social state. Though the argument may be illogical, the distinction drawn is very curious from our point of view.

> "*Archbishop.*   Wherefore do I this? so the question stands.
> Briefly to this end. We are all diseas'd;
> And, with our surfeiting, and wanton hours,
> Have brought ourselves into a burning fever,
> And we must bleed for it : of which disease
> Our late king, Richard, being infected, died.
> But, my most noble lord of Westmoreland,
> I take not on me here as a physician;
> Nor do I, as an enemy to peace,
> Troop in the throngs of military men :
> But rather shew a while like fearful war,
> To diet rank minds, sick of happiness;
> And purge the obstructions, which begin to stop
> Our very veins of life!"   *Act* iv., *Scene* 1.

In the following passage the same speaker refers to the surgical fact, that a broken bone after union becomes stronger than before.

> "*Archbishop.*   'Tis very true :—
> And therefore be assur'd, my good lord marshal,
> If we do now make our atonement well,
> Our peace will, like a broken limb united,
> Grow stronger for the breaking."   *Act* iv., *Scene* 1.

Falstaff's physiological essay on the character of Prince John is as replete with old medical theory as it is with wit.

> "*Falstaff.*   Good faith, this same young sober-blooded boy doth not love me : nor a man cannot make him laugh;—but that's no marvel, he drinks no wine. There's never any of these demure boys come to any proof; for thin drink doth so over-cool their blood, and

making many fish-meals, that they fall into *a kind of male green sickness;* and then, when they marry, they get wenches: they are generally fools and cowards;—which some of us should be too, but for inflammation. A good sherris-sack hath a two-fold operation in it. *It ascends me into the brain; dries me there all the foolish and dull and crudy vapours which environ it*: makes it apprehensive, quick, forgetive, full of nimble, fiery, and delectable shapes; which deliver'd o'er to the voice (the tongue), which is the birth, becomes excellent wit. The second property of your excellent sherris is,— *the warming of the blood; which, before cold and settled, left the liver white and pale,* which is the badge of pusillanimity and cowardice: but the sherris warms it, and *makes it course from the inwards to the parts extreme.* It illumineth the face; which as a beacon gives warning to all the rest of this little kingdom, man, to arm: and then *the vital commoners, and inland petty spirits, muster me all to their captain, the heart;* who, great and puffed up with his retinue, doth any deed of courage; and this valour comes of sherris: So that skill in the weapon is nothing without sack; for that sets it a-work: and learning, a mere hoard of gold kept by a devil, till sack commences it, and sets it in act and use. Hereof comes it, that Prince Harry is valiant: for the cold blood he did naturally inherit of his father, he hath, like lean, sterile, and bare land, manured, husbanded, and tilled, with excellent endeavour of drinking good, and good store of fertile sherris; that he is become very hot and valiant. If I had a thousand sons, the first principle I would teach them, should be,—to forswear thin potations, and addict themselves to sack." *Act* iv., *Scene* 3.

Thin drink and fish meals over-cool the blood, and occasion 'a kind of male green sickness'. The physiology of this opinion is unquestionably sound, for a low diet would, above all things, tend to impoverish the blood. The phrase ' a kind of male green sickness' obviously indicates that Shakespeare knew that green sickness, *chlorosis,* was a disease almost peculiar to women. He refers to its ordinary form in that most poetic passage of *Twelfth Night,* as " a green and yellow melancholy," which fed on the damask cheek of the love-sick virgin.

The remarkable medical word, inflammation, which was coined upon a false theory of the phenomena of that abnormal state of nutrition, which still, both in medical and common parlance, are expressed by this term, would appear to have been employed by Shakespeare to designate merely a state of excitement from strong drink. It is, indeed, the only place in which Shakespeare makes use of the word, and I am not aware that others have employed it in a non-medical sense. Milton uses it in the strictly medical sense.

> " Dire inflammation, which no cooling herb,
> Nor medicinal liquor can assuage."   *Samson Agonistes.*

The first of the two-fold operations of sack is founded upon a singular theory of Hippocrates, which will be best given in this place, by a quotation from the learned *History of Physic*, by Daniel Le Clerc, written in Shakespeare's century.

"*Of the Brain.* The brain is reckoned by Hippocrates among the glands, because it appeared to him of the same nature, being white, fryable, and spongy, as they were. And he believed, that the brain sucked up the superfluous humours of the body, like the other glands, which being all of a spongy nature, imbibe, says he, moisture easily.

" But there is this further of the brain ; that the head being hollow and round, draws incessantly, like a sort of cupping-glass, the moisture from the rest of the body, which rises in a vapour ; after which, it being over-charged, it sends it down to the lower parts, especially the glands, from whence come defluxions and catarrhs.

" Hippocrates, in some other places, makes the brain the seat of wisdom and understanding, although, as we have seen before, he lodges the soul, which is the same thing with the understanding, in the left ventricle of the heart."

The crudy vapours which environ the brain are thus explained as the moisture which rises to this organ "in the form of a vapour," and which being of a watery nature from thin potations, Sir John would, no doubt, think foolish, dull and crude, in comparison with the more stimulating and generous exhalations of a good 'sherris sack.' It will be observed that Shakespeare follows Hippocrates in attributing not only this humoral function, but also the intellectual function to the cerebral organ, or rather, in confounding the two together.

"The second property of your excellent sherris" has reference to another theory of Hippocrates, namely, that the veins, which were thought the only blood-vessels, had their origin in the liver. The Father of Medicine maintained that they come from the liver; the arteries from the heart. It appears, however, that in different parts of his works he expressed different opinions on the relation existing between the veins and the heart. The origin of the veins, however, in the liver is at least in one place decidedly expressed by him, and was by his successors developed into an article of physiological faith, which continued to be held even to Harvey's times. The following passage, from the biography attached to the Sydenham Society's edition of the *Works of Harvey*, states this fact very clearly.

"In ancient times, indeed, the veins were regarded, as they are esteemed by the vulgar at the present hour, as the principal vessels of the body; they only were once believed to contain true blood; the arteries were held to contain at best but a little blood, different from that of the veins, and mixed accidentally in some sort with the vital spirits, of which they are the proper conduits. In former times, farther,—times anterior to Harvey, whether more remotely or more nearly,—the liver, as the organ of the hæmapoësis, was regarded as the source of all the veins, or of all the proper blood-vessels; the heart, as the generator of heat and the vital spirits, was viewed as the mere cistern of the blood, whence it was propelled by the act of inspiration, and whither it reverted during the act of expiration, its flow to this part of the body or to that, being mainly determined by certain excitations there inherent or specially set up. By and by, however, the liver was given up as the origin of the venous system generally; but such anatomists as Jacobus Sylvius, Realdus Columbus, Bartholomæus Eustachius, and Gabriel Fallopius, may be found opposing Vesalius in regard to the origin of the vena cava, and asserting that it takes its rise from the liver, not from the heart, as the great reformer in modern anatomy had maintained."—*The Life of Harvey*, p. 54.

We must not overlook the very distinct terms in which Shakespeare, in this passage, refers to the motion of the blood, "and makes it course from the inwards, to the parts extreme."

" The vital commoners and inward petty spirits muster me all to their captain, the heart." This hypothesis, that the heart was the head quarters of the vital spirits which permeated the body through the arteries, adopted from Galen, was held, as Dr. Willis has shewn, even by those anatomists who have been put forward as rivals to the great discoverer of the heart's true function; thus Servetus, in the much discussed passage of the *Restitutio Christianismi*, says, " The vital spirit has its origin in the left ventricle, the lungs assisting especially in its generation; it is a subtile spirit.

Also Cæsalpinus, whose guesses at the heart's function have been put forward to detract from Harvey's originality, held that "the dilatation of the heart and arteries was due to an effervescence of the spirit."

The clearest, but most succinct, account which I have met with of the physiological opinions of the sixteenth century, is in that wonderful melange of learning, dirt, and humour, *The History of Garagantua and Pantagruel*, book iii., chapter 3. Rabelais, who was both a practising physician and a medical author, having translated and published some of the works both of Hippocrates and Galen, here condescends to place before the general public, and truly in the vernacular of his country, a concise account of the opinions which his brethren held it almost a matter of professional honour to conceal from the vulgar gaze under the cloak of a dead language. So far as I am able to judge, however, this clear sighted exposition is, in many respects, far in advance of the medical doctrines of the period, as might indeed have been expected from the almost miraculous insight of its author, whose disguise of buffoonery scarcely concealed a most unsafe originality of thought, and saved him from the dire penalties which would otherwise inevitably have attended it. In another passage which I have quoted under Coriolanus, Rabelais expressses the doctrine of the function of the liver which is implied in Falstaff's disquisition, namely, that the liver conveys blood through the veins for the good of the whole body.

"The intention of the founder of this microcosm is, to have a soul therein to be entertained, which is lodged there as a guest with its host, that it may live there for a while. Life consisteth in blood; blood is the seat of the soul;

wherefore the chiefest work of the microcosm is to be making blood continually.

" At this forge are exercised all the members of the body; none is exempted from labour, each operates apart, and doth its proper office. And such is their hierarchy, that perpetually the one borrows from the other, the one lends the other, and the one is the other's debtor. The stuff and matter convenient, which nature giveth to be turned into blood, is bread and wine. All kind of nourishing victuals is understood to be comprehended in these two, and from hence in the Gothish tongue is called companage. To find out this meat and drink, to prepare and boil it, the hands are put to work, the feet to walk and bear up the whole bulk of the corporal mass; the eyes guide and conduct all; the appetite in the orifice of the stomach, by means of a little sourish black humour, called melancholy, which is transmitted thereto from the milt, giveth warning to shut in the food. The tongue doth make the first essay, and tastes it; the teeth do chaw it, and the stomach doth receive, digest, and chilify it. The mesaraic veins suck out of it what is good and fit, leaving behind the excrements, which are, through special conduits for that purpose, voided by an expulsive faculty. Thereafter it is carried to the liver, where it being changed again, it by the virtue of that new transmutation becomes blood. What joy conjecture you, will then be found amongst those officers, when they see this rivulet of gold, which is their sole restorative? No greater is the joy of alchymists, when, after long travail, toil, and expense, they see in their furnaces the transmutation. Then is it that every member doth prepare itself, and strive anew to purify and to refine this treasure. The kidneys, through the emulgent veins, draw that aquosity from thence, which you call urine, and there send it away through the ureters to be slipped downwards ; where, in a lower receptacle, and proper for it, to wit, the bladder, it is kept, and stayeth there until an opportunity to void it out in his due time. The spleen draweth from the blood its terrestrial part, viz., the grounds, lees, or thick subtance settled in the bottom thereof, which you term melancholy. The bottle of the gall subtracts from thence all the superfluous choler, whence it is brought to another shop or work-house to be yet better purified and fined, that is, the heart, which by its agitation of diastolic and systolic motions so neatly subtilizeth and inflames it, that in the right side ventricle it is brought to perfection, and through the veins is sent to all the members. Each parcel of the body draws it then unto itself, and, after its own fashion, is cherished and alimented by it. Feet, hands, thighs, arms, eyes, ears, back, breasts, yea, all ; and then it is, that who before were lenders, now become debtors. The heart doth in its left-side ventricle so thinnify the blood, that it thereby obtains the name of spiritual ; which being sent through the arteries to all the members of the body, serveth to warm and winnow the other blood which runneth through the veins. The lights never cease, with its lappets and bellows, to cool and refresh it ; in acknowledgment of which good, the heart, through the arterial vein, imparts unto it the choicest of its blood. At last it is made so fine and subtle within the rete mirabile, that, thereafter, those animal spirits are framed and composed of it ; by means whereof, the imagination, discourse, judgment, resolution, deliberation, ratiocination, and memory, have their rise, actings, and operations."

This certainly is a nearer approach to Harvey's discovery

than any I have elsewhere met with in the physiology of the period, and might by a liberal interpretation be taken to imply, that what Shakespeare calls "the nimble spirits in the arteries," and "the vital commoners and inland petty spirits," was really blood which had been spiritualised or aerated in the lungs.

The origin of the old opinions appears to have been the following passage in Hippocrates' *Book on Aliments :* "The root of the veins is the liver, and the root of the arteries is the heart ; and from them blood and spirits are carried to all parts, and heat passes with the same."

In the following passage two similes are mixed with some want of clearness. The "venom of suggestion," or evil insinuations, acting as a ferment, might cause the contents of a closed barrel to expand, so that the vessel would leak but for the strength of its bonds. The supposed power of poison to swell and burst the body is expressed in several other passages.

"*King Henry.* Learn this, Thomas,
And thou shalt prove a shelter to thy friends ;
A hoop of gold, to bind thy brothers in :
That the united vessel of their blood,
Mingled with venom of suggestion,
(As, force perforce, the age will pour it in,)
Shall never leak, though it do work as strong
As aconitum, or rash gunpowder." *Act* iv., *Scene* 4.

When Romeo applies to the apothecary for poison, he asks for "soon speeding gear" which will kill "as violently as hasty powder fir'd." The above passage shows the poison which Shakespeare thought capable of this immediately fatal effect, aconite, which is indubitably one of the most virulent poisons with which, even at the present day, we are acquainted. Pereira says of it, "The root is undoubtedly one of the most fatal indigenous poisons," and of its alkaloid, aconitina, "in one case, one-fifteenth of a grain had nearly proved fatal;" and his editor, Dr. Taylor, says, "a dose of the tenth of a grain would probably destroy life with great rapidity. It is the most virulent poison known, not excepting hydrocyanic acid."—p. 695, vol. ii.

The king's illness is called an apoplexy, a term even now more loosely and vaguely employed by medical men than almost any other. It might be rightly applied to a sudden affection of the brain, caused by "the incessant care and labour of his mind;" but failing sight and giddiness of the brain might equally arise from failure of the heart's action; defective supply of blood to the brain, being attended with the same symptoms of its failing function, as interference with its due nutrition from congestion or pressure. The suspension of the respiratory movements so that the 'downy feather' stirred not, though it lay at the gates of breath, would indicate that the sudden illness, supervening on the shock of good news, was faintness and not apoplexy.

"*K. Henry,*   And wherefore should this good news make me sick?
Will fortune never come with both hands full,
But write her fair words still in foulest letters?
She either gives a stomach, and no food,—
Such are the poor, in health; or else a feast,
And takes away the stomach,—such are the rich,
That have abundance, and enjoy it not.
I should rejoice now at this happy news;
And now my sight fails, and my brain is giddy:
O me! come near me, now I am much ill.   [*Swoons*
    P. Humphrey.   Comfort, your majesty!
    Clarence.   O, my royal father!
    Westmoreland.   My sovereign lord, cheer up yourself, look up!
    Warwick.   Be patient, princes; you do know, these fits
Are with his highness very ordinary.
Stand from him, give him air; he'll straight be well.

M²

Cla. No, no; he cannot long hold out these pangs;
The incessant care and labour of his mind
Hath wrought the mure, that should confine it in,
So thin, that life looks through, and will break out.
   *   *   *   *
 War. Speak lower, princes, for the King recovers.
 P. Humph. This apoplexy will certain be his end.
 K. Henry I pray you, take me up, and bear me hence
Into some other chamber : softly, pray.
Let there be no noise made my gentle friends
Unless some dull and favourable hand
Will whisper music to my weary spirit.
  * * * * * *
    Enter PRINCE HENRY.
 P. Henry   Heard he the good news yet?
Tell it him.
 P. Humph. He alter'd much upon the hearing it.
 P. Hen. If he be sick
With joy, he will recover without physic.
   * * * *
     By his gates of breath
There lies a downy feather which stirs not:
Did he suspire, that light and weightless down
Perforce must move."   *Act* iv., *Scene* 4.

The quick recovery of intellectual powers shews that Prince Humphrey miscalled his father's illness in naming it an apoplexy. The whole scene describes the illness as faintness from exhaustion. It concludes with an expression of want of power of further speech, power and desire to think being retained; though it must be owned, that no reference had been made to pulmonary disease previous to the assertion that the lungs were wasted.

 "*K. Henry.* More would I, but my lungs are wasted so,
That strength of speech is utterly denied me." *Act* iv., *Scene* 4.

In the following passage Prince Henry's excuse for removing the crown affords another reference to the "tinct and multiplying medicine," the *aurum potabile,* as it was called by the old physicians, a term evidently in the poet's thought when he wrote the line in italics.

> "I spake unto the crown as having sense,
> And thus upbraided it: the care on thee depending,
> Hath fed upon the body of my father;
> Therefore, thou, best of gold, art worst of gold.
> Other, less fine in carat, is more precious,
> *Preserving life in med'cine potable;*
> But thou, most fine, most honour'd, most renown'd,
> Hast eat thy bearer up." *Act* iv., *Scene* 4.

KING HENRY V.

There is no small amount of medical knowledge in Mistress Quickly's account of Sir John's exit from the stage of life; knowledge, indeed, conveyed in language so quaintly humorous that it might easily be overlooked. The hostess, whose medical propensities we have before encountered, thus calls his old comrades to the reprobate knight's sick bed.

> "*Quickly.* As ever you come of women, come in quickly to Sir John: Ah, poor heart! he is so shaken of a burning quotidian tertian, that it is most lamentable to behold. Sweet men, come to him." *Act* ii., *Scene* 1.

The superstition is still prevalent among nurses that death takes place at the turning of the tide. The opinion that the 'parting' most often takes place after midnight can scarcely be called a superstition, for, if we remember rightly, it has been fairly backed by statistics. In that fatal physiognomy, the authority of which is recognised by the term *facies Hippocratica*, the very first sign is that given by Dame Quickly, "his nose was as sharp as a pen." Another of the dame's death signs, fumbling with the sheets and playing with flowers, &c., was given by the Father of Medicine as a symptom that "the man is delirious and will die," and the truth of his observation is still recognised, and his term *(carphologia)* is still used technically, to designate this action of picking or plucking at small objects.

"*Quickly.* Nay, sure, he's not in hell: he's in Arthur's bosom, if ever a man went to Arthur's bosom. 'A made a finer end, and went away, an it had been any christom child: 'a parted even just between twelve and one, e'en at turning o'the tide: for after I saw him fumble with the sheets, and play with flowers, and smile upon his fingers' ends, I knew there was but one way; for his nose was as sharp as a pen, and 'a babbled of green fields. How now, Sir John? quoth I: what, man! be of good cheer. So 'a cried out —God, God, God! three or four times: now I, to comfort him, bid him 'a should not think of God; I hoped there was no need to trouble himself with any such thoughts yet: So, 'a bade me lay more clothes on his feet: I put my hand into the bed, and felt them, and they were as cold as any stone; then I felt to his knees, and so upward, and upward, and all was cold as any stone."
Act ii., *Scene* 3.

"He smiled upon his fingers' ends, babbled of green fields; cried God, God, three or four times; talked of the whore of Babylon, and bade me lay more clothes on his feet."—What an exact picture is this of the half-conscious delirium of fatal exhaustion, attended with failing circulation until the limbs were "as cold as any stone." It is another of the aphorisms of Hippocrates that "in acute diseases, coldness of the extremities is bad;" and in a note to the Sydenham Society's edition of this author, Dr. Adams remarks: "Shakespeare's description of the death of Falstaff contains images which have always appeared to me to be borrowed (at second hand, no doubt,) from this and other passages of the present work." What a fine touch of nature there is in the reprobate old knight "babbling of green fields" in his last delirium; the impressions of early years, of innocent happiness flitting through his brain; the last of life's memories fading into the first, as the twilight of eve sometimes touches that of the morn. It is remarkable, what good sense and exact observation Shakespeare constantly puts into the mouths of his most vulgar characters.

The hostess acknowledges, indeed, that he raved about sack and women, "but then he was rheumatic, and talked of the whore of Babylon." Rheumatic, here of course, stands for lunatic, the dame being the antitype of Mistress Malaprop in the perverse application of words.

Does not Pistol refer to a fumigating apparatus for the venereal disease, in the powdering tub of infamy, from which Nym was to fetch Doll Tear-sheet; a tub, namely, in which the patient was exposed to fumes from powder of cinnabar, which, thrown upon a hot plate, or chafing-dish, would volatize and condense in the form of a powder on the body of the patient.

> "O hound of Crete, think'st thou my spouse to get?
> No; to the spital go,
> And from the powdering tub of infamy
> Fetch forth the lazar kite of Cressid's kind,
> Doll Tear-sheet she by name, and her espouse."
> *Act* ii., *Scene* 1.

The surgeons of Shakespeare's time, Clowes, Woodall, and Paré, although they appear to prefer inunction, speak of mercurial fumigation as if it were in common use. Woodall says, "Sinnabar, which is used in fumes for the pox, is a deadly medicine, half made of quicksilver, and half of brimstone by art of fire." Clowes describes mercurial fumigation by means "of certain trocheses or perfumes; the patient being placed under a canapie or pavilion in which the trocheses [composed of cinnabar and gums] are burnt on a chafing dish of coals." Ambrose Paré says, "some have devised a fourth manner of curing the *lues venerea*, which is suffitus or fumigations. They put the patient under a tent or canopy made close on every side, lest any thing should expire, and they put in unto him a vessel with hot coals, whereupon they plentifully throw cinnabaris, so that they may on every side enjoy the rising fume." In his chapter on the treatment of caruncules in the uretha, he describes and figures a "barrel fitted to receive the fume in." "You may put the patient naked into the barrel, so that he may sit upon a seate or boarde perforated, thus the patient shall easily receive the fume that exhales and none of it be lost, he covering and venting himself on every side." In Urquhart's translation of Rabelais, Friar John's sword is said to be "more rusty than the key-hole of an old powdering tub."—Book iii., c. 23. The original, however, scarce bears this meaning, "Il est par ma foy plus rouillé, que la claveure d'une vieil *charnier.*"

Poor Nell also meets with the same disaster as Doll, for Pistol smarting under his cudgelling exclaims,

"News have I, that my Nell is dead, i' the spital
Of malady of France ;   *Act* v., *Scene* 1.

The influence of mental satisfaction on the exhausted bodily organs, inspiring fresh alacrity and vigour into them, is thus maintained by the king.

"*K. Henry.* 'Tis good for men to love their present pains,
Upon example ; so the spirit is eased :
And, when the mind is quicken'd, out of doubt,
The organs, though defunct and dead before,
Break up their drowsy grave, and newly move
With casted slough and fresh legerity." *Act* iv. *Scene* 1.

In his comments upon the evils of greatness, the king asks plaintively whether ceremony will cure a fever.

" What drink'st thou oft, instead of homage sweet,
But poison'd flattery ? O, be sick, great greatness,
And bid thy ceremony give thee cure !
Think'st thou, the fiery fever will go out
With titles blown from adulation ?
Will it give place to flexure and low bending ?
Canst thou, when thou command'st the beggar's knee,
Command the health of it ? No, thou proud dream ;
That play'st so subtly with a king's repose." *Act* iv., *Scene* 1.

The king comments on sleep in the spirit of Abernethy, who advised his epicurean patient to live upon six-pence a day and earn it, since he finds it impossible to

" Sleep so soundly as the wretched slave ;
Who, with a body fill'd, and vacant mind,
Gets him to rest, cramm'd with distressful bread."
Act iv. *Scene* 1.

The pestiferous breath of the weltering battle field is the first example given by Ambrose Paré of "the corrupt and venomous air which may kill a man." "The air is infected and corrupted by the admixture of malign vapours arising from the unburied bodies of such as are slain in great conflicts."

" And those that leave their valiant bones in France,
Dying like men, though buried in your dunghills,
They shall be fam'd, for there the sun shall greet them,
And draw their honours reeking up to heaven ;
Leaving their earthly parts to choke your clime,
The smell whereof shall breed a plague in France."
Act iv., *Scene* 3.

KING HENRY VI. First Part.

The prayers of the church are still used for the sick, but in the olden time, their efficacy was not merely, as now, thought to be therapeutic, but morbific also. Gloster attributes the death of the king to this influence.

> "The church! where is it? Had not churchmen pray'd,
> His thread of life had not so soon decay'd;
> None do you like but an effeminate prince,
> Whom, like a school-boy, you may over-awe." *Act* i., *Scene* 1.

The glimmer of strong light as it appears to persons who are blind, but in whom the "thick drop serene" hath not quite quenched the orbs of vision, is finely used to point an argument in the following passage. A large proportion of those who have become blind can recognize the presence of a clear and shining light like that of the sun. I remember hearing a lecture on light, by Jonathan Hearder, the blind chemist, who, after displaying a series of beautiful experiments on the different sources of light, produced a blaze from electricity which almost blinded his audience, and of which, he himself said,—I can distinguish this, although the others have been invisible to me.

> "*Plantagenet.* The truth appears so naked on my side,
> That any purblind eye may find it out.
> *Somerset.* And on my side it is so well apparell'd,
> So clear, so shining, and so evident,
> That it will glimmer through a blind man's eye."
> *Act* ii., *Scene* 4.

The 'dying Mortimer' enumerates the symptoms of his decay—"the weak defects of age." He compares the condition of his limbs from long imprisonment, to those of a man 'new haled from the rack,' they are strengthless and numb. His senses fail, and his drooping limbs refuse support to the torpid body now scarce more than a 'lump of clay.'

> "Kind keepers of my weak decaying age,
> Let dying Mortimer here rest himself.—
> Even like a man new haled from the rack,
> So fare my limbs with long imprisonment:
> And these gray locks, the pursuivants of death,
> Nestor-like aged, in an age of care,
> Argue the end of Edmund Mortimer.
> These eyes, like lamps whose wasting oil is spent,
> Wax dim, as drawing to their exigent:
> Weak shoulders, overborne with burd'ning grief;
> And pithless arms, like to a wither'd vine
> That droops his sapless branches to the ground:
> Yet are these feet, whose strengthless clay is numb,
> Unable to support this lump of clay,
> Swift-winged with desire to get a grave,
> As witting I no other comforts have."   *Act* ii., *Scene* 5.

Some old superstition seems involved in this thought,

> "Civil dissension is a viperous worm
> That gnaws the bowels of the commonwealth."
> *Act* iii., *Scene* 1.

The description of the gradual destruction of a mortifying limb, a 'festered member,' in Exeter's prophecy of the result of the feud of the Roses, is as true to medical fact as it is terse and pointed.

> "This late dissension, grown betwixt the peers,
> Burns under feigned ashes of forg'd love,
> And will at last break out into a flame:
> As fester'd members rot but by degrees,
> Till bones, and flesh, and sinews, fall away,
> So will this base and envious discord breed."
> *Act* iii., *Scene* 1.

In the following, La Pucelle refers to the medical or surgical application of corrosive substances to eat or burn away diseased parts, which may not otherwise be remedied, as arsenical preparations are still used by empirics to corrode away cancerous growths, and as surgeons still employ corrosive acids to remove the surface of intractable ulcers.

> " Care is no cure, but rather corrosive,
> For things that are not to be remedied." *Act* iii., *Scene* 3.

The fighting woman in her appeal to Burgundy's patriotism, illustrates her thought by the mesenteric disease, "pining malady," of an infant.

> " As looks the mother on her lowly babe,
> When death doth close his tender dying eyes,
> See, see, the pining malady of France;
> Behold the wounds, the most unnatural wounds,
> Which thou thyself hast given her woeful breast!"
> *Act* iii., *Scene* 3.

A link in the pathological chain is evidently wanting in the illustration of the effects of boiling choler, which can only by a figure of speech find itself in the hollow passage of the voice.

> " *York.* Speak, Winchester; for boiling choler chokes
> The hollow passage of my prison'd voice." *Act* v., *Scene* 4.

The adaptation of the old theories to the pathology of the passions was necessarily difficult. The liver was thought the seat of passion, and superfluity of choler the result of its excitement, and the nerve symptoms arose from the boiling choler. It was the true pathology of passion upside down, the cart before the horse.

The effect of anxiety, alternations of hope and fear, on the general health is plaintively told by the poor king.

> " I feel such sharp dissension in my breast,
> Such fierce alarums both of hope and fear,
> As I am sick with working of my thoughts."
> *Act* v., *Scene* 5.

KING HENRY VI. SECOND PART.

Gloster excuses himself, on the plea of sudden indisposition, from reading throughout the disgraceful treaty, by which English possessions in France are given up to Queen Margaret's father.

> "Pardon me, gracious Lord;
> Some sudden qualm hath struck me at the heart,
> And dimm'd mine eyes, that I can read no further."
> *Act* i., *Scene* 1.

When the Protector Gloster makes arrangements for a duel with the cardinal, the latter uses in Latin, the two first words of the Scripture maxim, "Physician heal thyself."—

> "*Medice teipsum;*
> "Protector, see to't well, protect yourself." *Act* ii., *Scene* 1.

The king is exhorted, in medical phrase, to suppress the Irish rebellion in its early stage.

> "Send succours, lords, and stop the rage betime,
> Before the wound do grow incurable;
> For, being green, there is great hope of help."
> *Act* iii., *Scene* 1.

York being intrusted with the command of the forces for this expedition, and purposing to employ them for himself, says,

> "You put sharp weapons in a madman's hands." *Ibid.*

When the king swoons on hearing of Glosters death, Somerset proposes to recover him by a somewhat rough treatment, and in the position of the body certainly wrong.

"Rear up his body; wring him by the nose." *Act* iii., *Scene* 2.

Margaret appeals to the distressed king with a reference to a loathsome disease then common:

"What, dost thou turn away, and hide thy face?
I am no loathsome leper, look on me." *Act* iii., *Scene* 2.

When Warwick brings the king to "view the body" of Gloster, expressing his conviction that violent hands had been laid on his life, he describes the signs of a violent death, and especially of a death by strangulation, with a particularity which shews that the poet, whatever he might know of "crowner's quest law," was not ignorant of crowner's quest medicine.

"*Warwick.* See, how the blood is settled in his face!
Oft have I seen a timely-parted ghost,
Of ashy semblance, meagre, pale, and bloodless,
Being all descended to the labouring heart;
Who, in the conflict that it holds with death,
Attracts the same for aidance 'gainst the enemy;
Which with the heart there cools, and ne'er returneth
To blush and beautify the cheek again.
But see, his face is black, and full of blood;
His eye-balls further out than when he liv'd,
Staring full ghastly like a strangled man:
His hair uprear'd, his nostrils stretch'd with struggling;
His hands abroad display'd, as one that grasp'd
And tugg'd for life, and was by strength subdued.
Look on the sheets, his hair, you see, is sticking;
His well-proportion'd beard made rough and rugged,
Like to the summer's corn by tempest lodg'd.
It cannot be but he was murder'd here;
The least of all these signs were probable."
Act iii., *Scene* 2.

A reference to any work on medical jurisprudence will shew that the signs here specified are exactly those which must be looked for in death by strangulation, although, indeed, some important signs are omitted, especially marks of violence on the neck. Dr. Taylor says, that in persons strangled, "the face is more commonly livid and swollen, the eyes are congested [protruded?] and the pupils are dilated. . . . . A medical jurist ought to weigh all the circumstances connected with the position of the body. . . . The general lividity of the body, contraction of the fingers with clenching of the hands, and swelling and protrusion of the tongue, are the same in strangulation as in hanging." In Shakespeare's description, all these points have been attended to; the lividity of the face, the congestion of the eye-balls causing them to protrude, the hands in the condition of one that grasped, the position and condition of the body, the hair sticking to the sheets, and the beard rough and rugged; these particulars, taken together, testify to accurate knowledge of the appearances presented by this kind of violent death.

The earlier part of the above quotation is still more remarkable, since it expresses a pathological fact, which we should not have expected from Shakespeare, nor even from any medical man of his time. The pallid and pinched features, 'meagre, pale, and bloodless,' of the body after death, from any disease which has existed for some length of time, are referred to the fact that the blood has "descended to the labouring heart," "which with the heart there cools." The common condition of the heart after death filled with coagulated blood must have been known, if not observed, by the writer of this passage. We have seen that Shakespeare held the doctrine, which in his time, indeed, was universally prevalent among medical men, that the prime function of the heart and the arteries was to act as a reservoir to the vital spirits ; but this theory was by no means inconsistent with the above passage, since Galen, from whom it was adopted, and who had modified it from the teaching of Hippocrates, maintained that the blood did reach the right side of the heart, and came there in contact with the vital spirits which occupied the left side of the heart, through a supposed sieve-like structure of the septum. This passage should be compared with the equally remarkable one in *Measure for Measure:* " Why does my blood thus muster to my heart," &c. *Act* iii., *Scene* 4.

Queen Margaret, in parting with Suffolk, refers to the application of a corrosive substance to a wound of bad character, sphacelating or malignant as it might be, with the same surgical propriety as that used by La Pucelle in the first part.

" Away ! though parting be a fretful corsive, [corrosive]
It is appliant to a deathful wound." *Act* iii., *Scene* 2.

The terrible description of Cardinal Beaufort's death is a graphic picture of one form of acute delirium. We may well suppose it was brought on by remorse for the murder which he had recently committed; yet, although the cause of the disease may thus have been moral, the symptoms are those of phrenitis and not those of insanity. The acute nature of the disease, the existence of physical pain, the spectral hallucination, and the half consciousness indicated by allusions to his crime, belong to the delirium of phrenitis rather than to mania. The two forms of disease, indeed, do so run into each other, that cases occur, in which it is difficult for the most experienced physician to say whether they belong to the one or the other. For the reasons assigned, however, a diagnosis of the cardinal's sudden and grievous sickness can be fairly given. The symptoms are terribly true to some of the most painful cases which are brought under the physician's observation. The wretched patient gasps, and stares, and catches the air, blasphemes and curses, suffers the hallucination of the presence of his victim, now whispers to his pillow, now cries aloud. All this is in the description of Vaux.

" *Q. Margaret.* Whither goes Vaux so fast; what news,
        I pry'thee?
    Vaux. To signify unto his majesty
That Cardinal Beaufort is at point of death:
For suddenly a grievous sickness took him,
That makes him gasp, and stare, and catch the air,
Blaspheming God, and cursing men on earth.
Sometime, he talks as if Duke Humphrey's ghost
Were by his side: sometime, he calls the king,
And whispers to his pillow, as to him,
The secrets of his overcharged soul:
And I am sent to tell his majesty,
That even now he cries aloud for him."   *Act* iii., *Scene* 2.

In this instance, Shakespeare brings the frightful scene before the eyes of his audience, not merely to harrow up the soul, but doubtless also to shew what the death-bed of a murderer may be. In the dying man's first speech, mental horror and physical pain are joined in ghastly union. In his second speech, that half-retention of consciousness which exists in the delirium of phrenitis, but which is lost in that of acute mania, is strongly marked; and, while he displays the most vivid terror of eternal punishment, he defends himself from the supposed accusation of murder. In his agony he is athirst, and cries out, "give me some drink."

" *K. Henry.* How fares my lord? Speak, Beaufort, to thy
        sovereign.
    Cardinal. If thou be'st death, I'll give thee England's treasure
Enough to purchase such another island,

N

So thou wilt let me live, and feel no pain.
   K. Hen. Ah! what a sign it is of evil life,
When death's approach is seen so terrible!
   Warwick. Beaufort, it is thy sovereign speaks to thee.
   Car. Bring me unto my trial when you will.
Died he not in his bed? Where should he die?
Can I make men live, whe'r they will or no?—
O! torture me no more, I will confess.—
Alive again? Then show me where he is;
I'll give a thousand pounds to look upon him.—
He hath no eyes, the dust hath blinded them.—
Comb down his hair; look! look! it stands upright,
Like lime-twigs set to catch my winged soul!—
Give me some drink; and bid the apothecary
Bring the strong poison that I bought of him."
                                        Act iii., *Scene* 3.

Warwick, who detests the foul criminal, has coolness to observe and comment upon that horrible symptom of a painful death, which physicians call the 'sardonic grin.'

                  "See, how the pangs of death
Do make him grin!"

"He dies, and makes no sign" of hope on heaven's bliss, and the king orders his attendants to "close up his eyes," which, like those of his victim, would be "staring full ghastly." The dying man's cry for the strong poison which he had bought, suggests that this might have been the cause of his death, and that he had added the guilt of suicide to that of murder. The suddenness of his illness, and the amount of physical agony which he endured, agree with the supposition; and mental disturbance, as in King John's death scene, would be perfectly consistent with death from acrid or corrosive poison; but the fierce delirium appears rather that of sthenic inflammation of the brain, and is so accurately painted withal, that it is scarcely possible the author could have copied from anything but nature.

The line, "If thou be'st death, I'll give thee England's treasure," appears to have been founded on history or tradition. In the diary of John Ward, the medical Vicar of Stratford, is the following: "This Beaufort was the great Cardinal, who was reported to say on his death-bed, 'If all England could save his life, hee was able either by monie or policie to procure itt.'"—p. 177.

When Jack Cade's ruffians take Lord Say prisoner, comments are made upon the signs of ill health which he presents.

"*Say.* Long sitting to determine poor men's causes
Hath made me full of sickness and diseases.
Cade. Ye shall have a hempen caudle then, and the pap of hatchet.
Dick. Why dost thou quiver, man?
Say. The palsy, and not fear, provoketh me." *Act* iv., *Scene* 7.

Madness and brain-sickness are repeatedly imputed by the characters in this play to each other, and, in connection with this idea, Bedlam is often referred to; in one place being repeated in consecutive lines.

"*Clifford.* To Bedlam with him! is the man grown mad?
K. Henry. Ay, Clifford; a Bedlam and ambitious humour
Makes him oppose himself against his king." *Act* v., *Scene* 1.

The following, of course, refers to Telephus, whose wound, inflicted by Achilles, was only curable, according to the oracle, by that which made it. Achilles, to obtain the aid of the son of Hercules, in the Trojan war, effected the cure of his wound by applying to it rust, or rather verdigris, (for the weapon was of copper, or brass,) scraped from the head of the spear with which it had been inflicted.

"*York.* That gold must round engirt these brows of mine;
Whose smile and frown, like to Achilles' spear,
Is able with the change to kill and cure." *Act* v., *Scene* 1.

KING HENRY VI. THIRD PART.

The presence of blood in the heart is not dubiously referred to by Richard.

> "I cannot rest,
> Until the white rose that I wear, be dyed
> Even in the lukewarm blood of Henry's heart."
> *Act* i., *Scene* 2.

Richard, on hearing of his father's death, describes his rage and grief, in terms which, with poetic licence, describe the effects of emotion on the bodily functions. The degree of the body's moisture was an important point in old medicine.

> "*Richard.* I cannot weep; for all my body's moisture
> Scarce serves to quench my furnace-burning heart:
> Nor can my tongue unload my heart's great burden;
> For self-same wind, that I should speak withal,
> Is kindling coals that fire all my breast,
> And burn me up with flames that tears would quench.
> To weep is to make less the depth of grief."
> *Act* ii., *Scene* 1.

When Clifford, wounded to the death, has dragged himself from the battle, he refers to the mischief produced by the contact of air with the wounded surfaces.

> "The air hath got into my deadly wounds,
> And much effuse of blood doth make me faint."
> *Act* ii., *Scene* 6.

The Duke of Gloster, alluding to his brother Edward's incontinency, connects therewith its supposed pathological consequences, wasting of the marrow, bones, and all, and expresses the desire that he may become incompetent to beget issue.

> "*Gloster.* Ay, Edward will use women honourably.
> 'Would he were wasted, marrow, bones, and all,
> That from his loins no hopeful branch may spring,
> To cross me from the golden time I look for!"
> *Act* iii., *Scene* 2.

The influence of a woman's passions on the state of the fœtus, is dilated upon by Queen Elizabeth, when she has been informed that her husband has been taken prisoner.

> "*Q. Elizabeth.* Till then, fair hope must hinder life's decay.
> And I the rather wean me from despair,
> For love of Edward's offspring in my womb:
> This is it that makes me bridle passion,
> And bear with mildness my misfortune's cross.
> Ay, ay, for this I draw in many a tear,
> And stop the rising of blood-sucking sighs,
> Lest with my sighs or tears I blast or drown
> King Edward's fruit, true heir to the English crown."
> *Act* iv., *Scene* 4.

Warwick, when mortally wounded, recognizes that his hour is come, by signs which indicate minute observation of such modes of death.

> "My blood, my want of strength, my sick-heart shows,
> That I must yield my body to the earth."
>
> "These eyes, that now are dimm'd with death's black veil."
>
> "The wrinkles in my brows, now filled with blood."
>
> "Thou lov'st me not; for, brother, if thou didst
> Thy tears would wash this cold congealed blood
> That glues my lips, and will not let me speak."
> *Act* v., *Scene* 2.

The account which Gloster gives of his own birth is, that there was, what obstetricians call, a foot presentation, an event by no means unnatural, though it is here associated with another phenomenon, decidedly most improbable—namely, that he was born with teeth. The adaptation of his mind to the deformity of his body, concurs with Bacon's ill-natured theory: "Deformed persons are commonly even with nature;

for, as nature hath done ill by them, so do they by nature, being 'void of natural affection, and so they have their revenge on nature.'"

"Indeed, 'tis true, that Henry told me of:
For I have often heard my mother say
I came into the the world with my legs forward;
Had I not reason, think ye, to make haste,
And seek their ruin that usurp'd our right?
The midwife wonder'd; and the women cried,
'O, Jesus bless us, he is born with teeth!'
And so I was; which plainly signified
That I should snarl, and bite, and play the dog.
Then, since the heavens have shap'd my body so,
Let hell make crook'd my mind to answer it."
Act v., *Scene* 6.

RICHARD III.

The wish which Gloster expresses in *Henry VI.*, that his brother Edward were wasted, "marrow, bones, and all," appears to have its fulfilment at the beginning of this drama. The description of the kind of illness from which the king suffers, attended by weakness and melancholy arising from an evil diet, (a term courteously used to express an evil mode of life,) and resulting in his royal person being over-much consumed, comes as near to an admission that it is the result of debauchery, as the reticence of courtly speech will permit.

"*Hastings.* The king is sickly, weak, and melancholy,
And his physicians fear him mightily.
Gloster. Now, by Saint Paul, this news is bad indeed.
Oh! he hath kept an evil diet long,

    And over-much consum'd his royal person;
    'Tis very grevious to be thought upon.
    What, is he in his bed?"   *Act* i., *Scene* 1.

When Gloster arrests the funeral of King Henry, to pay his unnatural court to Anne, the latter describes a phenomenon which old superstition always attributed to the rencontre of a murderer with the body of his victim, and which used to be made use of as a sign of guilt.

    " O gentlemen, see, see! dead Henry's wounds
    Open their congeal'd mouths, and bleed afresh!
    Blush, blush, thou lump of foul deformity;
    For 'tis thy presence that exhales this blood
    From cold and empty veins, where no blood dwells;
    Thy deed, inhuman and unnatural,
    Provokes this deluge most unnatural."   *Act* i., *Scene* 2.

Anne, who uses her tongue with as much vehemence as her father did his sword, calls Gloster a 'diffused infection of a man,' meaning, either that his wickedness was diffused throughout his body, or that he diffused it around. To express her hatred more intensely, she spits at him, expressing the old belief in the poison of the toad, and the superstition respecting the basilisk, which Shakespeare refers to in several places.

    " *Gloster*. Why dost thou spit at me?
    Anne. 'Would it were mortal poison, for thy sake!
    Glo. Never came poison from so sweet a place.
    Anne. Never hung poison on a fouler toad.
Out of my sight! thou dost infect mine eyes.
    Glo. Thine eyes, sweet lady, have infected mine.
    Anne. 'Would they were basilisks, to strike thee dead!"
                              Act i., *Scene* 2.

Stanley excuses his wife's hostility to Gloster on the plea that ill health affects her temper.

    " Bear with her weakness, which, I think, proceeds
    From wayward sickness, and no grounded malice."
                              Act i., *Scene* 3.

The opinion is sound not to hold argument with an insane person.

> "*Dorset.* Dispute not with her, she is lunatic."
> Act i., Scene 3.

The tooth of a dog is elsewhere referred to as lacerating, but not lancing, the sore which it inflicts. Queen Margaret, with less knowledge, attributes the festering nature of such a wound to the venom of the tooth.

> " O Buckingham, beware of yonder dog ;
> Look, when he fawns, he bites ; and, when he bites,
> His venom tooth will rankle to the death."
> Act i., Scene 3.

In Clarence's account of his fearful dream, he refers to a sensation experienced in drowning.

> "Oh Lord ! methought what pain it was to drown !
> What dreadful noise of water in mine ears ! "
> Act i., Scene 4.

The word cordial is applied appropriately to its derivation and its application.

> "*K. Edward.* A pleasing cordial, princely Buckingham,
> Is this thy vow unto my sickly heart." Act ii., Scene 1.

The danger that a wound recently green or raw, and which has just been united, should break out or disunite, or at least suffer "likelihood of breach," or disunion, is the idea by which Buckingham illustrates the danger of traversing the country lately disturbed with civil war, with a large retinue.

> " *Rivers.* Why with some little train, my lord of Buckingham ?
> *Buck.* Marry, my lord, lest by a multitude,
> The new-heal'd wound of malice should break out ;
> Which would be so much the more dangerous,
> By how much the estate is green, and yet ungovern'd :
> * * *
> *Riv.* Yet, since it is but green, it should be put
> To no apparent likelihood of breach,
> Which, haply, by much company might be urged." Act ii. Scene 2

Gray, being led to the block, says of Richard's minions,

"A knot you are of damned blood-suckers."
Act iii., *Scene* 3.

A blood-sucker is the old medical word for leech, and a knot would be an appropriate term for a number of clustering leeches. In the *Second Part of Henry VI.*, the term of bloodsucker appears to mean the vampire bat, "the blood-sucker of sleeping men."

Gloster's fiendish plots spared neither the blood nor the honour of his kindred. He commands Buckingham to insinuate imputations against his own mother, by raising the medical question, which has so much puzzled even modern courts of law, of the natural duration of pregnancy.

"Tell them, when that my mother went with child
Of that insatiate Edward, noble York,
My princely father, then had wars in France;
And, by just computation of the time,
Found that the issue was not his begot;
Which well appeared in his lineaments,
Being nothing like the noble duke my father:
Yet touch this sparingly, as 'twere far off;
Because, my lord, you know my mother lives."
Act iii., *Scene* 5.

In the following passage, the "scars of infamy" may either mean those left by the branding iron, formerly used so much as a punishment, or the scars of an infamous disease. "Dark forgetfulness and deep oblivion" point to mental disease or decay, dementia.

"The noble isle doth want her proper limbs;
Her face defac'd with scars of infamy,
Her royal stock graft with ignoble plants,
And almost shoulder'd in the swallowing gulf
Of dark forgetfulness and deep oblivion."
Act iii., *Scene* 7.

Queen Elizabeth refers to the effect of tight-lacing on the heart, exactly as Paulina does in *The Winter's Tale*.

> "*Q. Eliz.* Ah! cut my lace asunder,
> That my pent heart may have some scope to beat,
> Or else I swoon with this dead-killing news."
> *Act* iv. *Scene* 1.

The cockatrice and the basilisk are synonyms. Ambrose Paré gives an engraving and history of the fabulous thing of whose existence he does not appear to doubt. Shakespeare generally uses the word basilisk, but in the following he employs the other term, and states the superstition.

> "O my accursed womb, the bed of death;
> A cockatrice hast thou hatch'd to the world,
> Whose unavoided eye is murderous!" *Act* iv., *Scene* 1.

It is doubtful whether Shakespeare intended in the following, a description of that accident, which is well known to obstetric physicians, the strangulation of the infant before its birth by the umbilical cord getting twisted around its neck. It may have had this meaning or it may not, as the Duchess appears to refer to an act of will on her part.

> "*K. Rich.* Who intercepts me in my expedition?
> *Duch.* Oh! she that might have intercepted thee,
> By strangling thee in her accursed womb,
> From all the slaughters, wretch, that thou hast done."
> *Act* iv., *Scene* 4.

The Duchess of York's description of her terrible son's nativity, infancy, childhood, and manhood, forms a graphic illustration of the maxim that no man was ever suddenly very wicked, and may well be commended to the study of those physicians who have recently invented, what they are pleased to call, 'moral idiotcy,' and who have humiliated the science of medicine by attempting to exonerate the guilt, and avert the punishment of murder, on arguments founded on no better grounds than that the infancy of the mature criminal had been thought "tetchy and wayward," and his school days "wild and furious." On these principles, the evidence of Richard the Third's mother would have been amply sufficient to prove that he was a moral idiot, and utterly irresponsible for the guilt of his actions. It might thus be urged, that with all his apparent force of will he had no free choice, but was himself the puppet of organization and of circumstance, and therefore, that all his crimes were inevitable. This question really resolves itself into one which the intellect of man has never yet been able to solve, namely, the origin of evil This at least, however, we are bound to acknowledge, that, if there be any fate in the production of evil, there is also a fated necessity in its punishment; and this practical distinction we must draw, that while a murder committed by a madman is a painful accident of his disease, a murder committed as the climax of a wicked life is a stupendous crime, towards which, neither knowledge nor ignorance, on our part, of the origin of evil, can justify any other feeling than that of abhorrence, or any other conduct than that of retributive justice. Richard himself held that his own bad actions were fated, and this doctrine of fatalism, with the contrary one of the grace, are stated in two lines between him and the queen.

"*K. Richard.* All unavoided is the doom of destiny:
Q. Eliz. True, when avoided grace makes destiny."
Act iv., *Scene* 4.

"*Duchess.* Art thou so hasty? I have staid for thee, God knows, in torment and in agony.

    K. Rich. And came I not at last to comfort you?
    Duch. No, by the holy rood, thou know'st it well,
Thou cam'st on earth to make the earth my hell.
A grevious burden was thy birth to me:
Tetchy and wayward was thy infancy.
Thy school-days, frightful, desperate, wild, and furious;
Thy prime of manhood, daring, bold, and venturous;
Thy age confirm'd, proud, subtle, sly, and bloody,
More mild, but yet more harmful, kind in hatred."
Act iv., *Scene* 7.

KING HENRY VIII.

Anne Bullen's enquiry of Lord Sands, whether the wildness he had from his father was madness, points to a knowledge of the hereditary character of this malady.

    " *Sands.* If I chance to talk a little wild, forgive me;
I had it from my father.
    Anne. Was he mad, Sir?
    Sands. Oh! very mad, exceeding mad, in love too:
But he would bite none."
Act i., *Scene* 4.

Wolsey is accused of having caused the insanity and death of one Dr. Pace.

    " *Campeius.* They will not stick to say, you envied him;
And, fearing he would rise, he was so virtuous,
Kept him a foreign man still; which so griev'd him,
That he ran mad, and died."
Act ii., *Scene* 2.

The king marries Ann Bullen without the privity of the great churchman, whose policy, thus thwarted, provokes the remark:

> "All his tricks founder, and he brings his physic
> After his patient's death; the king already
> Hath married the fair lady."   *Act* iii., *Scene* 2.

The idea of the body's exhaustion and repair, and the need of a busy man caring for his health, by alternating labour with repose or recreation, is contained in Wolsey's reply to the king respecting the occupation of his time.

> "For holy offices I have a time; a time
> To think upon the part of business, which
> I bear i'the state; and nature does require
> Her times of preservation, which, perforce,
> I, her frail son, amongst my brethren mortal,
> Must give my tendance to."   *Act* iii., *Scene* 2.

The history of Queen Catharine's sickness and death is drawn with great skill and delicacy. The poor deserted woman appears not to die from any positive disease, but from bodily debility, resulting from the heavy burden of grief and shame to which she had been subjected. The noble reticence of her character prevents any wild outburst of passion, and this suppression of the signs of feeling would all the more recoil upon the bodily strength. One of the surest signs of debility is well marked in the following.

> "*Griffith.* How does your grace?
> *Katherine.* O, Griffith, sick to death:
> My legs, like loaden branches, bow to the earth,
> Willing to leave their burden: Reach a chair;—
> So,—now, methinks, I feel a little ease.
>   *   *   *
> *Patience.* Do you note,
> How much her grace is alter'd on the sudden?
> How long her face is drawn? How pale she looks,
> And of an earthy cold? Mark you her eyes?
> *Grif.* She is going, wench; pray, pray."
>   *Act* iv., *Scene* 2.

The queen, however, revives sufficiently to sustain the

interview with Capuchius, who brings an affectionate message from the king, entreating her to take good comfort; which comfort, however, the queen says, comes too late, regretting it as gentle physic, which, in the early stage of disease, might have been remedial.

> "*Kath.* O my good lord, that comfort comes too late;
> 'Tis like a pardon after execution:
> That gentle physic, given in time, had cur'd me;
> But now I am past all comforts here, but prayers."
> *Act* iv., *Scene* 2.

In giving her noble message to her husband, she feels her strength quite fail her, and that symptom of fatal debility, so often noted by Shakespeare, is not omitted, "My eyes grow dim."

A minute account is given of Anne Bullen's childbed. It must have been rather curious when this play was represented, for Shakespeare's royal mistress to listen to the minute circumstances under which she first smelt the air, when, as Lear says, "we wawl and cry;" and how the lady gossip, who brought the king news that it was a girl, only got a hundred marks for it, payment, as she thought, for a groom.

> "*K. Henry.* Now, Lovell, from the queen what is the news?
> *Lovell.* I could not personally deliver to her
> What you commanded me, but by her woman
> I sent your message; who return'd her thanks
> In the greatest humbleness, and desir'd your highness
> Most heartily to pray for her.
> *King Hen.* What say'st thou? ha!
> To pray for her? what, is she crying out?
> *Lov.* So said her woman; and that her sufferance made
> Almost each pang a death.
> *K. Hen.* Alas, good lady!
> *Suffolk.* God safely quit her of her burden, and
> With gentle travail, to the gladding of
> Your highness with an heir!" *Act* v., *Scene* 1.

Gardiner, in the council held to accuse Cromwell, compares the protestant heresy to a contagious sickness, beyond the reach of medicine, the taint of which is likely to spread far and wide.

> "If we suffer
> (Out of our easiness, and childish pity
> To one man's honour) this contagious sickness,
> Farewell, all physic: And what follows then?
> Commotions, uproars, with a general taint
> Of the whole state." *Act* v., *Scene* 2.

He had before applied the same simile to Cromwell.

> "A most arch-heretic! a pestilence
> That does infect the land." *Act* v., *Scene* 1.

The introduction of Dr. Butts, the king's physician, has been commented on at page 55. Stowe, in his *Annals*, erroneously attributes the foundation of the College of Physicians to this person.

MACBETH.

When the witches had vanished from the eyes of Macbeth and Banquo, "as breath into the wind," the latter asks,

> "Were such things here as we do speak about?
> Or have we eaten of the insane root,
> That takes the reason prisoner?" *Act* i., *Scene* 3.

In the absence of any clue to the recognition of this root, it is satisfactory to be able to indicate the source from which there can be little doubt that Shakespeare borrowed the idea, namely, from Plutarch, a work, which it is certain that he closely studied. One of Shakespeare's own medical contemporaries, Sir Thomas Browne, quotes the following passage from Plutarch's *Life of Antonius*, remarking that "what plant this might be considerable (*i.e.*, to be thought of) from the symptoms and cure by wine."

"In the end they were compelled to live on herbs and roots, but they found few of them that men do commonly eat, and were enforced to taste of them that were never eaten before, among the which, there was one that killed them and made them lose their wits; for he that had once eaten of it his memory was gone from him, and he knew no manner of thing, but only busied himself in digging and hurling of stones from one place to another, as though it had been a great weight, and to be done with all possible speed. All the camp over were busily stooping to the ground, digging and carrying of stones from one place to another. But at last they cast up a great deal of choler and died suddenly, because they lacked wine, which was the only sudden remedy to cure that disease."—*Plutarch, in Vitâ Antonii.*

The horrible imaginings suggested to Macbeth, produce in his irritable constitution the bodily symptoms of nervous excitement so forcibly, as to attract his own attention to the disturbance of the bodily functions, and to the unusual manner in which palpitation of the heart shakes his frame.

"Why do I yield to that suggestion
Whose horrid image doth unfix my hair,
And make my seated heart knock at my ribs,
Against the use of nature? Presents fears
Are less than horrible imaginings:
My thought, whose murder yet is but fantastical,
Shakes so my single state of man, that function
Is smother'd in surmise; and nothing is,
But what is not." *Act* i., *Scene* 3.

Lady Macbeth's proposition to stupify Duncan's spongy officers with strong drink, describes the effects of the fumes of wine on the brain by a simile drawn from chemistry, then called the spagyric art. The brain, the seat of reason, shall become an alembic, or limbeck, a receptacle of fumes.

> " When Duncan is asleep,
> (Whereto the rather shall his day's hard journey
> Soundly invite him,) his two chamberlains
> Will I with wine and wassel so convince,
> That memory, the warder of the brain,
> Shall be a fume, and the receipt of reason,
> A limbeck only: when in swinish sleep
> Their drenched natures lie, as in a death."
> *Act* i., *Scene* 7.

The hallucination of the dagger is referred by Macbeth to its true pathological cause.

> " A dagger of the mind, a false creation,
> Proceeding from the heat-oppressed brain."
> *Act* ii., *Scene* 1.

Lady Macbeth does not trust to the fumes of wine to stupify the surfeited grooms, since she administers some narcotic, to an extent dangerous, but not fatal, to their lives.

> " I've drugged their possets
> That death and nature do contend about them,
> Whether they live, or die."   *Act* ii., *Scene* 2.

There are few subjects that Shakespeare has treated with more pathetic truthfulness than the distress arising from want of sleep; so much so, that the thought intrudes itself that he must, in his own person, have experienced this penalty of mental excitement exceeding the limits of health. In no place, however, is the description of sleep's restorative power delineated with such exquisite pathos as where Macbeth feels that he has murdered sleep; it is then that he exclaims,

o

> "Sleep, that knits up the ravell'd sleave of care,
> The death of each day's life, sore labour's bath,
> Balm of hurt minds, great nature's second course,
> Chief nourisher in life's feast." *Act* ii., *Scene* 2.

Macbeth's invitation to his guests

> "Now good digestion wait on appetite,
> And health on both!" *Act* iii., *Scene* 4.

contains the sound medical doctrine, that food taken with appetite promotes digestion, and that good digestion is needful to health.

The witches' cauldron receives only two ingredients for the composition of its hell-broth, which have any bearing on medicine. "Root of hemlock digged in the dark," points, like several other passages, to the importance attached by the old herbalists to the time and manner in which medicinal or poisonous plants were gathered. The "finger of birth-strangled babe" seems to indicate a knowledge of the accident of strangulation with the umbilical cord, to which the infant is liable during parturition.

The touching for the king's evil, which is so minutely described in this play, was performed by Edward the Confessor, the first of our kings who exercised this miraculous gift. He was, however, by no means the last, for the practice descended so near to these present times of unbelief as the life-time of Samuel Johnson, who was, himself, actually touched by the royal hand for this purpose. In this case we know that the remedy was not efficacious, for the scrofulous taint of the great moralist's constitution was as strong and as persistent as the superstitious bias of his mind, which, as this early incident seems to indicate, might derive its origin, like the physical disease, from hereditary predisposition. In the *Psychology of Shakespeare,* I have quoted Fuller's quaint account of this royal charlatanism, and of Queen Elizabeth's early dislike to it. The subject may be traced throughout old medical literature, the physicians being either sufficiently ignorant or sufficiently politic, not to doubt, or not to appear to doubt, the possession by our kings of this miraculous therapeutic power, which was valued by themselves as a proof of their legitimacy.

Primrose, on the Popular Error " of the curing of the King's-Evill by the toutch of the seventh sonne," argues, that as this "power of curing the King's-Evill is, by the blessing of God, granted to the Kings of Great Britaine and France," "this privilege is only vouchsafed to the aforesaid Kings, and if other men should attempt the same, it were too much rashnesse, and a grosse tempting of God."

" *Malcolm.*   Comes the king forth, I pray you?
  Doctor. Ay, Sir : there are a crew of wretched souls
That stay his cure: their malady convinces
The great assay of art : but, at his touch,
Such sanctity hath heaven given his hand,
They presently amend.
     Mal.   I thank you, doctor.
    Macduff. What 's the disease he means?
     Mal.   'Tis call'd the evil:
A most miraculous work in this good king ;
Which often, since my here-remain in England,
I have seen him do. How he solicits heaven,
Himself best knows : but strangely-visited people,
All swoln and ulcerous, pitiful to the eye,
The mere despair of surgery, he cures ;
Hanging a golden stamp about their necks,
Put on with holy prayers : and 'tis spoken,
To the succeeding royalty he leaves
The healing benediction. With this strange virtue,
He hath a heavenly gift of prophecy ;
And sundry blessings hang about his throne,
That speak him full of grace."   *Act* iv., *Scene* **3**.

Malcolm in medical phrase suggests revenge to comfort Macduff's grief.

"Let's make us med'cines of our great revenge,
To cure this deadly grief." *Act* iv., *Scene* 3.

The truthful representation of the phenomena of sleep-walking is a main element of the wonderful dramatic power in the scene where Lady Macbeth unconsciously confesses her guilt. The somnambulism does not occur every night, since the physician watches two nights before he is able to observe this great perturbation in nature.

"*Doct.* I have two nights watched with you, but can perceive no truth in your report. When was it she last walked?
Gentlewoman. Since his majesty went into the field, I have seen her rise from her bed, throw her night-gown upon her, unlock her closet, take forth paper, fold it, write upon 't, read it, afterwards seal it, and again return to bed; yet all this while in a most fast sleep.
Doct. A great perturbation in nature! to receive at once the benefit of sleep, and do the effects of watching. * * *
Gent. Lo you, here she comes! This is her very guise; and, upon my life, fast asleep. Observe her; stand close.
Doct. How came she by that light?
Gent. Why, it stood by her: she has light by her continually; 'tis her command.
Doct. You see, her eyes are open.
Gent. Ay, but their sense is shut.
Doct. What is it she does now? Look how she rubs her hands.
Gent. It is an accustomed action with her, to seem thus washing her hands; I have known her continue in this a quarter of an hour.
Lady M. Yet here's a spot," &c. *Act* v. *Scene* 1.

The physiology of sleep-walking is not very clearly understood even now, and, certainly, little could be added to the description of its phenomena which we receive from Shakespeare. The eye is open, but its sense is shut, at least its sense of discriminating perception. To what extent the senses are obscured in somnambulism is a curious and unresolved problem. It is probable that Lady Macbeth saw the little hand, which all the perfumes of Arabia could not sweeten, though with hallucinated mind she saw it blood-spotted. It is to be remarked that the hallucinations of dreams appeal to all the senses, so that the test of reality which Shakespeare has himself proposed, the verification of one sense by that of others, would not be valid. The "damned spot" is an hallucination, not of the organ of vision, but of the cerebral centre of the sense; the smell of blood is equally a false testimony of the cerebral centre of the sense of smell; and the words which she seems to hear from her lord, "a soldier and afraid," indicate that the cerebral hallucination of sense is complete. The hallucinations of the waking state, rarely, if ever, appeal to all the senses at the same time, and thus afford a curious distinction to the hallucinations, if they can be so called, of dreams. The muscular movements, both vocal and general, in sleep-walking, are not automatic as they have been called, but definitely directed by these hallucinations of the cerebral centres of sense.

When the doctor of physic, who seems to be a sensible, though somewhat timid, man, declines to attempt any treatment of the case saying, "this disease is beyond my practice," he appears to have been deterred by the fear of being mixed up with terrible state secrets, " Foul whisperings are abroad," &c. We cannot agree with him in his opinion, " more needs she the divine than the physician," for the wretched queen is at this time clearly in a state of disease, and inaccessible to a divine, whose sacred office could only be available when the perturbations of physical nature had been allayed by physical means.

The doctor does not appear to have given up his patient, for two scenes later we find Macbeth asking his opinion.

"How does your patient, doctor?
 Doctor. Not so sick, my lord,
As she is troubled with thick-coming fancies,
That keep her from her rest.
 Macb. Cure her of that:
Canst thou not minister to a mind diseas'd;
Pluck from the memory a rooted sorrow;
Raze out the written troubles of the brain;
And, with some sweet oblivious antidote,
Cleanse the stuff'd bosom of that perilous stuff,
Which weighs upon the heart?
 Doct. Therein the patient
Must minister to himself.
 Macb. Throw physic to the dogs, I'll none of it.—
Come, put mine armour on: give me my staff:—
Seyton, send out. Doctor, the thanes fly from me;—
Come, Sir, despatch:—If thou could'st, doctor, cast
The water of my land, find her disease,
And purge it to a sound and pristine health,
I would applaud thee to the very echo,
That should applaud again.—Pull't off, I say—
What rhubarb, senna, or what purgative drug,
Would scour these English hence?" *Act* v., *Scene* 3.

"Some sweet oblivious antidote" has been supposed by commentators to have been suggested by Spencer's description of Nepenthe, or by Virgil's of the effects of Lethe. It is more likely, I think, to refer to the "drowsy syrups" mentioned by Iago. In Shakespeare's time, narcotics were commonly administered in syrups as a vehicle, a mode of pharmacy of which traces still remain.

Macbeth's expression, 'throw physic to the dogs,' has been quoted to sustain the opinion that Shakespeare himself despised the aid of medicine; an opinion which is utterly refuted by the manner in which, throughout the plays, he speaks of physic, and represents the character of the physician. When occasion demands, he can represent a starved apothecary, as in *Romeo and Juliet;* or a Dr. Caius, ridiculous in clipped English and love-sickness; but he always represents the character of the physician in a generous and beneficent, even, dignified garb. This is the case with Lady Macbeth's physician, and, to a still greater extent, with the physicians in *Lear* and *Cymbeline.* Macbeth had some reason to say, 'throw physic to the dogs, I'll none of it,' because the doctor, frightened at the terrible secrets of which he had unwittingly become cognizant, and looking upon Lady Macbeth as a great criminal, had declared himself unable to minister to minds diseased. Macbeth, moreover, was in the most impetuous state of combative excitement, and he would throw physic to the dogs, because it could not do the one thing he had at heart at the time, the overthrow of his enemies, and the establishment of his power. The medical form in which this task is proposed, is one of the most remarkable examples of Shakespeare's use of medical similes. The doctor is called upon first to diagnose the disease of the body politic, in the manner which, as we have seen, was then common among physicians; he is to 'cast the water of the land,' and thus to find her disease; that being found, he must treat the diseased land, and purge it to a sound and pristine health. What purgative will do this? Is it rhubarb, senna, or what else? Who will remove the obstructions which are at least evident, and scour these English hence? This conversation is held while Macbeth is putting on his armour with impetuous haste, and it is hard to say whether his earnest demand for some sweet oblivious antidote for the sorrow and trouble written in the brain of his queen, or whether his figurative invitation that the doctor should turn statesman, and cleanse the land with purgatives, most indicate the bias to medical turns of thought. Just before this scene, one of Macbeth's opponents expresses the same thought in the same form, namely, that the common-weal is sick, and requires purgation.

"*Caithness.*   Well, march we on,
To give obedience where 'tis truly ow'd:
Meet we the medicine of the sickly weal;
And with him pour we, in our country's purge,
Each drop of us."   *Act* v. *Scene* 2.

Macbeth relies more upon charms than upon medicine, but the last charm turns out to be an equivocation on an event brought about by medical art.

"*Macbeth.*   I bear a charmed life, which must not yield
To one of woman born.
   Macduff.   Despair thy charm;
And let the angel whom thou still hast serv'd
Tell thee, Macduff was from his mother's womb
Untimely ripp'd."   *Act* v., *Scene* 7.

The removal of the fœtus from the mother's womb, named Cæsarian after Rome's greatest soldier, who is said to have entered the world like Macduff, may be performed after the mother's death, or before, in the hope of saving both lives. The mode of expression, 'untimely ripped,' seems to indicate that the first of these was the manner in which Macduff saw the light. In *Cymbeline*, the name given to the infant, Posthumus, indicates that he was born after the death of his mother. The mother in the vision uses the same term as Macduff, "ripped."

"*Sicilius.*   I died, whilst in the womb he stay'd
                Attending Nature's law.   *   *
   Mother. Lucina lent me not her aid,
                But took me in my throes;
            That from me was Posthumus ripp'd,
                Came crying 'mongst his foes,
            A thing of pity!"   *Act* v. *Scene* 4.

CORIOLANUS.

The current of medical thought which runs through this play is broad and strong. Menenius' version of Æsop's fable is thorougly medical in its description of the bodily functions, while, as in so many other references of this kind, the poet applies the doctrines of physiology to the theory of government and statesmanship. In this instance, the simile appears rather misapplied, since the rulers of a nation would be the brain and the hands, rather than the stomach of the body politic. This misapplication, however, is explained by the circumstances of the discussion, namely, that the disaffected mob accuse the Senate, that they "suffer us to famish, and their storehouses are crammed with grain." Menenius, with quiet humour, describes the slow manner in which the process of digestion is carrried on. "Your most grave belly was deliberate, not rash," it is the shop and storehouse of the whole body, which, after first receiving the general food, sends it "through the rivers of blood, even to the court the heart." The flow of blood *to* the heart, thus distinctly stated, was a fact well known and recognized in Shakespeare's time. It was the flow of blood *from* the heart, and round again in a circle to the heart, that is, the *circulation* of the blood, which was not known to Shakespeare or to any other person before Harvey's immortal discovery. The flow of the blood "through the cranks and offices of man" is a singular expression. 'Offices' appear to mean functions, put for their organs, and 'cranks' mean bendings, or turnings, and, no doubt, refer to the elbows or turns in the blood vessels. The word, an uncommon one, is used in *Venus and Adonis*, in which the course of a hunted hare is described. "He cranks and crosses with a thousand doubles."

'The strongest nerves' appears to be used in the sense of sinews or tendons, a sense in which Shakespeare uses the word nerve generally, perhaps universally.

The idea that the flour of the food for the nourishment of the body is separated from the refuse or bran which remains in the stomach, again leads back the mind to the plethoric storehouse of the senators on which the discussion hinges.

"*Menenius.* There was a time, when all the body's members
Rebell'd against the belly; thus accus'd it:—
That only like a gulf it did remain
I' the midst o' the body, idle and unactive,
Still cupboarding the viand, never bearing
Like labour with the rest; where the other instruments
Did see, and hear, devise, instruct, walk, feel,
And mutually participate; did minister
Unto the appetite and affection common
Of the whole body. The belly answered,—
   Citizen. Well, Sir, what answer made the belly?
   Men. Sir, I shall tell you.—With a kind of smile,
Which ne'er came from the lungs, but even thus,
(For, look you, I may make the belly smile
As well as speak,) it tauntingly replied
To the discontented members, the mutinous parts
That envied his receipt; even so most fitly
As you malign our senators, for that
They are not such as you—
   Cit. Your belly's answer: What!
The kingly-crowned head, the vigilant eye,
The counsellor heart, the arm our soldier,
Our steed the leg, the tongue our trumpeter,
With other muniments and petty helps
In this our fabric, if that they—
   Men.   What then?

'Fore me, this fellow speaks!—What then? What then?
 Cit. Should by the cormorant belly be restrain'd,
Who is the sink o' the body,—
 Men.   Well, what then?
 Cit. The former agents, if they did complain,
What could the belly answer?
 Men.   I will tell you;
If you'll bestow a small (of what you have little,)
Patience a while, you'll hear the belly's answer.
 Cit. You are long about it.
 Men.   Note me this, good friend;
Your most grave belly was deliberate,
Not rash like his accusers, and thus answer'd,
'True is it, my incorporate friends,' quoth he,
'That I receive the general food at first,
Which you do live upon: and fit it is;
Because I am the storehouse, and the shop
Of the whole body; But if you do remember,
I send it through the rivers of your blood,
Even to the court, the heart, to the seat o' the brain,
And through the cranks and offices of man:
The strongest nerves, and small inferior veins,
From me receive that natural competency
Whereby they live: and though that all at once,
You, my good friends,' (this says the belly,) 'mark me,—
 Cit. Ay, Sir; well, well.
 Men.   'Though all at once cannot
See what I do deliver out to each;
Yet I can make my audit up, that all
From me do back receive the flour of all,
And leave me but the bran.' What say you to't?
 Cit. It was an answer: How apply you this?
 Men. The senators of Rome are this good belly,
And you the mutinous members." *Act* i., *Scene* 1.

Rabelais uses this same fable of Æsop to illustrate the social miseries which would result if the world should be filled with a rascally rabble of people that would not lend; his hero, in the witty classification of men into those who borrow and those who lend, decidedly belonging to the former category, and being as decidedly inimical to all who did not belong to the latter. Malone refers to this fable as it is told by Camden, in his *Remains*, (A.D. 1605,) and remarks, that "Shakespeare appears to have had Camden as well as Plutarch before him." Rabelais, however, appears to me by far the more probable model, on account of the physiological dress in which he invests the fable, which Camden merely repeats after Æsop. Rabelais had been translated before 1775, and Mr. Upton observes on the expression in *Lear*, " Nero is an angler in the lake of darkness," that Rabelais says " Nero was a fiddler in hell and Trajan an angler." But, independently of this coincidence, it is very improbable that Shakespeare would omit to make acquaintance with a mind so congenial to more than one phase of his own as that of Rabelais, whose version of the fable is as follows :

"It would prove much more easy in nature to have fish entertained in the air, and bullocks fed in the bottom of the ocean, than to support or tolerate a rascally rabble of people that will not lend. These fellows, I vow, I do hate with a perfect hatred ; and if, conform to the pattern of this grievous, peevish, and perverse world which laudeth nothing, you figure and lighten the little world, which is man, you will find in him a terrible justling coyle and clutter. The head will not lend the sight of his eyes to guide the feet and hands ; the legs will refuse to bear up the body ; the hand will leave off working any more for the rest of the members ; the heart will be weary of its continued motion for the beating of the pulse, and will no longer lend his asssistance ; the lungs will withdraw the use of their bellows ; the liver will desist from convoying any more blood through the veins for the good of the whole ; the bladder will not be indebted to the kidneys, so that the urine thereby will be totally stopped. The brains, in the interim, considering this unnatural course, will fall into a raving dotage, and withhold all feeling from the sinews, and all motion from the muscles. Briefly, in such a world without order and array, owing nothing, lending nothing, and borrowing nothing, you would be a more dangerous conspiration than that which Æsop exposed in his apologue. Such a world will perish undoubtedly; and not only perish, but perish very quickly. Were it Æsculapius himself, his body would immediately rot, and the chafing soul, full of indignation, take its flight."

When Menenius has finished his argument with the mob, Marcius breaks in upon them with another medical simile by no means so complimentary as the former one.

> "What's the matter, you dissentious rogues,
> That, rubbing the poor itch of your opinion,
> Make yourselves scabs?" *Ibid.*

He follows it up with another, the general truth of which, however, may be questioned.

> "Your affections are
> A sick man's appetite, who desires most that
> Which would increase his evil." *Ibid.*

The haughty warrior rallies his flying soldiers with yet another medical simile.

> "*Marcius.* All the contagion of the south light on you!
> You shames of Rome!—you herd of—Boils and plagues
> Plaster you o'er; that you may be abhorr'd
> Further than seen, and one infect another
> Against the wind a mile!" *Act* i., *Scene* 4.

The boils or plagues invoked would appear to refer to the boils or bubos of the plague, the strength of whose infection is thus fancifully exaggerated.

When Marcius himself is severely wounded he bravely makes light of it.

> "The blood I drop is rather physical
> Than dangerous to me." *Act* i., *Scene* 5.

A subsequent disparagement of his wounds draws from his colleague a reply, referring to a natural event in wounds, and also to an old mode of treatment.

> "*Marcius.* I have some wounds upon me, and they smart
> To hear themselves remember'd.
> *Cominius.* Should they not,
> Well might they fester 'gainst ingratitude,
> And tent themselves with death." *Act* i., *Scene* 9.

Wounds not remembered might well fester from neglect, or if not remembered and not tented according to the surgical practice of the time, they might well be supposed to run the risk of ending fatally, or in medical periphrasis "tent themselves with death." The tent mentioned here, and in many other passages, is, of course, the substance made of lint or flax, which in the rough surgery of the olden time, was habitually thrust into wounds.

Cominius continuing to argue against Marcius' overstrained modesty, refers to the manner in which suicide was thought preventable in the olden time.

> "If 'gainst yourself you be incensed, we'll put you
> (Like one that means his proper harm) in manacles."
> *Act* i., *Scene* 9.

The loss of blood, however, has its effect on the haughty man, causing physical and mental debility.

> "*Lartius.* Marcius, his name?
> *Coriolanus* By Jupiter, forgot!—
> I am weary; yea, my memory is tir'd.—
> Have we no wine here?" *Ibid.*

When Menenius receives a letter from his friend Marcius, now surnamed Coriolanus, he describes the health preserving effect of the pleasure it affords him, in terms which convey the poet's high appreciation of Galen, the great medical authority of his own day. The reference, however, implies a trifling anachronism, inasmuch Galen did not live until nearly six hundred years after the time of Menenius. Shakespeare was wilfully reckless of anachronisms, like the king who was above grammar. He expresses as much in the playful sneer of Lear's fool. "This prophecy shall Merlin make; for I live before his time." "An estate of seven years' health," appears a medical thought conveyed in a legal form.

"A letter for me? It gives me an estate of seven years' health; in which time I will make make a lip at the physician: the most sovereign prescription in Galen is but empiric physic, and, to this preservative, of no better report than a horse-drench. Is he not wounded? He was wont to come home wounded."
Act ii., *Scene* 1.

In the following, commentators suppose that "rapture" means some sort of fit. Shakespeare uses "rapt" to express a condition resembling ecstasy, as in Macbeth,

"Your prattling nurse
Into a rapture lets her baby cry."   *Act* ii., *Scene* 1.

Coriolanus' abhorrence of "the rank-scented many," leads him to denunciate the weak counsels of the Senate, who incline to give them some share of power, "mingling them with us." This to his aristocratic pride would be like wilfully catching the measles, an old term for leprosy. "And to *meselle* houses of that same lond."—*R. Brunne.* "Rise ye dede men, clense ye mesels."—*Wiclif*, quoted by *Richardson*.

> " As for my country I have shed my blood,
> Not fearing outward force, so shall my lungs
> Coin words till their decay, against those measels,
> Which we disdain should tetter us, yet sought
> The very way to catch them." *Act* iii., *Scene* 1.

The 'wish,' which Coriolanus attributes to the senators of his own faction, was quite contrary to the practice of the medical men in Shakespeare's day, who were in the habit of refusing to compromise their reputation by entering upon the treatment of sick persons whom they judged to be incurable. Thus Fuller speaks of a physician of the highest eminence, who studiously kept himself out of the way of being employed by James I. in the treatment of the Prince of Wales, whose early decease he had prognosticated.

> " To jump a body with a dangerous physic
> That's sure of death without it." *Ibid.*

The violent tribune's retort to Menenius' exhortation to temperance, when he wishes to execute mob-law upon the hero, conveys the same medical maxim as that referred to in *Much Ado*, namely, " for to strange sores strangely they strain the cure." Brutus puts the same maxim in an inverted form, both the one and the other, however, being evidently founded upon the maxim of Hippocrates, that extreme diseases need extreme remedies.

> "*Menenius.* Be that you seem, truly your country's friend,
> And temperately proceed to what you would
> Thus violently redress.
>   *Brutus.*   Sir, those cold ways,
> That seem like prudent helps, are very poisonous
> Where the disease is violent :—Lay hands upon him,
> And bear him to the rock." *Ibid.*

When Coriolanus has beaten back the Ædiles and the

people, his friends entreat him to retire, in another reference to the old form of surgery which treated wounds with tents.

> "Leave us to cure this cause:
> *Men.*   For 'tis a sore upon us
> You cannot tent yourself."   *Ibid.*

A string of surgical similes is maintained. The enemy compares Coriolanus to a disease which must be cut away; the friend compares him to a limb affected with curable disease which it would be fatal to amputate; and then with versatile thought leaving this idea, he compares him to a gangrened foot whose former service it would be ingratitude to forget.

> "*Sicinius.* He's a disease, that must be cut away.
> *Menenius.* O, he's a limb, that has but a disease;
> Mortal, to cut it off; to cure it, easy.
> What has he done to Rome that's worthy death?
> Killing our enemies? The blood he hath lost,
> (Which, I dare vouch, is more than that he hath
> By many an ounce,) he dropp'd it for his country:
> And, what is left, to lose it by his country,
> Were to us all, that do't, and suffer it,
> A brand to the end o' the world.
> *Sic.*   This is clean kam.
> *Brutus.* Merely awry: when he did love his country,
> It honour'd him.
> *Men.*   The service of the foot
> Being once gangren'd, is not then respected
> For what before it was—
> *Bru.*   We'll hear no more:—
> Pursue him to his house, and pluck him thence;
> Lest his infection, being of catching nature,
> Spread further."   *Act* iii., *Scene* 1.

Menenius persuades submission to the sentence of banishment, because

> "The violent fit o' the time craves it as physic
> For the whole state."   *Act* iii., *Scene* 2.

P

Coriolanus compares the breath and the love of the people to two causes of disease, the marsh miasma, and, as in *Henry V.*, to putrifying bodies.

> "You common cry of curs! whose breath I hate
> As reek o' the rotten fens, whose loves I prize
> As the dead carcases of unburied men
> That do corrupt my air, I banish you." *Act* iii., *Scene* 3.

Volumnia, no doubt, refers to the cutaneous eruptions common in plague as the "red pestilence." "The red plague rid you," in the *Tempest*, and the "tokened pestilence," in *Antony and Cleopatra*, refer to the same symptoms. The tokens, *i. e.*, of death, included, however, more than the red eruption.

> "Now the red pestilence strike all trades in Rome,
> And occupations perish!" *Act* iv., *Scene* 1.

The activity and vigour of a state of war is paradoxically preferred to peace, as if the former were a state of health, and the latter of disease. Hamlet makes peace the time of health, though of plethoric health which ripens into war. Apoplexy is here confounded with lethargy, which is described as proceeding by the degrees, mulled, deaf, sleepy, insensible. The term apoplexy is used rather loosely by Shakespeare in many places, but always to signify an affection of the brain; whereas, modern physicians have most absurdly used the same term for sudden diseases of other organs, and thus speak and write of apoplexy of the lungs and apoplexy of the liver.

> "*1st Servant.* Let me have war, say I: it exceeds peace as far as day does night; it's spritely, waking, audible, and full of vent. Peace is a very apoplexy, lethargy: mulled, deaf, sleepy, insensible."
> *Act* iv., *Scene* 5.

It has been said that the fate of the battle of Leipsic turned upon a badly cooked cutlet, which gave Napoleon a fit of indigestion. Menenius so fully recognizes the alliance between the stomach and the brain, that he will not throw away a chance by asking grace for his country from his triumphal and revengeful friend, except at a time when, upon physiological grounds, good digestion has filled the veins and warmed the blood, and fairly paved the way to generosity of feeling.

> "*Menenius.* I'll undertake it:
> I think he'll hear me. Yet, to bite his lip,
> And hum at good Cominius, much unhearts me.
> He was not taken well; he had not din'd:
> The veins unfill'd, our blood is cold, and then
> We pout upon the morning, are unapt
> To give or to forgive; but when we have stuff'd
> These pipes, and these conveyances of our blood,
> With wine and feeding, we have suppler souls
> Than in our priest-like fasts: therefore I'll watch him
> Till he be dieted to my request,
> And then I'll set upon him." *Act* v., *Scene* 1.

JULIUS CÆSAR.

The charm against sterility, referred to by Cæsar, is copied from Plutarch, who describes the feast *Lupercalia*, in which "noble young men run naked through the city striking in sport whom they meet in their way with leather thongs," which blows were supposed to have the effect attributed to them by Cæsar.

> "The barren, touched in this holy chase,
> Shake off their steril curse."
> *Act* i., *Scene* 2.

Cassius's description of Cæsar's fever is rather meagre from our point of view, compared with many of Shakespeare's medical descriptions. The symptoms given are, that this god did shake, his lips lost their colour, his eyes their lustre, and he did groan, and was afflicted with thirst, and his spirit was beaten down, as that of the bravest must be under sickness.

> "He had a fever when he was in Spain,
> And, when the fit was on him, I did mark
> How he did shake: 'tis true, this god did shake:
> His coward lips did from their colour fly;
> And that same eye, whose bend doth awe the world,
> Did lose its lustre: I did hear him groan:
> Ay, and that tongue of his, that bade the Romans
> Mark him, and write his speeches in their books,
> Alas! it cried, 'Give me some drink, Titinius,'
> As a sick girl."
> *Act* i., *Scene* 2.

Casca's description of Cæsar's epilepsy is as terse as it well can be. He fell down, foamed at the mouth, and was speechless.

"The rabblement hooted, and clapped their chapped hands, and threw up their sweaty night-caps, and uttered such a deal of stinking breath because Cæsar refused the crown, that it had almost choked Cæsar; for he swooned, and fell down at it: and for mine own part, I durst not laugh, for fear of opening my lips, and receiving the bad air.
 Cassius. But, soft, I pray you: What? Did Cesar swoon?
 Casca. He fell down in the market-place, and foamed at mouth, and was speechless.
 Brutus. 'Tis very like: he hath the falling sickness."
Act i., *Scene* 2.

When Portia claims to participate in the mental disquiet of her husband, and he excuses his restlessness on the ground of ill health, she refutes him, with a good knowledge of the rules of regimen.

"I should not know you, Brutus. Dear my lord,
Make me acquainted with your cause of grief.
 Brutus. I am not well in health, and that is all.
 Portia. Brutus is wise, and were he not in health,
He would embrace the means to come by it.
 Bru. Why, so I do:—Good Portia, go to bed,
 Por. Is Brutus sick? and is it physical
To walk unbraced, and suck up the humours
Of the dank morning? What, is Brutus sick;
And will he steal out of his wholesome bed
To dare the vile contagion of the night,
And tempt the rheumy and unpurged air
To add unto his sickness? No, my Brutus;
You have some sick offence within your mind."
Act ii., *Scene* 1.

Brutus, still hesitating to share the secrets of his heart with the too inquisitive woman, attempts to console her with the assurances of his love.

> " *You are my true and honourable wife,*
> *As dear to me as are the ruddy drops*
> *That visit my sad heart.*"   *Ibid.*

On these three lines, a short essay, the only one bearing upon Shakespeare's physiological opinions I have anywhere been able to find, has been written by Mr. Thomas Nimmo, and has been published in the second volume of the *Shakespeare Society's Papers*. Mr. Nimmo considers that this passage "contains, what I cannot view otherwise than a distinct reference to the circulation of the blood, which was not announced to the world, as is generally supposed, until some years after the death of Shakespeare." Assuming the truth of this, he argues either that the Play was not written so early as 1603, the date fixed by Mr. Collier, or that "Shakespeare had been made acquainted by Harvey himself, with his first notions on the subject." . . . "Is it then impossible that Harvey, a young medical practitioner, may have become acquainted with Shakespeare, may have become intimate with him, and may have acquainted him with those great ideas by which also he hoped to become famous." In some comments on the article, Mr. T. J. Pettigrew satisfactorily disposes of Mr. Nimmo's suggestion: "There is no evidence that Shakespeare knew Harvey; and, as Shakespeare died in 1616, when the first ideas of Harvey upon the subject were promulgated at the college, he could not, through that medium, have been acquainted with it; but if the date of 1603, as given by Mr. Collier, as the period at which the play of Julius Cæsar was written, be the correct one, it is quite clear that Shakespeare could not have then known Harvey, for he must at that time have been abroad, and, whatever may have been his reflections upon the discovery of the existence of valves in the veins, there are no traces in any of his writings to shew that he had then entertained any particular views upon the nature of the circulation."

Shakespeare might indeed have known Harvey, as he

no doubt was intimate with many of the leading minds of the age; but, in addition to the fact, that Harvey's first notice of his discovery was made in the year of Shakespeare's decease, Mr. Nimmo's suggestion is easily refuted from the other writings of the poet, with which it seems probable that Mr. Nimmo had not made himself acquainted. There are several passages in the plays, in which the presence of blood in the heart is quite as distinctly referred to, as in this speech of Brutus; but the passages quoted in these pages from *Love's Labour Lost*, and from the *Second Part of Henry IV.*, distinctly prove that Shakespeare entertained the Galenical doctrine universally prevalent before Harvey's discovery, that, although the right side of the heart was visited by the blood, the function of the heart and its proper vessels, the arteries, was the distribution of the vital spirits, or, as Biron calls them, "the nimble spirits in the arteries." Shakespeare believed indeed in the flow of the blood. "the rivers of your blood," which went "even to the court, the heart;" but he considered that it was the liver, and not the heart which was the cause of the flow. There is not, in my opinion, in Shakespeare, a trace of any knowledge of the circulation of the blood. Surely the temple of his fame needs not to be enriched by the spoils of any other reputation!

The sickness of Ligarius, which he discards at the bidding of Brutus, "I here discard my sickness," would seem not to have been a pretended one, since Cæsar refers to its nature and effect.

> "Cæsar was ne'er so much your enemy
> As that same ague which hath made you lean."
> *Act* ii., *Scene* 3.

In the quarrel between Brutus and Cassius, the former says,

> " You shall digest the venom of your spleen,
> Though it do split you." *Act* iv., *Scene* 3.

This seems again to convey the old false notion that poison always swells the body.

Portia's mode of committing suicide is as remarkable as it is obscure.

> "*Brutus.*   Impatient of my absence;
> And grief, that young Octavius with Mark Antony
> Have made themselves so strong;—for with her death
> That tidings came;—With this she fell distract,
> And, her attendants absent, swallow'd fire."
> *Act* iv., *Scene* 4.

Messala may well say, "For certain she is dead, and by strange manner." Shakespeare, however, took the fact from Plutarch. "She determining to kill herself (her parents and friends carefullie looking to her to kepe her from it) tooke hotte burning coles, and cast them into her mouth, and kept her mouth so close, that she choked herselfe."

In Antony's eulogium on Brutus, the theory of the old physicians, that life is composed of the four elements (see *Twelfth Night*), is alluded to.

> " His life was gentle; and the elements
> So mix'd in him that nature might stand up,
> And say to all the world, 'This was a man.'"
> *Act* v., *Scene* 5.

This old theory is the subject of the 44th and 45th Sonnets.

ANTONY AND CLEOPATRA.

Cleopatra, with the idea that she would like to sleep away the time of her lover's absence, calls for mandragora, as a soporific.

> "*Cleopatra.* Charmian,—
> *Charmian.* Madam.
> *Cleo.* Ha, ha!—
> Give me to drink mandragora.
> *Char.*   Why, madam?
> *Cleo.* That I might sleep out this great gap of time
> My Antony is away."   *Act* i., *Scene* 5.

Shakespeare refers to this drug, a second time, in *Othello*, and in exactly the same sense. Iago observing of his master whose peace of mind has been for ever destroyed by jealousy

> "No poppy nor mandragora,
> Nor all the drowsy syrups of the world,
> Shall med'cine thee to that sweet sleep
> Which thou ow'dst yesterday."

Mandragora appears to have been extensively used as a narcotic in the olden time. It was prescribed by Hippocrates. Salmon, quoting Schroder, says, that it is seldom used inwardly. The plant is the *atropia mandragora*, and it was chiefly brought from Italy; the root, the leaves, and the apples were used medicinally, and, according to Salmon, it is "wonderfully narcotic and soporific." The root of the plant is forked, and was supposed to bear resemblance to the form of a man, hence called 'anthropomorphon;' thus arose the remarkable saying that when the plant was plucked from the ground, it emitted a groan like that of a human being in pain. Shakespeare refers, in two passages, to the supposed human shape of the mandrake, in the *Second Part of Henry IV.;* and in two other passages he refers to the superstition respecting its groan. The plant, therefore, is referred to in the plays, altogether, six times, and it is markworthy that on the two occasions where its real medicinal properties are the occasion of its mention, the Latin term, mandragora is used; the vulgar appellative, mandrake, being employed on the occasions where the vulgar superstition is alluded to.

"Would curses kill as doth the mandrakes' groan?"
Henry VI., 2nd *Part, Act* iii., *Scene* 2.

"And shrieks like mandrakes torn out of the earth,
That living mortals hearing them run mad."
Romeo and Juliet, Act iv., *Scene* 5.

The penalty, however, seems to have been attached to the act of pulling the root from the earth, and, in ancient times, it was evaded by fastening a dog to the plant, and whipping the animal, who, in efforts to escape, drew forth the root.

The reference made here to Antony, as the great medicine whose tinct has gilded his messenger, no doubt refers to gold, which among our superstitious forefathers was emphatically considered the great medicine; the allusion is the same as that of "the tinct and multiplying medicine" found in *All's Well that Ends Well.*

"*Cleo.* How much unlike art thou Mark Antony!
Yet, coming from him, that great medicine hath
With his tinct gilded thee." *Act* i., *Scene* 5.

The effect of a voluptuous life upon the character, through the influence of the body, and especially of the brain, is described by Pompey.

"Tie up the libertine in a field of feasts;
Keep his brain fuming; Epicurean cooks
Sharpen with cloyless sauce his appetite;

>That sleep and feeding may prorogue his honour,
>Even till a Lethe'd dullness!" *Act* ii., *Scene* 1.

Here is another allusion to 'green sickness,' referring, as in *Henry IV.*, to a man.

>"Cæsar is sad; and Lepidus,
>Since Pompey's feast, as Menas says, is troubled
>With the green-sickness." *Act* iii., *Scene* 2.

The "tokened pestilence," means the plague or pestilence in which "the Lord's tokens," *(Love's Labour Lost,)* or the "death's tokens," *(Troilus and Cressida,)* have appeared, indicating, according to the old belief, that there was no hope of recovery.

>"*Enobarbus.* How appears the fight?
>*Scarus.* On our side like the token'd pestilence,
>Where death is sure." *Act* iii., *Scene* 8.

One would suppose that the poet must have seen a wound of the shape here so minutely described.

>"*Antony.* Thou bleed'st apace.
>*Scarus.* I had a wound here that was like a T,
>But now 'tis made an H." *Act* iv., *Scene* 7.

Cæsar laments over the death of Antony as if his life had been a part of his own existence, yet a diseased part, which it was needful to lance.

>"Oh Antony!
>I've follow'd thee to this; but we do lance
>Diseases in our bodies." *Act* v., *Scene* 1.

Cleopatra threatens suicide by starvation and watchfulness, a very efficient means, as alienist physicians too well know. The singular mode of suicide which she did adopt, by the bite of the asp, "the pretty worm of Nilus that kills and pains not," is a much more congenial form of death to the voluptuous character of the woman, who had made a study "of easy ways to die."

"*Cæsar.*   The manner of their deaths?
I do not see them bleed.
    Dolabella.   Who was last with them?
    1 *Guard.* A simple countryman, that brought her figs:
This was his basket.
    Cæs.   Poison'd them.
    1 *Guard.*   O Cæsar,
This Charmian liv'd but now; she stood, and spake:
I found her trimming up the diadem
On her dead mistress; tremblingly she stood,
And on the sudden dropp'd.
    Cæs.   O noble weakness!—
If they had swallow'd poison, 'twould appear
By external swelling; but she looks like sleep,
As she would catch another Antony
In her strong toil of grace.
    Dol.   Here, on her breast,
There is a vent of blood, and something blown,
The like is on her arm.
    1 *Guard.* This is an aspic's trail: and these fig-leaves
Have slime upon them, such as the aspic leaves
Upon the caves of Nile.
    Cæs.   Most probable
That so she died; for her physician tells me
She hath pursued conclusions infinite
Of easy ways to die."   *Act* v., *Scene* 2.

Cæsar's comments upon the bodies of the queen and her women repeats the old notion that poison produces swelling of the body.

No book appears to me to convey a more faithful impression of the opinions prevalent among the class of medical men we should call general practitioners in the seventeenth century, than the *Diary of the Rev. John Hall, Vicar of Stratford upon Avon*, who studied medicine at the University, and afterwards at "Barber Chyrurgeons Hall," and practised it more or less professionally in conjunction with his clerical duties. This diary, which extends from 1648 to 1679, is about equally divided into medical and ecclesiastical notes. As this diary commenced thirty years after

Shakespeare's death, and as it emanated from a learned man, who had made medicine the study of his life, we might expect that it would be considerably in advance of Shakespeare's knowledge of medicine. We find, however, in the notes, far more to illustrate than to refute the opinions of the medical vicar's immortal townsman. Thus, in the subject of swelling of the body from poison, Ward writes: "When one was poisoned at Coventrie, hee was taken upp out of his grave; but as the apothecarie said the earth would keep him from swelling, so that no judgement could bee made thereby; but being opened, they found the poison in his stomach."

It is curious that Shakespeare makes Cleopatra apply the aspic both to the breast and to the arm, since we find a discussion in old Primrose's *Popular Errors*, on this point. Primrose does not appear to have read Shakespeare, or with his love of reference he would certainly have shewn it. In his chapter on the mountebank's antidote, he says: "And now the story of *Cleopatra* comes to my minde. *Petrus Victorius* blames the painters, that paint *Cleopatra* applying the aspe to her paps, seeing it is manifest out of *Plutarch*, in the *Life of Antonius*, and out of *Plinie* likewise, that she applyed it to her arme. *Zonaras* relates that there appeared no signe of death upon her, save two blew spots on her arme. *Cæsar* also in her statute which he carryed in triumph, applyed the aspe to her arme: For in the armes there are great veines and arteries, which doe quickly and in a straight way convey the venome to the heart, whereas in the paps the vessels are slender, which, by sundry circumvolutions onely, do lead to the heart."

CYMBELINE.

The conversation between the queen and the physician, Cornelius, contains several note-worthy points on the subject of poisons;—the herbalist practice of gathering flowers while the dew is on them;—the conscientious scruple of the physician to give the queen slow and deadly poisons;—the queen's excuse that, in order to amplify her judgment or knowledge from herbs to more potent agents, she wishes to try the effects of these deadly compounds upon worthless animals, and to experiment upon antidotes;—the reply of the good and sensible man that to inflict pain on brutes hardens the heart, and that to experiment in this manner with poisons is not without danger to the health.

"*Queen.* Whiles yet the dew's on ground, gather those flowers;
Make haste: Who has the note of them? * *
Now, master doctor; have you brought those drugs?
    Cornelius. Pleaseth your highness, ay: here they are, madam:
But I beseech your grace, (without offence—
My conscience bids me ask;) wherefore you have
Commanded of me these most poisonous compounds,
Which are the movers of a languishing death;
But, though slow, deadly?
    Queen.   I wonder, doctor,
Thou ask'st me such a question: Have I not been
Thy pupil long? Hast thou not learn'd me how
To make perfumes? distil? preserve? yea, so,
That our great king himself doth woo me oft
For my confections? Having thus far proceeded,
(Unless thou think'st me devilish,) is't not meet
That I did amplify my judgment in
Other conclusions? I will try the forces
Of these thy compounds on such creatures as
We count not worth the hanging, (but none human,)

<pre>
      To try the vigour of them, and apply
      Allayments to their act ; and by them gather
      Their several virtues and effects.
          Cor.   Your highness
      Shall from this practice but make hard your heart :
      Besides, the seeing these effects will be
      Both noisome and infectious."   Act i., Scene 6.
</pre>

The annals of criminal jurisprudence shew that this excuse of the queen's is one of the readiest and most common among those who deal with poisons for the purpose of murder. In the great trial of the horrible poisoner Palmer, it was argued that the strychnine he had bought was for the purpose of poisoning dogs ; but there was no proof that he had used any part of the drug for this purpose, or it is possible that this vulgar Borgia might thus have evaded his doom.

Cornelius penetrates the character of the queen, and suspecting her wicked intentions, gives her a narcotic, something that will stupify and dull the sense for a while, but will not prove poisonous.

<pre>
          " Cornelius. I do not like her. She doth think she has
      Strange lingering poisons : I do know her spirit,
      And will not trust one of her malice with
      A drug of such damn'd nature : Those she has
      Will stupify and dull the sense awhile :
      Which first, perchance, she'll prove on cats and dogs ;
      Then afterward up higher ; but there is
      No danger in what show of death it makes,
      More than the locking up the spirits a time,
      To be more fresh, reviving."   Ibid.
</pre>

A crisis in the plot of the play hinges upon the operation on Imogen of this narcotic, the supposed powers of which appear to have been exactly the same as that given by Friar Lawrence to Juliet for the purpose of simulating death. Modern medicine is acquainted with no drug having the property to produce for a while the show of death, and yet to leave the powers of life so unharmed, that the subject of them shall be " more fresh, reviving."

The meaning of the following passage is thought obscure by the commentators. It would be plain enough but for the word "emptiness;" but as it is more difficult to vomit on an empty, than on a full stomach, this word seems used merely to augment the expression. Iachimo is comparing the excellence of Imogen with the sluttery of her husband's supposed mistress.

> " Sluttery, to such neat excellence oppos'd,
> Should make desire vomit emptiness,
> Not so allur'd to feed." *Act* i. *Scene* 7.

Imogen, desiring her lord's content in all things, except his absence from her, wishes that to be "medicinable," or to have the property of medicine.

> " Let that grieve him—
> Some griefs are med'cinable; that is one of them,
> For it doth physick love." *Act* iii. *Scene* 2.

The idea in the following seems to be, that the wife, impatient to meet her lord, longs for counsel to do so, in words quicker than the ears can receive them; as excess of light may blind, so may rapidity of sound smother the sense of hearing.

> " Say, and speak thick;—
> Love's counsellor should fill the bores of hearing
> To the smothering of the sense." *Ibid.*

When Imogen strives not to permit her sickness to engross attention, her excuse conveys a reproach on the fancied illnesses of those on whom the influences of city life have conferred the curse of hypochondria.

> "So sick I am not;—yet I am not well:
> But not so citizen a wanton, as
> To seem to die, ere sick." *Act* iv., *Scene* 2.

Posthumus, life-weary and in prison, compares his state with that of a man clinging to life in the agony of painful disease. The gout, however, is not a good form of disease for this illustration, since there are few of those who suffer from it who "groan in perpetuity."

> "Yet am I better
> Than one that's sick o' the gout: since he had rather
> Groan so in perpetuity, than be cur'd
> By the sure physician, death, who is the key
> To unbar these locks." *Act* v., *Scene* 4.

The wicked queen, who bore down all with her brain, is struck with disease of the brain, when her schemes fail. She lies "upon a desperate bed" from the effects of

> "A fever with the absence of her son;
> A madness, of which her life's in danger." *Act* iv., *Scene* 3.

Towards the end of the play we learn the fatal result, "with horror, madly dying," though, like the death of Constance and of Lady Macbeth, it is hidden from view.

Shakespeare sometimes places before his audience scenes of death, whose terror can hardly be exceeded, as that of King John and Cardinal Beaufort; but the innate delicacy, which is not inconsistent with much verbal grossness, prevents him from so exhibiting a woman.

Cymbeline's reflection upon a physician announcing the death of his patient would seem to convey no exalted opinion of an art which could not always save life, if it were not accompanied by the full admission of the highest purpose to which medicine can ever pretend, namely, to prolong life.

>"*Cornelius.*   Hail, great king!
>To sour your happiness, I must report
>The queen is dead.
>   *Cymbeline.*   Whom worse than a physician
>Would this report become? But I consider,
>By medicine life may be prolong'd, yet death
>Will seize the doctor too.—How ended she?
>   *Cor.*   With horror, madly dying, like her life,
>Which, being cruel to the world, concluded
>Most cruel to herself."   *Act* v., *Scene* 5.

The queen's confession, which the king credits on the recognized legal ground, because "she spoke it dying," informs us that the physician's aid failing her, she had obtained poison from some other source.

>   "She did confess she had
>For you a mortal mineral; which, being took,
>Should by the minute feed on life, and, ling'ring,
>By inches waste you."   *Ibid.*

This belief in slow poisoning was general in olden time, although no better founded on fact than the belief that persons burst with poison, or that narcotics could, like an alarum clock, be set for a certain number of hours. Ambrose Paré's third chapter on poisons is on the subject, "Whether there be any such Poysons as will kill at a set time?" a question which, on the authority of Theophrastus, he answers in the negative, grounding his own opinion on the different operations of all drugs on "man's different natures in complexion and temper." "For in such (for example sake) as have the passages in their arteries more large, the poyson may more readily and speedily enter into the heart, together with the aire that is continually drawn into the body."

"Some poysons, more readily perform their parts, others more slowly, yet may you find no such as will kill in set limits of time, according to the will and desire of men; for that some kill sooner or later than others, they do this not of their own or proper nature, as physicians rightly judge, but because the subject on which they light, doth, more or less, resist or yield to their efficacie."

The name given to Cymbeline's physician is worthy of note. Cornelius was the name of the physician to Charles V., who gained European reputation by curing the Emperor of gout and general ill habit of body. It seems more probable, therefore, that Shakespeare adopted the name from this source, than from the more classic one of Cornelius Celsus. The physicians in *Lear* and *Macbeth* are not honoured with names. Henry the Eighth's physician, Dr. Butts, however, is named, though, if Goodall be correct, with the error of the final letter, "s" instead of "e." Dr. Caius, in *The Merry Wives of Windsor*, was probably named after the eminent physician to Queen Elizabeth, though the dramatic character bears no shade of resemblance to the learned and wealthy physician, who left the noblest monument with the shortest epitaph on record; the former being the College founded by him at Cambridge, and the latter the inscription on his tomb in the chapel of that College, "Fui Caius."

TROILUS AND CRESSIDA.

Troilus, in the same speech, refers to his love both as an ulcer and a wound.

> "Pour'st in the open ulcer of my heart
> Her eyes, her hair, her cheeks, her gait, her voice;
> * * * * *
> But, saying thus, instead of oil and balm,
> Thou lay'st in every gash that love hath given me
> The knife that made it." *Act* i., *Scene* 1.

In the description of Ajax, gout is alluded to as a disease of the joints, and especially of the joints of the hands.

> "*Alexander.* He is melancholy without cause, and merry against the hair: he hath the joints of every thing; but everything so out of joint, that he is a gouty Briareus, many hands and no use; or purblinded Argus, all eyes and no sight." *Ibid.*

Agamemnon begins his address to the council of war with an allusion to jaundice as the physical effect of grief.

The resemblance which he traces in the checks and disasters in the veins of action, to knots in the pine which render the vein of the wood tortuous, would seem to be derived from the tortuous knots so common in the veins of the legs, known to medical men as varices.

> "Princes,
> What grief hath set the jaundice on your cheeks?
> The ample proposition that hope makes
> In all designs begun on earth below,
> Fails in the promis'd largeness; checks and disasters
> Grow in the veins of actions highest rear'd;
> As knots, by the conflux of meeting sap,
> Infect the sound pine, and divert his grain
> Tortive and errant from his course of growth."
> *Act* i., *Scene* 3.

In the following passage, the old belief in planetary influence on diseases is expressed.

> " And therefore is the glorious planet, Sol,
> In noble eminence enthron'd and spher'd
> Amidst the other ; whose med'cinable eye
> Corrects the ill aspects of planets evil,
> And posts, like the commandment of a king,
> Sans check, to good and bad. But when the planets,
> In evil mixture, to disorder wander,
> What plagues, and what portents ! " *Ibid.*

The want of subordination and discipline produces, what Ulysses calls, a social fever, the diagnosis of which being given, Agamemnon invites an exposition of the proper treatment.

> " *Ulysses.* So every step,
> Exampled by the first pace that is sick
> Of his superior, grows to an envious fever
> Of pale and bloodless emulation :
> And 'tis this fever that keeps Troy on foot,
> Not her own sinews. To end a tale of length,
> Troy in our weakness stands, not in her strength.
> *Nestor.* Most wisely hath Ulysses here discover'd
> The fever whereof all our power is sick.
> *Agamemnon.* The nature of the sickness found, Ulysses,
> What is the remedy ? " *Ibid.*

Ulysses, commenting upon the mimicry with which Patroclus disparages Nestor's age, describes the symptoms of senile disease, rather than the faint defects of age.

> " And then, forsooth, the faint defects of age
> Must be the scene of mirth ; to cough, and spit,
> And with a palsy, fumbling on his gorget,
> Shake in and out the rivet." *Ibid.*

The malignant buffoonery of Thersites constantly avails itself of offensive allusions to disease. In the following, the double meaning attributed to boils running with matter is obvious.

"And those boils did run? Say so,—did not the general run? were not that a botchy core?" *Act* ii., *Scene* 1.

The use of the old surgical appliance, the tent, is here distinctly indicated as being thrust to the bottom of the wound.

"*Hector.* Modest doubt is call'd
The beacon of the wise, the tent that searches
To the bottom of the worst." *Act* ii., *Scene* 2.

Thersites logically concludes, that painful nodes are the most appropriate curse for those who fight for a lewd woman.

"After this, the vengeance on the whole camp! or, rather, the bone-ache! for that, methinks, is the curse dependent on those that war for a placket." *Act* ii., *Scene* 3.

The very objectionable *casus belli* of the Greeks is here again stated, and another medical curse imprecated.

"All the argument is, a cuckold and a whore. A good quarrel to draw emulous factions, and bleed to death upon! Now the dry *serpigo* on the subject! and war and lechery confound all!"
Ibid.

The *serpigo* is mentioned in *Measure for Measure*, erroneously, indeed, as a possible case of death. It appears to have been a term widely used by old medical authors for any creeping skin disease. The disease, however, to which it was most frequently applied, was the vesicular disease now called *herpes circinatus*, which certainly could not be called dry. The term *serpigo* was also frequently applied to creeping forms of *impetigo* and *psoriasis*, and to the latter of these especially, a dry scaly eruption, the term of the text would be perfectly appropriate.

The following contains the correction of a vulgar anatomical error.

"*Ulysses.* The elephant hath joints, but none for courtesy: His legs are legs for necessity, not for flexure." *Act* ii., *Scene* 3.

In Sir Thomas Browne's *Enquiries into Vulgar and Common Errors*, the first Chapter, Book 3, is on the subject "That an elephant hath no joints. The first shall be of the elephant, whereof there generally passeth an opinion it hath no joints, and this absurdity is seconded with another, that being unable to lie down, it sleepeth against a tree." "This conceit is not the daughter of later times, but an old and gray-headed error," says the commentator on Browne; it was derived from Ctesias the first Greek who saw and described an elephant, and it was controverted by Aristotle.

The digestive maxim of, "after dinner sit awhile," was not entertained by Patroclus, who, speaking for his chief to the princes of their afternoon call, says,

"He hopes it is no other
But, for your health and your digestion sake,
An after-dinner's breath." *Act* ii., *Scene* 3.

Ulysses, speaking of the intense pride of Achilles, treat it as a disease, in which his mental, and his active or corporeal parts, rage in fatal commotion.

" Imagin'd worth
Holds in his blood such swoln and hot discourse,
That, 'twixt his mental and his active parts,
Kingdom'd Achilles in commotion rages,
And batters down himself: What should I say?
He is so plaguy proud, that the death-tokens of it
Cry—'No recovery.'" *Ibid.*

These marks which were held to be of such fearful import, are called "The Lord's tokens," in *Love's Labour Lost*, *Act* v., *Scene* 2; and are again referred to as a fatal symptom in

Antony and Cleopatra, "The tokened pestilence where death is sure."

The following is the account which Woodall gives of these cutaneous marks, and of the effect which the belief in their fatal character had upon the patients in whom they appeared.

"Of the markes or spots, commonly, though neither properly nor always truely called, God's Tokens." "The fourth apparent outward signe of the Plague is, the markes or spots appearing upon the skinne, usually called God's Tokens, but not as being ever certaine tokens of the pestilence, and so of death to the patient, as vulgarly they are taken to be, by ignorant people in their unexpert conjectures and opinions, for that it is daily manifest, many have spots of severall formes and colours, when venomous feavours raigne, and yet have not the plague: and again many have suspitious and fearefull spots, which the vulgar tearme God's Tokens, and recover and live many years after; myself have cured not a few in that kind, that are now, to God's glory, living; these spots are upon some bodies like flea bitings, in others larger, in some againe as big as a penny. In some bodies there are very many, and sometimes they are like frecles, and they are most commonly found upon the breast, and sometimes upon the backe, armes, and legges of the patients; they are in some of a colour blewish, or of a sad red, and some are like lead colour, and others purple, some are of a pale blew, and these spots are ever without paine: but the very appearance of any spots, to any in the plague, cause sudden fear to the patient; which, though the markes be insensible, yet through sudden feare, they produce faintings, swoundings, trembling of the heart, and death following thereupon, although neither the patient feele paine as is said, neither alwayes the Artist can judge, by reason hee seeth just cause of sudden death to his patient, the reason being secret with God, as inwardly afflicting mankind, *de præscientia Dei,* namely of the foreknowledge of God: so much of the markes, spots, or tokens, in some appearing in the disease of the Plague."—p. 333.

Troilus describes one symptom of his passion.

"My heart beats thicker than a feverous pulse,
And all my powers do their bestowing lose."
Act iii., *Scene* 2.

The symptoms of fever are referred to in many other passages: in Cassius' description of Cæsar's fever; by King John, who threatens the citizens of Angiers, with his cannon, "to make a shaking in your walls;" in *Macbeth,* "after life's fitful fever," "as if the earth was feverous and did shake;" and again, in the almost same words in *Coriolanus,* "as if the world were feverous and did tremble." Old medical writers called ague 'the fever,' and it is still called 'intermittent fever' and the 'marsh fever.' It is evident from the above expressions that Shakespeare often used the term in this sense. He, however, also applied it in the sense more usually accepted at the present time to designate common infectious fever: see the speech of the archbishop in the *Second Part of Henry IV., Act* iv., *Scene* 1, "A burning fever" brought on by surfeiting, and "we must bleed for it;" and in *Henry V., Act* iv., *Scene* 1, "Think'st thou thy fiery fever will go out." In *Timon,* typhus seems referred to, as "potent and infectious fevers;" and the fever of drunkards, "till the high fever seethe your blood to froth."

The advice of Patroclus to his patron expresses an old

superstition about self-inflicted wounds, and the imperceptible manner in which the poison of ague may infect the system.

> "Those wounds heal ill that men do give themselves:
> Omission to do what is necessary
> Seals a commission to a blank of danger;
> And danger, like an ague, subtly taints
> Even then when we sit idly in the sun." *Act* iii., *Scene* 3.

The woman's longing, here mentioned, is probably that of child-bearing women, to which so much superstitious importance has been attached.

> "*Achilles.* I have a woman's longing,
> An appetite that I am sick withal." *Ibid.*

In the following, Thersites quibbles on the word tent.

> "*Patroclus.* Who keeps the tent now?
> *Thersites.* The surgeon's box, or the patient's wound."
> *Act* v., *Scene* 1.

The malevolent buffoon, no longer satisfying himself as before with a single disease, the bone-ache or the dry serpigo, imprecates in the following curse a whole nosology.

> "Now the rotten diseases of the south, the guts-griping, ruptures, catarrhs, loads o'gravel i'the back, lethargies, cold palsies, raw eyes, dirt-rotten livers, wheezing lungs, bladders full of imposthume, sciaticas, lime-kilns i' the palm, incurable bone-ache, and the rivell'd fee-simple of the tetter, take and take again such preposterous discoveries!" *Act* v., *Scene* 1.

This is the only place in all the dramas where such a list of diseases is given, unless we allow the maladies of Petruchio's horse to enter into competition.

By the 'rotten diseases of the south' were probably meant that disease which the English called 'the French disease,' and the French called 'the Neapolitan disease.' 'Loads of gravel in the back,' of course refer to gravel in the kidneys, which would be attended by pain in the loins; it would, however, require some medical knowledge to refer this pain to its true cause. 'Lethargy' is frequently confounded by medical men of the time, and by Shakespeare himself, with apoplexy, and 'cold palsies' are the old medical term for chronic paralysis. 'Dirt-rotten livers' indicate a pathological state, as distinguished from a named disease, a state, moreover, by no means of common occurrence. The same may be said of 'bladders full of imposthume,' or chronic inflammation of the bladder, with muco-purulent discharge. One can only guess that 'lime-kilns i' the palm' was meant to designate that condition of chronic gout in the joints of the hands, in which, what are called chalk stones are formed; it might, however, be objected that these would appear not in the palm, but in the knuckles, and, therefore, this explanation is only tendered for want of a better. 'The rivelled fee-simple of the tetter,' or shrivelled, as we should now write it, points to the intractable ring-worm. Altogether, this nosological catalogue indicates a degree of pathological knowledge by no means of that superficial kind, which every observant man possesses; such as that, for instance, indicated in the next comparison which Thersites uses, "Thou green sarsenet flap for a sore eye."

Shakespeare sometimes confuses the idea of an organ and its function, but the two are very carefully distinguished by Troilus expressing belief in the constancy of his mistress.

> " That doth invert the attest of eyes and ears,
> As if those organs had deceptious functions,
> Created only to calumniate." *Act* v., *Scene* 2.

The use of the term nerve and sinew in this play is to be noted; Agamemnon is called,

"Thou great commander, nerve and bone of Greece."
Act i., *Scene* 3.

Hector exhorts Troilus

"Let grow thy sinews 'till their knots be strong."
Act v., *Scene* 3.

Achilles says of Troy, when he has slain Hector,

"Here lies thy heart, thy sinews, and thy bone."
Act v., *Scene* 9.

In the first of these lines, the word nerve appears to be used in the sense to which we now restrict the word sinew, and in the second, the word sinew appears to be used for muscle. Knots in the veins, or varices, are spoken of in this play, but there are no such things as knots in the sinews proper, while knots of muscles or knotted muscles would be perfectly appropriate to express the confirmation of this tissue. Shakespeare, throughout the plays, nowhere uses the word muscle in its anatomical sense. The third of these lines illustrates the meaning of the word nerve as sinew, in the first line; a sense in which, with one or two doubtful exceptions, Shakespeare appears always to have made use of the word nerve; for instance, "as hardy as the Nemean lion's nerve,"—*Hamlet;* and in the 120*th Sonnet,*

"Needs must I under my transgression bow,
Unless my nerves were brass or hammered steel."

It is certain that this erroneous use of the word is borrowed from Hippocrates, and unless it can be shewn to have been common to other writers of Shakespeare's time, it would add much to the other weighty evidence contained in his writings, that he was conversant with the works of the Father of Medicine; the copy of an obsolete error being stronger evidence to this effect, than the adoption of that which in his day was still recognized as truth, and therefore, was more likely to have been received at second hand. It would not have been needful for Shakespeare to have read Hippocrates in the Greek, since several translations of his works, or portions of his works, were then in existence. The use of the word nerve by Hippocrates, and those who came after him, is thus stated by Le Clerc: "The Greek anatomists that came after Hippocrates, distinguished three sorts of parts which were before confounded; the Nerves called $\nu\epsilon\tilde{\upsilon}\rho a$, which are the passages of the animal spirits, which communicate sense and motion to all parts of the body; the tendons, $\tau\acute{\epsilon}\nu o\nu\tau\epsilon\varsigma$, which come from the muscles, and serve to contract or extend the members or the ligaments; $\sigma\upsilon\nu\delta\epsilon\sigma\mu o\iota$, which serve peculiarly to strengthen the articulations of the bones. Hippocrates has given the first of these names indifferently to all the three parts; so that $\nu\epsilon\tilde{\upsilon}\rho o\nu$, nerve, did as well and as often signifie in him a tendon and a ligament. He seems sometimes to mean by it, a nerve, though, according to Galen, Hippocrates uses generally the word $\tau o\nu o\varsigma$ in that signification."

Cassandra predicting the death of Hector mentions the white appearance of the eyes, in persons dying from hæmorrhage.

"Look, how thou diest! look, how thine eye turns pale!
Look, how thy wounds do bleed at many vents!"
Act v., *Scene* 3.

The farewell words of Pandarus have a curious reference to his vocation, and to the old-fashioned sweating treatment of the malady incurred in it. In old times the public stews were under the jurisdiction of the Bishop of Winchester.

"My fear is this,—
Some gulled goose of Winchester would hiss;
Till then I'll sweat, and seek about for eases;
And at that time bequeath you my diseases."
Act v., Scene 11.

ROMEO AND JULIET.

The distinction between a man who is born blind and one who becomes blind is, that

"He, that is strucken blind, cannot forget
The precious treasure of his eyesight lost." *Act* i. *Scene* 1.

The precocity of southern women, and the effect well recognised among medical men, of early child-bearing upon the health, are noted by Capulet. Lady Capulet was a mother at Juliet's age.

"My child is yet a stranger in the world,
She hath not seen the change of fourteen years;
Let two more summers wither in their pride,
Ere we may think her ripe to be a bride.
   Paris. Younger than she are happy mothers made.
   Capulet. And too soon marr'd are those so early made."
Act i., Scene 2.

Benvolio's epigram, and his fence of wit with Romeo, contain remarks of medical interest. The assertion that one pain is lightened by another's anguish is a well known fact, often acted upon in the treatment of disease by blisters, cauteries, &c. "One desperate grief cures with another's anguish," is not, as might seem, a mere repetition, but rather the expression of another medical fact; that some forms of diseases give way on the supervention of others; thus, it is well known, that some disorders give way on the supervention of consumption, and, which is perhaps yet more to the point, the old belief is still widely credited, that ague will cure consumption. Consumptive people are still sent to aguish districts, in order that they may take the new infection of the less fatal disease.

"*Benvolio.* Tut, man! One fire burns out another's burning,
One pain is lessen'd by another's anguish;
Turn giddy, and be holp by backward turning:
One desperate grief cures with another's languish:
Take thou some new infection to the eye,
And the rank poison of the old will die.
   Romeo. Your plantain leaf is excellent for that.
   Ben. For what, I pray thee?
   Rom.   For your broken shin.
   Ben. Why, Romeo, art thou mad?
   Rom. Not mad, but bound more than a madman is:
Shut up in prison, kept without my food,"
Whipp'd, and tormented, and—Good e'en, good fellow."
Act i., *Scene* 2.

One does not see the connection of Romeo's plantain leaf with Benvolio's medical philosophy. The surgical virtue of this leaf is also spoken of by Costard, in *Love's Labour Lost*. Romeo's description of the treatment of madmen goes some points beyond that of Rosalind, "a dark house and whip," since starvation is added, and the poor wretch is to be tormented, plagued, and teased into excitement probably; perhaps more would have been added, but for the interruption. There can be little doubt, from the sometimes painful, and sometimes ludicrous manner in which the treatment of madmen is referred to by Shakespeare, that he felt its cruelty and folly.

The nurse's little piece of domestic medicine, putting wormwood to her nipple to wean the infant at the time of the earthquake, is quaintly in character.

> "When it did taste the wormwood on the nipple
> Of my dug, and felt it bitter, pretty fool!
> To see it tetchy, and fall out with the dug."   *Act* i. *Scene* 3.

In Mercutio's account of the queen of dreams, the following passage is not very intelligible to any knowledge we at present possess of the parasitic inhabitants of maid's fingers, the only one inhabiting there with which we are acquainted being, the *acarus scabiei*, being an animal invisible to the naked eye, and, under the microscope, more like a lobster than a worm.

> "Her wagoner a small grey-coated gnat,
> Not half so big as a round little worm
> Prick'd from the lazy finger of a maid."   *Act* i., *Scene* 4.

In the writings of an eminent surgeon of Shakespeare's day, the following passage occurs, which proves that Mercutio's illustration was in perfect accord with medical opinion.

"We commonly call them worms, which many women, sitting in the sunne shine, can cunningly picke out with nedles, and are most common in the handes."—*A Compendious Chyrurgerie*, by John Banester, A.D. 1585, p. 465.

The blisters on ladies' lips, *herpes labialis*, occasioned by bad breath and indigestion from trashy food, is sound medical doctrine, best illustrated by Shakespeare's own maxim, "things sweet in taste are in digestion sour."

> "O'er ladies' lips, who straight on kisses dream :
> Which oft the angry Mab with blisters plagues,
> Because their breaths with sweetmeats tainted are."   *Ibid.*

The old herbalist doctrine, that every plant, and indeed, every natural substance, has its proper medicinal virtue, is more fully expressed by Father Laurence while gathering his baleful weeds and medicinal flowers, than in any other of the references to this subject that are scattered through the plays. The constant revolution of nature in birth and death, in nutrition and decay here also expressed, is fully established by modern science, so that the old thought of the circle of life is no longer a vague idea but a proved and established fact.

The herbalist reflection, on the intermixture of good and evil, of malignant and benignant power in different parts of the same plant, may find an illustration in the laurel tribe.

"Now ere the sun advance his burning eye,
The day to cheer, and night's dank dew to dry,
I must upfill this osier cage of ours,
With baleful weeds, and precious-juiced flowers.
The earth, that's nature's mother, is her tomb;
What is her burying grave, that is her womb:
And from her womb children of divers kind
We sucking on her natural bosom find;
Many for many virtues excellent,
None but for some, and yet all different.
O, mickle is the powerful grace, that lies
In plants, herbs, stones, and their true qualities;
For nought so vile that on the earth doth live,
But to the earth some special good doth give;
Nor aught so good, but, strain'd from that fair use,
Revolts from true birth, stumbling on abuse:
Virtue itself turns vice, being misapplied;
And vice sometime 's by action dignified.
Within the infant rind of this weak flower
Poison hath residence, and medicine power:
For this, being smelt, with that part cheers each part;
Being tasted, slays all senses with the heart."
Act ii., *Scene* 3.

Mercutio's quaint picture of a drivelling idiot, lolling up and down, and exercising the magpie faculty of concealment upon some bauble to which he attaches value, could scarcely be more tersely expressed.

"This drivelling love is like a great natural, that runs lolling up and down to hide his bauble in a hole." *Act* ii., *Scene* .4

The effects attributed to the narcotic given by the friar to Juliet are impossible, and can only be referred to the great ignorance and superstition respecting the effects of poisons which prevailed in the olden time, when the most enlightened medical men could believe that life might be insidiously taken away by such means as poisoned gloves and poisoned torches, and when it was a subject, as we have shewn, of scientific disputation whether poisons could be set to operate, or, to use Juliet's expression, 'tempered' to produce their effects a long time or a short time after.

"*Friar Laurence.* Take thou this phial, being then in bed,
And this distilled liquor drink thou off:
When, presently, through all thy veins shall run
A cold and drowsy humour, which shall seize
Each vital spirit; for no pulse shall keep
His natural progress, but surcease to beat:
No warmth, no breath, shall testify thou liv'st;
The roses in thy lips and cheeks shall fade
To paly ashes; thy eyes' windows fall,
Like death, when he shuts up the day of life;
Each part, depriv'd of supple government,
Shall stiff, and stark, and cold, appear like death:
And in this borrow'd likeness of shrunk death
Thou shalt remain full two and forty hours,
And then awake as from a pleasant sleep." *Act* iv., *Scene* 1.

The effects promised are represented to have been produced, for passionate old Capulet, who, when he thought his disobedient daughter alive, had no better term for her than 'You green-sickness carrion,' finds her cold, pale, and stiff.

> "*Capulet.* Ha! let me see her:—Out, alas! she's cold:
> Her blood is settled, and her joints are stiff;
> Life and these lips have long been separated."
> *Act* iv., *Scene* 5.

Romeo's description of the starved apothecary's shop, while it testifies to the author's faithful observation of detail, cannot be said to shew any medical knowledge; nor ought this to be expected, since such knowledge would have been quite out of character in Romeo. If Friar Laurence had visited the shop, doubtless his observations upon the poor wretch to whom it belonged, and on the shop itself, would have been widely different, and probably full of medical knowledge. The condition of affairs described is certainly very unlike that of the London "coach-keeping apothecaries" as they are commented upon by writers of the period, and whose lucrative business could well bear comparison with the gains of the learned and authentic fellows of the college, by whom they were treated with such authoritative contempt. The trade in physic could not have been a bad one, if Decker, in his *Gull's Hornbook*, had any grounds for the following advice. "How a gallant should behave himself at an ordinary: You may rise during dinner time to ask for a closestool, protesting to all the gentlemen that it costs you an hundred pounds a year in physic, besides the annual pension which your wife allows her doctor."

> "*Romeo.* I do remember an apothecary,—
> And hereabouts he dwells,—which late I noted
> In tatter'd weeds, with overwhelming brows,
> Culling of simples; meagre were his looks,
> Sharp misery had worn him to the bones:
> And in his needy shop a tortoise hung,
> An alligator stuff'd, and other skins
> Of ill-shap'd fishes; and about his shelves
> A beggarly account of empty boxes,
> Green earthen pots, bladders, and musty seeds,

Remnants of packthread, and old cakes of roses,
Were thinly scatter'd to make up a show." *Act* v. *Scene* 1.

Mr. Steevens points out that Shakespeare derived the circumstance of the apothecary's shop, from Painter's translation of the Italian novel on which the drama is founded: "———beholding an apotecary's shop of lyttle furniture, and like store of *boxes* and other thynges requisite for that science, thought that the very poverty of the master apothecarye would make him wyllyngly yelde to that whych he pretended to demande." Malone shews, by a quotation from Nashe, that in Shakespeare's time a stuffed alligator made part of the furniture of an apothecary's shop; and Steevens refers to the third plate of Hogarth's Marriage a-la-Mode, and to his own personal observation, to shew that the custom has been handed down to a recent period.

In Romeo's demand for a rapid poison, he expresses the thought that it will act upon the blood, or being conveyed by means of the blood, "disperse itself through all the veins." The opinion does not seem to have existed that these rapid poisons could act upon the nervous system.

" *Romeo.* Come hither, man.—I see that thou art poor:
Hold, there is forty ducats: let me have
A dram of poison; such soon-speeding gear
As will disperse itself through all the veins,
That the life-weary taker may fall dead,
And that the trunk may be discharg'd of breath
As violently, as hasty powder fir'd
Doth hurry from the fatal cannon's womb." *Act* v., *Scene* 1.

A curious act of authority to prevent the spread of pestilence is described by Friar John.

"The searchers of the town,
Suspecting that we both were in a house
Where the infectious pestilence did reign,
Seal'd up the doors, and would not let us forth."
Act v., *Scene* 2.

Romeo, in the tomb, expresses the still prevalent opinion of lighting (not lightning) before death.

> "How oft when men are at the point of death,
> Have they been merry? which their keepers call
> A lightning before death." *Act* v., *Scene* 3.

The word 'merry,' however, scarcely describes the condition to which this expression refers, which rather means that when a man has been in a state of delirium or aberration of mind, his mental faculties become collected and alert for a short period before his decease. This phenomenon does undoubtedly, although rarely, take place.

TIMON OF ATHENS.

Apemantus, who, in his malignant humour, strongly resembles Thersites, is like him also in his readiness to imprecate disease. He begins by wishing the comforts of chronic rheumatism to the supple parasites.

> "Aches contract and starve your supple joints."
> *Act* i., *Scene* 1.

The connection between the flow of the blood and bodily warmth, and the decrease of both in old age, are expressed by Timon.

> "These old fellows
> Have their ingratitude in them hereditary:
> Their blood is cak'd, 'tis cold, it seldom flows:

"'Tis lack of kindly warmth, they are not kind;
And nature, as it grows again toward earth,
Is fashion'd for the journey, dull, and heavy."

Act ii., *Scene* 2.

The comments of Flaminius upon his master's false friend express the idea, that food, after it has been converted to the nutriment of the body, supplies either reinforcement to diseased or to healthy function. Perhaps there is no medical opinion which of late years has undergone a larger and more important development, than the relationship existing between the nutrition of the body and a state of health or of disease, and it may perhaps be said, without exaggeration, that the highest expression of modern medical science is to trace the conditions of development and decay, of health and of disease, in the varying states of nutrition. Of course, so broad a view as this could not be attributed either to Shakespeare or to the most enlightened physician of his time, but the following passage clearly expresses the opinion, which, at that time, was much in advance of professional knowledge, that additions to the nutriment of the body may either increase and foster a state of disease, or may invigorate the healthy functions so as to expel disease. Which of these events took place would depend upon the state of the body and the kind of disease. Thus, there is an old proverb, which commands us "to feed a cold, and starve a fever;" it may, however, be quoted rather as a vulgar error, than as a condensed expression of true knowledge, which would be better expressed by the concise saying of that able physician, the late Dr. Graves of Dublin, who, when walking with Dr. Stokes through St. Patrick's cathedral, remarked, "When I die, let this be my epitaph: *He fed fever.*"

> "Thou disease of a friend, and not himself!
> Has friendship such a faint and milky heart,
> It turns in less than two nights? O you gods,
> I feel my master's passion! This slave
> Unto this hour has my lord's meat in him:
> Why should it thrive, and turn to nutriment,
> When he is turn'd to poison?
> O, may diseases only work upon't!
> And, when he's sick to death, let not that part of nature
> Which my lord paid for, be of any power
> To expel sickness, or prolong his hour!" *Act* iii. *Scene* 1.

Timon's own injunction to the thieves may serve as an illustration of the manner in which, in one condition of the body, diseases only may work upon the very material which in another condition, is doubtless of "power to expel sickness," for if the subtle blood of the grape can add fuel to disease in high fever, its power in low fever to expel disease is equally unquestionable.

> "Here's gold: Go, suck the subtle blood of the grape,
> Till the high fever seeth your blood to froth,
> And so 'scape hanging. Trust not the physician;
> His antidotes are poison, and he slays
> More than you rob." *Act* iv., *Scene* 3.

The following passage expresses a practice among physicians of Shakespeare's day, which seems very strange and inhuman to us, namely, that they would not only not undertake the treatment of diseases of which they thought there was little chance of cure, but that they would throw up the treatment of a case which they had already undertaken when the patient's condition appeared hopeless.

Lord Bacon, in his work on *The Advancement of Learning*, comments severely upon this practice of the physicians of his day. "In the enquiry of diseases, they do abandon the cures of many, some as in their nature incurable, and others as past the period of cure; so that Sylla and the triumvirs never proscribed so many men to die, as they do by their ignorant edicts; whereof numbers do escape with less difficulty than they did in the Roman proscriptions. Therefore I will not doubt to note as a deficience, that they enquire not the perfect cures of many diseases, or extremities of diseases; but pronouncing them incurable, do enact a law of neglect, and exempt ignorance from discredit. Nay, farther, I esteem it the office of a physician not only to restore health, but to mitigate pain and dolours; and not only when such mitigation may conduce to recovery, but when it may serve to make a fair and easy passage."

"*Sempronius.* Must I be his last refuge? His friends, like physicians,
Thrice give him o'er; Must I take the cure upon me?"
Act iii., *Scene* 3.

An old-fashioned surgical remedy is referred to by Alcibiades.

"Is this the balsam, that the usuring senate
Pours into captains' wounds? Banishment?"
Act iii., *Scene* 5.

The nosological point of Timon's terrible curse on Athens is somewhat generalised under the heading of infectious fevers, the disease of lust and liberty, (that is, of libertinism,) and an infectious skin disease under the title of general leprosy; cold sciatica is indeed particularised, but it may be supposed to be given as a type of the chronic diseases of age.

"Plagues, incident to men,
Your potent and infectious fevers heap
On Athens, ripe for stroke! Thou cold sciatica,
Cripple our senators, that their limbs may halt
As lamely as their manners! Lust and liberty
Creep in the minds and marrows of our youth;

> That 'gainst the stream of virtue they may strive,
> And drown themselves in riot! Itches, blains,
> Sow all the Athenian bosoms; and their crop
> Be general leprosy! Breath infect breath;
> That their society, as their friendship, may
> Be merely poison!" *Act* iv., *Scene* 1.

The aid of the sun in the production of malaria is invoked. The medical propriety of the term 'rotten humidity' could not be surpassed, since it is one of the recognized laws of malaria, that a due proportion of heat, moisture, and decomposition should combine to generate it. Excessive heat, or excessive cold, an amount of humidity which inundates vegetation and prevents rottenness, or a want of humidity which dries up a country and prevents decay, are one and all adverse to the production of malaria. Hence it is that agues occur chiefly in the spring and fall, when there is enough both of sun and moisture to produce rotten humidity. Shakespeare has the same thought in *Henry IV.*, "Worse than the sun in March this praise doth nourish agues."

> "*Timon.* O blessed breeding sun, draw from the earth
> Rotten humidity; below thy sister's orb
> Infect the air!" *Act* iv., *Scene* 3.

Timon, in his adjuration to Alcibiades, expresses very distinctly the opinion so often alluded to in the plays, that diseases are dependent upon planetary influence.

> "Be as a planetary plague, when Jove
> Will o'er some high-vic'd city hang his poison
> In the sick air: Let not thy sword skip one."
> *Act* iv., *Scene* 3.

The converse of this wish is the idea expressed by Marcellus, in *Hamlet*, speaking of Christmas time.

> "The nights are wholesome, then no planets strike."

The supposed aid of astrology to medicine here indicated was by no means a mere vulgar error; thus the Rev. John Ward, the clerical physician of Shakespeare's own parish, quaintly reports the opinion of the great herbalist on this point, "Nick Culpepper says, that a physitian without astrologie is like a pudden without fat."

The most fearful invocation, however, of the mad misanthropist is the one which he addresses to the rapacious courtesans, including, as it does, a complete list of the secondary effects of venereal virus.

> "*Timon.* Consumptions sow
> In hollow bones of man: strike their sharp shins,
> And mar men's sparring. Crack the lawyer's voice,
> That he may never more false title plead,
> Nor sound his quillets shrilly: hoar the flamen
> That scolds against the quality of flesh,
> And not believes himself: down with the nose,
> Down with it flat; take the bridge quite away
> Of him, that his particular to foresee,
> Smells from the general weal: make curl'd-pate ruffians bald;
> And let the unscarr'd braggarts of the war
> Derive some pain from you: Plague all;
> That your activity may defeat and quell
> The source of all erection.—There's more gold:—
> Do you damn others, and let this damn you,
> And ditches grave you all!" *Act* iv., *Scene* 3.

Among all these symptoms of "the malady of France," the only ambiguous one is the first, in which the word consumption seems to be somewhat indefinitely applied, as it is in the next scene, where Timon says, "Consumption catch thee!" It seems most probable, that 'consumptions in the hollow bones' means disease of the bones of the cranium, which form that which may essentially be called, the hollow bone of the body. Disease of these bones we know to have been terribly frequent in the olden time, when the treatment of syphilis consisted mainly in the administration of mercury.

Painful nodes on the shin-bones are, no doubt, meant by the expression, 'strike their sharp shins,' and in connexion with this symptom, it may either be that 'mar men's sparring' means, that they would prevent men from using those kicks on the shins, which form part of the movements of attack and defence in wrestling; or that the aching nodes may prevent men spurring on horseback. Venereal ulcerations of the larynx are next referred to; "Crack the lawyer's voice," &c. The priest is made to bear the mark of infamy still more in public, in the white scaly skin disease to which Timon, in the earlier part of the scene, applies the very same epithet, 'hoar,' old English for white, as hoar frost, "Make the hoar leprosy adored."

The next symptom applies to that hideous disfigurement of chronic syphilis, loss of the nose; even its structure is referred to, "take the *bridge* quite away." The fearful list of the effects of chronic syphilis is concluded by impotence and baldness; the last of which is especially remarkable, as it was not observed to be a symptom of the complaint until a date shortly before Shakespeare wrote. It will be instructive to compare his list of symptoms with the following, from Hamilton's *History of Medicine*, which perhaps contains, the most complete list to be found in any medical author of the period.

"Nicholas Brassa's work on syphilis is one of the best of the age, founded almost wholly upon his own experience, and evincing a thorough acquaintance with his subject. His description of the symptoms which accompany this dreadful complaint, and make it distinct from every other, is complete, but it should be remembered that the whole of the morbid train which he describes is not to be expected to occur in the same individual. The following brief enumeration of the symptoms he details, may serve to give some idea of the appearance assumed by the complaint at that period:—Hard pustules on the head and forehead; pains in the head and limbs, especially in the thighs, which increase at night; in one subject, whom he dissected in 1524, he found a congestion of white pus among the muscles of the thigh; abscesses both in the thighs and other parts; ulcers . . .; nodes; painful tubercules; tumours on the joints; cracks and scales on the hands and feet; a crust over the whole body as in leprosy; relaxation of the uvula; ulcers in the mouth, fauces, and epiglottis, which do not proceed to suppuration; erosion of the cartilages of the larynx; caries of the bones; buboes which, when brought to suppurate, remove the complaint; and a falling off of the hair of the head and the beard. His mention of this last symptom fixes the period at which he wrote, which could not have been earlier than 1536, since we learn from Fallopius, that the loss of the hair was not observed to be a symptom of the complaint before that date, when the disorder had been known for about forty years. In the catalogue of symptoms, exhibiting, it must be confessed, a sufficiently frightful picture of this loathsome complaint, one only, which is now one of the commonest attendants upon syphilis, is wanting, namely, gonorrhœa; which, as Fallopius, upon whose information we may rely, also acquaints us, did not appear during the first forty years after its introduction, Fernelius being the first to notice it. Had such a symptom fallen under the notice of so attentive an observer as Brassa, we may feel assured he would not have omitted it."

This description of syphilis published, as it appears, some time subsequently to 1536, and the best that, up to that time, had been published, is less complete, as an enumeration of symptoms, than that of Shakespeare; for while it contains some symptoms, which are not those of syphilis, as abscesses in the thighs, and relaxation of the uvula, it omits two important particulars which the dramatist mentions, namely, impotence and loss of the nose. It is to be observed, moreover, that, while Brassa jumbles together, what are called the primary and the secondary symptoms of the disease, Shakespeare, in this remarkable passage, mentions the secondary forms of the disease only. That this is from knowledge and not from ignorance is very certain, since, in an earlier passage of the same scene, he refers to the primary symptoms.

" She, whom the spital-house and ulcerous sores
Would cast the gorge at, this embalms and spices."

It has been impossible to shirk this repulsive subject, for in Shakespeare's time, both the novelty and the ravages of this disease attracted to it a larger share both of public and professional attention than any other disease, except, perhaps, the epidemics which were at that time so frequent and so fatal; and however free from gloss is the manner in which Shakespeare has here spoken of the diseases which dog immorality and disgust innocence, it was needful for the elucidation of our subject to examine this passage in detail and with care, for there is really no other passage throughout the plays which appears to carry with it so strong a proof of the medical knowledge of the author.

The wide prevalence and the horrible nature of these 'rotten diseases of the south' are referred to in *Hamlet*, in the grave-digging scene.

"*Hamlet.* How long will a man lie in the earth ere he rot?
Clown. I'faith, if he be not rotten afore he die
(As we have many pocky corses now-a-days
That will scarce hold the laying in;)
He will last for some eight year, or nine year;
A tanner will last you some nine year."

In Wunderlich's *History of Medicine*, p. 80, it is recorded that Girtanner had reckoned up 263 separate treatises which had been written on this disease before the end of the sixteenth century; a fact significant of the attention and anxiety which it excited in the profession.

If Shakespeare disgusts the delicacy of the present age by the undisguised manner in which he treats this subject, it must be admitted that he presents it in a form little calculated to delude or to mislead, but that, on the contrary, he paints the morbid features of libertinism in all their truthful hideousness, from which a young man might derive the same kind of lesson, as that of temperance, which the Spartan fathers endeavoured to teach their children, by presenting to their observation the repulsiveness of drunkenness in the person of their helots.

That the disease was held to be eminently disgraceful, is obvious from such expressions as "the powdering tub of infamy;" and from the care taken to conceal it, as in the following passage from Hamlet, which sounds very like the professional experience of a physician; the adjective, of course, points to the disease as 'the malady of France.'

>"*King.*   But, so much was our love,
>We would not understand what was most fit;
>But, like the owner of a foul disease,
>To keep it from divulging, let it feed
>Ev'n on the pith of life."

Timon thus refers to the cure of this disorder, in his exhortation to the courtesans to spread sin and misery.

>" Give them diseases,   *   *   *   *
>   *   *   *   *   season the slaves
>For tubs and baths; bring down rose-cheeked youth
>To the tub-fast, and the diet."   *Act* iv., *Scene* 3.

The tub mentioned twice in this sentence is, no doubt, the powdering tub, whose use is referred to in *Henry V*, " The powdering tub of infamy," used in the spital. This tub is also mentioned in *Measure for Measure*, in the lewd conversation between the Clown and Lucio.

>" *Clown.* Troth, sir, she hath eaten up all her beef, and she is herself in the tub.
>*Lucio.* Why, 'tis good; it is the right of it: it must be so: ever your fresh whore, and powdered bawd."

The baths referred to were, probably, sweating baths, which were greatly used in the treatment of this disease; thus we read in Astruc's learned work, that Jasper Torella, an eminent physician and medical author, and also Bishop of Justinia, who flourished in the early part of the sixteenth century, says that the cure of this disease, which he calls pudendagra, depends, in the first place upon diet and potions, in the second upon bathing and local applications, and especially on the use of the stove or sudatory, the hot air or sweating bath; and in the third place on liniments containing a small proportion of quicksilver. But, although the sweating bath played so great a part in the treatment of *lues*, the secretions of the skin were also systematically stimulated by what were called sweating decoctions and sweating drinks, composed of sassafras and guaiacum, so that Pandarus might well refer to sweating as the principal remedy for the disease. "Till then I'll sweat, and seek about for eases." Guaiacum and sassafras were the main ingredients in these sudorific medicines. Ward humorously indicates the abundant use of the latter, by saying that an apothecary, whenever his wife was talkative, set her to beat sassafras.

The following passage, from Woodall, shews that the surgeons of Shakespeare's time adopted a particular diet in the treatment of *lues*, which was known and distinguished, par excellence, as *the* diet; and it is this diet, no doubt, which is referred to by Timon with the affix of the definite article.

"*Of the Dyet Pot.* The Dyet Pot is not alone to be used in cases of dyet drinke, seething for the Pox and not otherwise; for as a learned doctor upon occasion lately reasoned, there is difference between *the Dyet* and *a Dyet*, though in both kinds there is even, *quot homines tot sententiæ*, so many men so many minds. Wherefore concerning descriptions of several dyet drinks for the Pox, I will refer the Surgeon's mate to other authors: for in truth I must defer that point to fitter opportunity; I mean till I write toutching the cure of that disease."—*Woodall*, p. 23.

I have not anywhere found that the old surgeons recommended fasting during the treatment, and therefore cannot explain the word tub-fast; the most they did was to enjoin a liquid and moderate diet; thus, during inunction, Ambrose Paré orders, "Yet, if the patient shall be weak, you may some houre before the unction, give him some gelley, the yolke of an egge, or some broath made of meate, boiled to pieces, but very sparingly, lest nature, intent upon the concoction of solid meats, or in great quantity, should bee drawn away from that which we intend."

The following is the diet and treatment laid down as proper in this disease by the medical rector of Sratford: " Diet in the pocks is to be drying, as oat cakes, biscuits, a few raisins, now and then a bit of veal may bee permitted them; purge, let blood, sweat six or seven mornings together."—p. 279. There are numerous references in Ward's *Diary* to different forms and uses of diet: thus he speaks of "dyet drinks of sarza and guaiacum in stew-pots."—p. 250. " The inch dyet, wherein we eat by drammes, and drink by spoonfuls, more perplexeth the mind than cureth the bodie."—p. 254. " A dyet bag of many ingredients," into which one of the consulting physicians merrily recommended them to put a haycock. —p. 381.

Although Timon speaks under the title of leprosy, of the lepra of syphilis, which is known to us to be not contagious, he also recognizes the contagious form of the disease, to which the term was more strictly applied.

" *Timon.* All villains that do stand by thee are pure.
Apemantus. There is no leprosy but what thou speak'st.
Timon. If I name thee.—
I'll beat thee,—but I should infect my hands." *Act* iv., *Scene* 3.

It must, however, be remembered that in Shakespeare's time, the secondary forms of syphilis were erroneously thought to be contagious in the highest degree.

Thus Erasmus, quoted by Astruc, says: "*G. A.* But you forget, this evil is propagated many ways besides that of copulation, as by kissing, talking together, touching each other, drinking together. For such is the spiteful nature thereof, that it is never better pleased than when it can spread its poison to others without advantaging itself. *P. E.* If it be thus, let no one suffer his barber to come near him to mow down his beard; or, for safety, let every man shave himself. *G. A.* But if, by way of security, what if each of them were to keep his lips close, and not speak a word till the barber has done and is gone about his business? *P. E.* That won't do, because the infection may be taken in by the nostrils. *G. A.* I have a remedy for that. *P. E.* Pray what? *G. A.* To do as the chemists, wear a mask with glass eyes that may let in the light, and a tube also that may be fastened from under the arms, by which the air may pass to and from the mouth and nostrils. *P. E.* This is well enough, if we had nothing to fear from a touch of his fingers, from his linen, and from his comb and scissors."

A perusal of Astruc's learned work instructs me, that I have probably been wrong in the opinion expressed in an earlier page, that the French crown referred to in *Measure for Measure*, *All's Well that Ends Well*, and *Midsummer Night's Dream*, was the common venereal *rupia*, since it appears that there was a particular form of venereal skin disease which was called "*le chapelet*," a technical term which would be anglicised into "crown." "The skin," says Astruc, "is troubled with hard, callous, circular tubercles or pustules. They are frequently to be found, too, about the forehead and temples, and behind the ears, where, being disposed in order, they form the figure of a crown, and are commonly called by the French, *le chapelet*."—*Treatise on the Venereal Diseases*, by John Astruc, M.B.

In the following, Timon appears to refer to the old superstition that a lie produces a blister on the tongue, though in the malice of his rage, he imprecates the minor punishment on truth, and the old surgery of cauterization on falsehood.

> "*Timon.* Thou sun, that comfort'st, burn!—Speak, and be hang'd:
> For each true word, a blister! and each false
> Be as a caut'rizing to the root o' the tongue,
> Consuming it with speaking!" *Act* v., *Scene* 2.

HAMLET.

In the Oxford edition the word 'blood' is substituted in the following passage for 'head' as it occurs in other editions, with the utmost advantage, as it would appear, to the sense. The presence of the blood in the heart was, as we have shewn, well known to Shakespeare.

> "The *blood* is not more native to the heart,
> The hand more instrumental to the mouth,
> Than is the throne of Denmark to thy father."
> *Act* i., *Scene* 2.

The opinion of Laertes is so far true, that contagious fevers are certainly contracted with greater facility in youth, than either in infancy or in age.

> "The canker galls the infants of the spring,
> Too oft before their buttons be disclose'd;
> And in the morn and liquid dew of youth
> Contagious blastments are most imminent." *Act* i. *Scene* 3.

The following quotation has already been commented upon, as appearing to confirm the evidence of other passages, that Shakespeare entertained the medical opinion of his day, that the arteries were used for the transmission of the vital spirits.

" *Hamlet.*   My fate cries out,
And makes each petty artery in this body
As hardy as the Nemean lion's nerve."   *Act* i., *Scene* 4.

"Each vital spirit," spoken of by Friar Laurence in *Romeo and Juliet,* (see page 242,) as under the influence of poison when the pulse ceases to beat, has an obvious reference to the same theory.

Shakespeare is not wholly responsible for the impossible manner of the murder which the ghost describes, since he but adheres to the story as given in the tale of Saxo-Grammaticus. Commentators, probably led by the similarity of sound, have been satisfied to suppose that the juice of cursed hebenon is the juice of henbane; but henbane is by no means a virulent poison; and the word is much more likely to have been a generic name for poison producing *hebetudo animi.* The leperous distilment doubtless means, a juice or distilment supposed to be capable of producing leprosy.

" *Ghost.* . Brief let me be :—Sleeping within mine orchard,
My custom always in the afternoon,
Upon my secure hour thy uncle stole,
With juice of cursed hebenon in a vial,
And in the porches of mine ears did pour
The leperous distilment; whose effect
Holds such an enmity with blood of man,
That, swift as quicksilver, it courses through
The natural gates and alleys of the body ;
And, with a sudden vigour, it doth posset
And curd, like eager droppings into milk,
The thin and wholesome blood : so did it mine ;
And a most instant tetter bark'd about,
Most lazar-like, with vile and loathsome crust,
All my smooth body.
Thus was I, sleeping, by a brother's hand,
Of life, of crown, and queen, at once despatch'd."
                                        Act i., *Scene* 5.

In the players' representation of the murder, the poison

which has these effects, impossible to any natural substance, is represented to be a compound, endued with its virus by the ceremonial of witchcraft.

> " Thou mixture rank, of midnight weeds collected,
> With Hecate's ban thrice blasted, thrice infected,
> Thy natural magic and dire property,
> On wholesome life usurp immediately." *Act* iii., *Scene* 2.

The manner in which Laertes traces the effect of Hamlet's supposed disappointment in love, represents a physiological chain of events which can often be observed in the development of insanity from a moral cause. The moral shock first produces fasting, either from disgust of food, pre-occupation of mind, or wilful abstinence; the supply of nutriment cut off, loss of sleep results, partly from this cause and partly from the moral cause itself; general physical debility follows, accompanied by disturbance of the cerebral functions and the development of mania, so that he, who "first fell into a sadness" as the natural and not morbid result of disappointed affection, passes through a period of physical disturbance into a state of disease of the brain at the opposite pole of emotion, namely, mania—" The madness wherein now he raves." The power of ethnological insight here indicated is remarkable.

> "*Polonius.* And he, repulsed, (a short tale to make,)
> Fell into a sadness; then into a fast;
> Thence to a watch; thence into a weakness;
> Thence to a lightness; and, by this declension,
> Into the madness whereon now he raves,
> And all we mourn for." *Act* ii., *Scene* 2.

Hamlet refers to the tent used as a probe, as if he would thrust it to the sensitive part of a wound.

> " I'll tent him to the quick! if he but blench,
> I know my course!" *Act* ii., *Scene* 2.

In the following play upon the double meaning of the word 'choler,' the medical sense is most prominent, and the rational treatment of carrying off the excess of bile by purgation is alluded to.

"*Guildenstern.* The king, Sir—
Hamlet. Ay, Sir, what of him?
Guil. Is, in his retirement, marvellously distempered.
Ham. With drink, Sir?
Guil. No, my lord, rather with choler.
Ham. Your wisdom should show itself more richer, to signify this to his doctor; for, for me to put him to his purgation, would, perhaps, plunge him into far more choler." *Act* iii., *Scene* 2.

In Hamlet's defence of his sanity, his appeal to the pulse has been thought to mean that it had not that rapidity which exists generally in mania; perhaps, the expression, 'temperately keep time,' would be more rightly referred to its regularity than to its rapidity; but, however this may be, it is certain that the last phrase, 'makes as healthful music,' refers to its regularity, since medical men even now speak of the rythm of the heart's action, and the rythm of the pulse, in this sense. The simile with which he concludes, forcibly calls to mind a burrowing ulcer leaving thin edges of unhealthy skin, which the surgeon in vain attempts to film over with superficial applications, and to effect the cure of which, he finds it actually essential 'to tent to the quick,' and even to apply a corsive, (or corrosive,) like that referred to by Queen Margaret.

"*Hamlet.* Ecstasy!
My pulse, as yours, doth temperately keep time,
And makes as healthful music: It is not madness,
That I have uttered: bring me to the test,
And I the matter will re-word; which madness
Would gambol from. Mother, for love of grace,
Lay not that flattering unction to your soul,

> That not your trespass, but my madness, speaks:
> It will but skin and film the ulcerous place;
> Whiles rank corruption, mining all within,
> Infects unseen."   *Act* iii. *Scene* 4.

There is an amusing story told of a medical man, who, in spite of a one-sided education, was a most useful member of Parliament, that in attempting to quote one of the above lines, he said,

> " Lay not that flattering ointment to your chest."

In describing the signs of Hamlet's terror, the queen calls the hair an excrement,

> " Your bedded hair, like life in excrements,
> Starts up, and stands on end."   *Act* iii., *Scene* 4.

The hair is called "valour's excrement," in the *Merchant of Venice;* and Autolycus, in *Winter's Tale,* says of his false beard, that he will "pocket up his pedlar's excrement." Shakespeare in this did not deviate from either scientific or common usage. Decker says, "Why should the chins and lips of old men lick up that excrement which they violently clip away from the heads of young men?" and Ray in the *Creation,* quoted by Richardson, says, "The hair, which though it be esteemed an excrement;" also Howell, "Hair but an excrementitious thing."

The following saying of the king's tallies still more closely with the aphorism of Hippocrates than that of the friar in *Much Ado about Nothing.*

> " Diseases, desperate grown,
> By desperate appliance are reliev'd,
> Or not at all."   *Act* iv., *Scene* 3.

The aspect of a recent scar, and the technical word for it, *cicatrix,* are here given, though Shakespeare gives to the latter a false quantity.

> "Since yet thy cicatrice looks raw and red
> After the Danish sword." *Act* iv., *Scene* 3.

The word hectic is peculiarly appropriate here, as a chronic fever produced by irritation.

> "The present death of Hamlet. Do it, England;
> For like the hectic in my blood he rages,
> And thou must cure me." *Ibid.*

Hamlet's comparison of needless war to an imposthume is excellent on both sides.

> "This is the imposthume of much wealth and peace;
> That inward breaks, and shows no cause without
> Why the man dies." *Act* iv., *Scene* 4.

War has been stated by cynical statists to be man's natural condition, and peace but the period of exhaustion and recruitment. Shakespeare does not go quite so far as this, but he looks upon war as a disease produced by that state of the body in which health becomes rank and plethoric; a state expressed by the king in this passage, in which, however, pleurisy has been written for plethory.

> "For goodness, growing to a pleurisy,
> Dies in his own too-much." *Act* iv., *Scene* 7.

Imposthumes, or aposthumes, for the word is written by our old surgical writers both ways indifferently, had a wide meaning; indeed according to Ambrose Paré's classification of them into five species, the name appears to have included every thing which could be called 'a swelling against nature:' phlegmons, pustules, erysipelas, œdema, scirrhus, carbuncle, scrofulous swellings, &c. The term, moreover, appears to have been used for any collection of purulent fluid. Thus in the *Three Exact Pieces* of Leonard Phioravant, Knight and Doctor of Physick, (A.D. 1652), there is a chapter on Inward Impostumes. "These imposthumes inwardly, are evill to know, and uncertain to cure, because the patient himself cannot tell in what place they be, though he feel the pain : and, therefore, all that we reason of in that matter may be to the contrary. For where a man cannot see with the eye, nor touch with the hand, the matter is doubtful whether it be, or no : and, therefore, it is best to say little."

The medical Parson Ward also says in his *Diary*,—"Matthias Carnax affirms that he found many ulcers and apostems in the heart."—p. 256. And again, "Gill told mee of a woman that had an apostheme about the side, and his master intended to trepan her on one of the ribs ; whether it canne be : I suspected itt to be a ly."—p. 266

The use of the word, therefore, by Hamlet is most appropriate ; an abscess of the liver breaking into the peritoneum, or an empyema producing suffocation by opening into the lungs, would have exactly the effect which he describes.

A spendthrift sigh hurts by easing, as every one knows who has adopted this method to cure a stitch in the side, which, being caused by a slight cramp of the intercostal muscles, is cured, like other cramps, by the muscle being violently stretched.

" And then this *should* is like a spendthrift sigh,
That hurts by easing. But, to the quick o'the ulcer."
Act iv., *Scene* 7.

The description which Laertes gives of the weapon-poison refers to the herbalist opinion of the influence of the moon.

" I bought an unction of a mountebank,
So mortal, that but dip a knife in it,
Where it draws blood, no cataplasm so rare,
Collected from all simples that have virtue
Under the moon, can save the thing from death." *Ibid.*

LEAR.

Kent, in rebuking the king's anger for his advice, says,

> "Kill thy physician, and thy fee bestow
> Upon the foul disease." *Act* i., *Scene* 1.

Lear cursing Goneril says,

> "The untented woundings of a father's curse
> Pierce every sense about thee!" *Act* i., *Scene* 4.

Untented appears to mean, 'not to be tented,' wounds the bottom of which is not to be reached.

"A cure for kibes or chilblains" is given in Phioravant, and no doubt this is the meaning attached to it here, and also in *Hamlet*.

> "*Fool.* If a man's brains were in his heels, wer't not in danger of kibes." *Act* i., *Scene* 5.

Kent, railing at the steward, says,

> "A plague upon your epileptic visage!
> Smile you at my speeches as I were a fool?"
> *Act* ii., *Scene* 2.

The offence given seems to have been an idiotic simper, and the intimate relationship of epilepsy with idiotcy, makes the observation, "epileptic visage," appropriate.

Lear, in the excitement of his rage, makes use of the following remarkable expression,

> "O, how this mother swells up toward my heart!
> *Hysterica passio!* Down, thou climbing sorrow,
> Thy element's below." *Act* ii., *Scene* 4.

It might, at first sight, appear that this use of a strictly technical term was not properly applied to one of the male sex; but, although hysteria far most frequently attacks women, and the term itself, indeed, is derived from the female organization, both ancient and modern physicians recognize the fact that the symptoms which are called hysterical are frequently observed in men. Old physicians constantly call hysteria the rising of the mother, *Mater pro matrix.* In Dr. Hall's *Century of Cases*, the mother is constantly used for hysterical affections: thus, " The fits of the mother often afflicted her, of which she was not delivered till she shed tears."—p. 148. The following quotation, however, is as explanatory as can be desired. " There is another disease which people term the *Rising of the lights*, and I am of his opinion, that it is the same with what they call *Hysterica passio*, or, *The mother*, because it seizeth upon women, (though men too sometimes have somewhat like it,) and it is evident enough, since *Dr. Highmore*, a very industrious learned man, hath sufficiently shewn, that the *lungs* are the part principally affected with that which hitherto hath been called a *Fit of the mother.*"—*Medela Medicinæ; a Plea,* &c., by M. N., Med. Lond. [*i.e.*, Dr. Nedham] A.D., 1665, p. 48.

While Lear is still able to contend against his rage, he finds the following medical excuse for the conduct of his son-in-law.

> " No, but not yet:—may be, he is not well:
> Infirmity doth still neglect all office,
> Whereto our health is bound; we are not ourselves,
> When nature, being oppress'd, commands the mind
> To suffer with the body: I'll forbear;
> And am fallen out with my more headier will,
> To take the indispos'd and sickly fit
> For the sound man." *Act* ii., *Scene* 4.

He curses Goneril as a disease in himself, comparing her,

it would appear, to those fatal signs which were called the death-tokens in the plague.

> "But yet thou art my flesh, my blood, my daughter;
> Or, rather, a disease that's in my flesh,
> Which I must needs call mine: thou art a boil,
> A plague-sore, an embossed carbuncle,
> In my corrupted blood." *Ibid.*

Lear enunciates a truth often observed in compound diseases, though here the greater malady is that of the mind.

> "But where the greater malady is fix'd,
> The lesser is scarce felt." *Act* iii., *Scene* 4.

The web and pin, or the 'pin and web,' as it is called in the *Winter's Tale*, was an old name for cataract.

> "*Edgar.* This is the foul fiend Flibbertigibbet: he begins at curfew, and walks till the first cock; he gives the web and the pin, squints the eye, and makes the hare-lip." *Ibid.*

The poor mad king has a medical idea of the origin of his daughter's wickedness.

> "*Lear.* Then let then anatomize Regan; see what breeds about her heart: Is there any cause in nature, that makes these hard hearts?" *Act* iii., *Scene* 6.

After Gloster's eyes have been so cruelly trodden out, a servant says,

> "I'll fetch some flax, and whites of eggs,
> To apply to his bleeding face. Now, heaven help him."
> *Act* iii., *Scene* 7.

White of eggs was a frequent application of the old surgeons, and, in *Banister's Surgery*, the whites of eggs spread upon flax is noted as a good application.

Lear asks for a perfume as from an apothecary, who, in the olden time, was the recognised perfumer as well as drug vendor.

> "Give me an ounce of civet, good apothecary,
> To sweeten my imagination." *Act* iv., *Scene* 6.

The physician's treatment of Lear belongs rather to mental than physical disease; he, however, gives his patient some narcotic herbs to produce sleep.

> "*Physician.* There is means, madam:
> Our foster-nurse of nature is repose,
> The which he lacks; that to provoke in him,
> Are many simples operative, whose power
> Will close the eye of anguish." *Act* iv., *Scene* 4.

The physician's bearing is honest and self-reliant, and the honourable treatment he receives marks the esteem of the author for his calling.

The gradual sickening of Regan, from the poison she has taken, is true to nature, and favourably contrasts with the descriptions of impossible effects from poison so abundant in the plays.

OTHELLO.

Desdemona's father, unable to give credence to her love for a middle-aged man of colour on any other supposition, attributes it to the use of charms, love-philtres, or aphrodisiac drugs, the belief of the power of which was common in Shakespeare's time, and is said to be still prevalent throughout the south of Europe. Falstaff's kissing-comfits and eryngoes belong to the same category; Decker refers to the latter in the same sense, "Good cheer, the very eryngo-root of gluttony," he says, helps to draw "the coach of lechery."

"*Brabantio.*   Are there not charms
By which the property of youth and maidenhood
May be abused?"   *Act* i., *Scene* 1.

" Judge me the world, if 'tis not gross in sense,
That thou hast practised on her with foul charms;
Abused her delicate youth with drugs, or minerals,
That waken motion."   *Act* i., *Scene* 2.

" She is abus'd, stol'n from me, and corrupted
By spells and medicines bought of mountebanks."
                                    Act i., *Scene* 3.

              " I therefore vouch again
That with some mixtures powerful o'er the blood,
Or with some dram conjur'd to this effect
He wrought upon her."   *Ibid.*

Roderigo gives a reason for contemplated suicide in medical form of speech.

" It is a silliness to live when to live is torment; and then we have a prescription to die when death is our physician." *Ibid.*

Iago's exposition, of what may be called medical metaphysics, describes human conduct as the result of the oscillating balance of reason and desire, and attributes virtue and vice to the wise or foolish management of the body and exercise of the will. It contains one expression which, with a degree of probability not more overstrained than that which attributes to Shakespeare the knowledge of Harvey's great discovery, by a literal reading, would lead to the conclusion that he had anticipated Linnæus' theory of the sexes of plants. No other author I know of, uses the word "gender" in any other sense than to mark the attributes of sex; while he himself uses it in this sense in several passages, as "the numbers of the genders"—*Merry Wives.* But he also uses it to designate a kind or species, as in *Hamlet*—" The great love the general gender bear him." It is probable, therefore, that it is in this sense the word is used by Iago, and, that Shakespeare had not necessarily any idea of the sexual physiology of plants which the great Swedish natutalist developed into a system; and thus also when he refers, in other places, to the sex of plants, that it is merely a poetical metaphor; as, for instance, when in *Midsummer Night's Dream* he says, "The female ivy so enrings the barky fingers of the elm;" in *Romeo and Juliet*, "Among fresh female buds shall you this night inherit at my house;" in the *Winter's Tale*, "Pale primroses that die unmarried."

"*Iago.* Virtue? a fig! 'tis in ourselves, that we are thus, or thus. Our bodies are our gardens; to the which our wills are gardeners: so that if we will plant nettles, or sow lettuce; set hyssop, and weed up thyme: *supply it with one gender of herbs, or distract it with many*; either to have it sterile with idleness, or manured with industry; why, the power and corrigible authority of this lies in our wills. If the balance of our lives had not one scale of reason to poise another of sensuality, the blood and baseness of our natures would conduct us to most preposterous conclusions: but we have reason to cool our raging motions, our carnal stings, our unbitted lusts: whereof I take this, that you call love, to be a sect or scion." *Act* i., *Scene* 3.

Iago's argument, that Othello will become weary and disgusted with his bride, is illustrated by a medical simile. She is to him, at present, as luscious as locusts, which the Oxford editor quotes from *Ludolfus* to be "*Suavis valde nec non salubris est cibus;*" the "locusts and wild honey," indeed of St. John's diet. When wearied of her she will disgust his taste like *coloquintida* (colocinth or bitter apple).

"These Moors are changeable in their wills; fill thy purse with money. The food that to him now is as luscious as locusts, shall be to him shortly as bitter as coloquintida." *Act* i., *Scene* 3.

The motive of Iago's machinations is envy and jealousy,

the last of which, he likens in its effect to a corrosive mineral poison.

> "For that I do suspect the lusty Moor
> Hath leap'd into my seat; the thought whereof
> Doth, like a poisonous mineral, gnaw my inwards."
> *Act* ii., *Scene* 1.

He advises Cassio to petition Desdemona's good offices with her husband for the pardon of his drunken broil.

> "This broken joint, between you and her husband, entreat her to splinter; and, my fortunes against any lay worth naming, this crack of your love shall grow stronger than it was before."
> *Act* ii., *Scene* 3.

Splints, or splinters, as these surgical appliances were called, are used both to broken bones, and to joints which have been recently dislocated. The first part of this sentence seems to imply their use to the latter purpose, but the second part points to a crack, as in a broken bone.

Iago, in appeasing the impatience of his dupe, refers to the gradual cure of wounds as by granulation.

> "How poor are they that have not patience!
> What wound did ever heal but by degrees?"
> *Act* ii., *Scene* 3.

The devilish philosophy of Iago can find no better illustration than slow poison for the fatal mischief he has effected on his master's peace of mind. If jealousy, like a poisonous mineral, gnawed his own vitals, that which he has instilled into the Moor, is a slow poison, not, indeed, felt at first, but acting by degrees on the blood. The effect, in the utter loss of that "which knits up the tangled sleeve of care," of that which the most powerful narcotics known cannot reproduce, neither poppy, whose juice is opium, nor mandragora, which Cleopatra calls for to sleep away the absence of her imperial lover, nor all the syrups in which narcotics were then usually administered.

> "The Moor already changes with my poison:
> Dangerous conceits are, in their natures, poisons,
> Which, at the first, are scarce found to distaste;
> But, with a little act upon the blood,
> Burn like the mines of sulphur.—I did say so:—
> Look, where he comes! Not poppy, nor mandragora,
> Nor all the drowsy syrups of the world,
> Shall ever medicine thee to that sweet sleep
> Which thou ow'dst yesterday." *Act* iii., *Scene* 3.

When the slow poison of Othello's jealousy verges upon its outbreak, he says to Desdemona,

> " Give me your hand: This hand is moist, my lady,
>   * *   * *   *
> This argues fruitfulness, and liberal heart;
> Hot, hot, and moist: This hand of yours requires
> A sequester from liberty." *Act* iii., *Scene* 4.

This sign of warmth is repeated in the *Venus and Adonis*

> " With that she seizeth on his sweating palm,
> The precedent of pith and livelihood."

It appears to express an old opinion that "a moist palm indicates a hot liver," one, however, which Primrose considered a vulgar error, and to the refutation of which he devoted a chapter.

The general disturbance of the bodily health, and especially of the nervous system from some trifling local irritation, is well expressed by Desdemona.

> " Men's natures wrangle with inferior things,
> Though great ones are their object. 'Tis even so;
> For let our finger ache, and it indues
> Our other healthful members ev'n to a sense
> Of pain." *Act* iii., *Scene* 4

Othello's mind is so terribly over-wrought, that it re-acts

T

upon the body until he is described as falling into a trance. Iago's designation of this as an epilepsy, of which it is the second fit, appears a mere falsehood. It is to be observed, however, that Shakespeare's knowledge of epilepsy here goes farther than in *Julius Cæsar*, since he describes the maniacal excitement which so often follows the fit.

> "*Iago.* My lord is fallen into an epilepsy;
> This is his second fit; he had one yesterday.
> *Cas.* Rub him about the temples.
> *Iago.* No, forbear:
> The lethargy must have his quiet course:
> If not, he foams at mouth: and, by and by,
> Breaks out to savage madness. Look, he stirs."
> Act iv. Scene 1.

When Cassio has been persuaded to withdraw himself, Iago applies to the patient himself the truthful and correct designation of his morbid state.

> "I shifted him away,
> And laid good 'scuse upon your ecstasy." *Ibid.*

The lunar theory of lunacy, from which the term, is definitely expressed by Othello.

> "It is the very error of the moon
> She comes more nearer earth than she was wont,
> And makes men mad." *Act* v., *Scene* 2.

Othello compares the tears, which flow in his dread remorse, to the gum of Arabia; probably not gum arabic, but myrrh is meant.

> "Of one, whose subdu'd eyes,
> Albeit unused to the melting mood,
> Dropt tears as fast as the Arabian trees
> Their medicinal gum." *Ibid.*

PERICLES.

Pericles directs a sarcasm at the proverbial dislike which doctors have to physic.

> "*Pericles.* Thou speak'st like a physician, Helicanus;
> Who minister'st a potion unto me,
> That thou would'st tremble to receive thyself."
> *Act* i., *Scene* 2.

He describes his shipwrecked condition by a term which has puzzled the commentators, "thronged up with cold," very expressive of a condition which cold would produce, as if a man were pressed or squeezed together by it. "Thronged up," however, is a midland counties' vulgarism; 'thronged up with work,' being a term often used to express the being overwhelmed with work.

> " A man throng'd up with cold; my veins are chill,
> And have no more of life than may suffice
> To give my tongue that heat to ask your help."
> *Act* ii., *Scene* 1.

The dependence of life upon the blood is referred to in the king's pledge.

> " Wishing it so much blood unto your life."
> *Act* ii., *Scene* 3.

And again in the estimate of the prince's love.

> " Even as my life, or blood that fosters it."
> *Act* ii., *Scene* 5.

Ceremon, an Ephesian lord, who practises as a physician, states the reasons why he prefers the "virtue and cunning," or power and knowledge of this art to honour and wealth. The word "infusions" is used ambiguously, perhaps erroneously, for the "true qualities," which Ceremon, like Friar Laurence in *Romeo and Juliet,* finds in "plants, herbs, stones." He calls physic a secret art, which, however, he bases both on authority and on experience, 'my practise;' he is both dogmatist and empiric. He hints at a knowledge of the *vis medicatrix,* the cures of nature. Shakespeare had good precedent for making a lord practise physic. The medical Marquis of Dorchester has been mentioned at page 30. Another medical peer was also Shakespeare's contemporary. "Edmund, Earl of Derby, who died in Queen Elizabeth's days, was famous for chirurgerie, bone-setting and hospitalitie."—Ward's *Diary,* p. 161.

" *Ceremon.* I held it ever,
Virtue and cunning were endowments greater
Than nobleness and riches: careless heirs
May the two latter darken and expend;
But immortality attends the former,
Making a man a god. 'Tis known, I ever
Have studied physic, through which secret art,
By turning o'er authorities, I have
(Together with my practice,) made familiar
To me and to my aid, the bless'd infusions
That dwell in vegetives, in metals, stones;
And I can speak of the disturbances
That nature works, and of her cures; which gives me
A more content in course of true delight
Than to be thirsty after tottering honour,
Or tie my pleasure up in silken bags,
To please the fool and death." *Act* iii., *Scene* 2.

The means used by Ceremon to recover the queen from her apparent state of death, by stimulants from the boxes in the closet, by warmth and friction, "the fire and the cloths," are exactly those which would be adopted in such a case. Music also is employed, as with Lear, to arouse the mind into a state of wakeful attention.

> "For look, how fresh she looks!—They were too rough
> That threw her in the sea. Make a fire within;
> Fetch hither all my boxes in my closet.
> Death may usurp on nature many hours,
> And yet the fire of life kindle again
> Her overpressed spirits. I have heard
> Of an Egyptian, had nine hours lien dead,
> By good appliance was recovered.
> Well said, well said; the fire and the cloths.—
> The rough and woeful music that we have,
> Cause it to sound, 'beseech you.
> The vial once more—How thou stirr'st, thou block!—
> The music there.—I pray you, give her air:—
> Gentlemen,
> This queen will live: nature awakes; a warmth
> Breathes out of her; she hath not been entranc'd
> Above five hours. See how she 'gins to blow
> Into life's flower again!" *Ibid.*

In stating that a man who had "nine hours lien dead," had been recovered, the poet has, no doubt, lapsed into a looseness of expression, really intending that the man had lain nine hours as dead, or with the appearance of death. Even Homer sometimes nods, and Shakespeare could no more intend to bring a dead man to life again, than he could have intended to describe the men who had been killed at the battle of St. Alban's as still exercising the functions of life.

> "And dead men's cries do fill the empty air."
> *Henry* VI., *Part* 2.

Pericles is in a state of melancholy, his distemperature displaying itself by long-continued silence and abstinence.

> "A man, who for this three months hath not spoken
> To any one, nor taken sustenance,
> But to prorogue his grief." *Act* v., *Scene* 1.

It is thought that the sweet harmony of a beautiful and skilful musician may "make a battery through his deafened parts," that is, attract his attention and win some words from him; and, although the courtiers fear that all will be effectless, the remedy is tried under the promise,

> "If that thy prosperous and artificial feat
> Can draw him but to answer thee in aught,
> Thy sacred physic shall receive such pay
> As thy desires can wish."
> *Ibid.*

The remedial employment of music is thus represented a second time in this play.

When Pericles finds his daughter in the fair musician, he questions her bodily presence.

> "But are you flesh and blood?
> Have you a working pulse? and are no fairy-motion?"
> *Ibid.*

—

TITUS ANDRONICUS is the only one of Shakespeare's plays which contains no passages referring to medical subjects.

—

VENUS AND ADONIS.

The vulgar remedy, prescribed for the fainting fit into which Henry VI. falls when he hears of the death of Gloster, is applied to the goddess for the same purpose. The term, "holds her pulses hard," is obscure.

> "He wrings her nose, he strikes her on the cheeks,
> He bends her fingers, holds her pulses hard;
> He chafes her lips."

On the following lines on the lips of Adonis, an edition of Mr. Knight's has this note; "The custom of strewing houses with fragant herbs was universal at a period when the constant recurrence of the plague habituated families to the use of what they considered preventives." The passage also refers to the old pretence of predicting pestilence from the aspect of the heavenly bodies; one form of medical astrology.

> "Long may they kiss each other, for this cure!
> O never let their crimson liveries wear!
> And as they last, their verdure still endure,
> To drive infection from the dangerous year!
> That the star-gazers, having writ on death,
> May say, the plague is banish'd by thy breath."

The Goddess of Love accuses the Mistress of the Moon that, with the desire "to mingle beauty with infirmities," she has made the youth subject to the tyranny of disease, "of mad mischances and much misery;"

> "As burning fevers, agues pale and faint,
> Life-poisoning pestilence, and frenzies wood,
> The marrow-eating sickness, whose attaint
> Disorder breeds by heating of the blood;
> Surfeits, imposthumes, grief, and damn'd despair,
> Swear Nature's death for framing thee so fair."

The distinction here drawn between fever and ague is noteworthy, since Shakespeare usually employs the words as synonymous. "Wood," applied to frenzies, means mad. It is used by Shakespeare in this sense, in *Midsummer Night's Dream*, and *Henry VI. 1st Part*, "raging wood." In Beaumont and Fletcher's *Gentle Shepherdess* is the expression, "bitten by wood-dog's venomed tooth." The Anglo-Saxon was 'wod,' the Scotch still use 'wud.'

The effect of fear on the heart is described in a metaphor strikingly resembling the very remarkable one used by Angelo in *Measure for Measure;* the idea, however, is here expressed with far less force and exactness. Angelo makes the heart a king, and the blood his subjects; here the heart is a captain, and the 'feeling parts' are soldiers.

> "This dismal cry rings sadly in her ear,
>   Through which it enters to surprise her heart;
> Who, overcome by doubt and bloodless fear,
>   With cold-pale weakness numbs each feeling part;
> Like soldiers, when their captain once doth yield,
> They basely fly, and dare not stay the field."

The heroic surgery of an English queen to her husband's poisoned wound, was like that which Adonis' hounds employ.

> "And there another licking of his wound,
> 'Gainst venom'd sores the only sovereign plaster."

That disturbance of the brain frequently causes imperfect performance of the function of sight, and especially the phenomenon of double vision, is a fact not generally known beyond the limits of the medical profession; yet it is here stated very distinctly.

> "Upon his hurt she looks so steadfastly,
>   That her sight dazzling, makes the wound seem three;
> And then she reprehends her mangling eye,
>   That makes more gashes where no breach should be;
> His face seems twain, each several limb is doubled,
> For oft the eye mistakes, the brain being troubled."

THE RAPE OF LUCRECE.

That the veins become turgid under the influence of passionate emotion might be taught by common observation. The point worthy of notice in the description of Tarquin's state as he stands by his yet sleeping victim is, that the veins are supposed to act independently of the heart, an idea quite in accordance with the physiology of the period.

> "For standing by her side,
> His eye, which late this mutiny restrains,
> Unto a greater uproar tempts his veins;
> And they, like straggling slaves for pillage fighting,
>   Obdurate vassals, fell exploits affecting,
> In bloody death and ravishment delighting,
>   Nor children's tears, nor mother's groans respecting,
>   Swell in their pride, the onset still expecting;
> Anon his beating heart, alarum striking,
> Gives the hot charge, and bids them do their liking."

The beneficial use of poisonous substances in pharmacy, and the correction of one quality by others in medicinal compounds, is thus pointedly stated.

> "The poisonous simple sometimes is compacted
> In a pure compound; being so applied,
> His venom in effect is purified."

The following line is nearly identical with Gaunt's observation in *Richard II.*, "Things sweet in taste prove in digestion sour."

> "His taste delicious, in digestion souring."

The invocation of Lucrece to "hateful vaporous and foggy night," expresses the often repeated opinion of the unwholesome nature of night air, an opinion very naturally prevalent in an undrained aguish country. The 'musty' vapours of night are not now so poisonous, here at least, as they are represented in many passages of Shakespeare, but the doctrine still holds good in aguish countries, where night may yet fitly be appealed to to send her poisonous clouds, that they may

> "With rotten damps ravish the morning air;
> Let their exhal'd unwholesome breaths make sick
> The life of purity,"

After Tarquin's crime is consummated, the wretched lady personifies and rails upon Opportunity which wrought his success and her ruin. She asks of Opportunity "When wilt thou—

> "Give physic to the sick, ease to the pained?
> The poor, lame, blind, halt, creep, cry out for thee,
> But they ne'er meet with Opportunity.
>
> The patient dies while the physician sleeps;
> The orphan pines while the oppressor feeds;
> Justice is feasting while the widow weeps;
> Advice is sporting while infection breeds:
> Thou grant'st no time for charitable deeds:
> Wrath, envy, treason, rape, and murder's rages,
> Thy heinous hours wait on them as their pages."

"Give physic to the sick, ease to the pained," is the counterbuff to Macbeth's "Throw physic to the dogs," which has been quoted to prove Shakespeare's low estimate of medicine; although it clearly means no more than Romeo's "Hang up philosophy unless philosophy can make a Juliet." The opinion here obviously inferred is, that physic can relieve the sick, and that the patient will not die if the physician do not sleep. The line, "advice is sporting while infection breeds," describes the old-world carelessness of medical men in prophylactic hygiene, sanatory science, as it is now somewhat loosely called. There can be no greater proof of the disinterestedness of the medical profession than the devotion of its sons to this branch of their science, which, aiming at the prevention of disease in the mass, has been developed almost entirely by themselves in opposition to the stubborn prejudices of the public. Advice here means medical opinion, as in *Henry VI., 2nd Part,* " I hope your lordship goes abroad by advice." And again, " With good advice and little medicine."

Lucrece's suicide, a sacrificial oblation to the chastity of her married life, is effected by stabbing herself. The description of the condition of the blood is very remarkable.

" And bubbling from her breast, it doth divide
In two slow rivers, that the crimson blood
Circles her body in on every side,
 Who like a late-sack'd island vastly stood
 Bare and unpeopled, in this fearful flood.
Some of her blood still pure and red remain'd,
And some look'd black, and that false Tarquin stain'd.
About the mourning and congealed face
Of that black blood, a watery rigol goes,
 Which seems to weep upon the tainted place:
 And ever since, as pitying Lucrece' woes,
 Corrupted blood some watery token shows;
And blood untainted still doth red abide,
Blushing at that which is so putrefied."

The phenomenon which attends the coagulation of blood in the separation of the serum from the clot is obviously referred to in the " watery rigol " which surrounds the "congealed face of that black blood." Knowledge of this separation of blood into clot and serum is also evident from the line " Corrupted blood some watery token shows," although the theory of its production is, of course, merely poetic. We scarcely yet can be said to know to what physical cause it really is due, although curiously enough the most recent theory attributes it to what may be called the first stage of corruption, the development of ammonia. That the dramatist had observed the different colour of the two kinds of blood is evident; but that he should know the cause of it was not to be expected, since even Harvey attributed the difference between bright and dark blood to the size of the opening from which it flows, "when it flows from a small orifice, it is of a brighter hue,—for then it is strained as it were, and the thinner and more penetrating portion only escapes."—*Second Disquisition.* Harvey attributed the coagulation of the blood to the very cause here assigned by Shakespeare. "As it [the blood] lives and is a very principal animal part, consisting of these juices mingled together, it is an animated *similar* part, composed of a body and a vital principle. When this living principle of the blood escapes, however, in consequence of the extinction of the native heat, the primary substance is forthwith corrupted and resolved into the parts of which it was formerly composed; first into cruor, afterwards with red and white parts, those of the red parts that are uppermost being more florid, those that are lowest being black. Of these parts, moreover, some are fibrous and tough (and these are the uniting medium of the rest,) others ichorous and serous, in which the mass of coagulum is wont to swim. Into such a serum does the blood almost wholly resolve itself at last. But these parts have no existence severally in living blood; it is in that only which has become *corrupted* and is resolved by death that they are encountered."—*On Generation.* Thus Harvey's opinion of the life in the blood is as positive as Shakespeare's. In the same work he says, "I maintain that the living principle resides primarily and principally in the blood."

SONNETS.

The 34th sonnet contains the following medical allusion.

> " For no man well of such a salve can speak,
>   That heals the wound, and cures not the disgrace :
>   Nor can thy shame give physic to my grief."

The old medical theory, that "our life is made up of the four elements" (see *Twelfth Night*), is referred to in the 44th and 45th Sonnets ; in the former to earth and water ;

> " The other two, slight air and purging fire,
>   Are both with thee, wherever I abide ;
> The first my thought, the other my desire,
>   These present-absent with swift motion slide.
> For when these quicker elements are gone
>   In tender embassy of love to thee,
> My life, being made of four, with two alone
>   Sinks down to death, oppress'd with melancholy ;
> Until life's composition be recur'd
>   By those swift messengers return'd from thee,
> Who even but now come back again, assur'd
>   Of thy fair health, recounting it to me :
> This told, I joy ; but then no longer glad,
> I send them back again, and straight grow sad."

The 111th Sonnet has a couplet alluding to the use of vinegar in the plague. Ambrose Paré, in his chapter on " What drinke the patient infected with Plague ought to use," insists on the use of oxymel (vinegar and honey), oxycrate (lemon-juice and syrup), tart cider, juleps of sorel, &c. Mr. Collier's note is " Potions of eysel, *i.e.*, potions of vinegar, for which " eysel," esill, or eyesel, was the old name."

> " Whilst, like a willing patient, I will drink
>   Potions of eysel, 'gainst my strong infection."

The following medical Sonnet, the 118th, is founded upon the old fashion of physicking to prevent sickness. Periodical abstraction of blood and periodical purgation for the purpose of preserving health, were not out of vogue in country districts within my own memory. Bacon, in his *Essay on the Regimen of Health*, says, "If you fly physic in health alltogether, it will be too strange for your body when you need it; if you make it too familiar it will work no extraordinary effect when sickness cometh. I commend rather, some diet for certain seasons, than frequent use of physic, except it be grown into a custom, for those diets alter the body more, and trouble it less." He would, therefore, have been delighted with the wisdom of the physician whose personal practice is recorded by Ward. "I have heard of a physician that used constantly to fast, or else bee drunk once every month, for the preservation of his health."—p. 267.

"Like as, to make our appetites more keen,
 With eager compounds we our palate urge:
As, to prevent our maladies unseen,
 We sicken to shun sickness, when we purge;
Even so, being full of your ne'er-cloying sweetness,
 To bitter sauces did I frame my feeding,
And, sick of welfare, found a kind of meetness
 To be diseas'd, ere that there was true needing.
Thus policy in love, to anticipate
 The ills that were not, grew to faults assured,
And brought to medicine a healthful state,
 Which, rank of goodness, would by ill be cured;
But thence I learn, and find the lesson true,
Drugs poison him that so fell sick of you."

The use of distilled medicines and the appearance of the alembic (the limbeck of Lady Macbeth,) are referred to in the 119th Sonnet.

"What potions have I drunk of syren tears,
 Distilled from limbecks, foul as hell within."

The following may allude either to the protruded eye-ball, the eye "staring full ghastly" of madding fever, or to the obliquity of the eye, the 'squiny' of Lear, which is also common in this form of disease. The latter would seem to agree best with the meaning of the passage, "Bear thine eyes straight," in the 140th Sonnet.

"How have mine eyes out of their spheres been fitted,
In the distraction of this madding fever!"

The 140th Sonnet has the following reference to the habitual practice of physicians to sooth and flatter with hope of recovery, those patients to whom the knowledge that there was no hope would be likely to aggravate the disease. Ward says of the contrary practice, "A physician told a father that his sonne was a dead man: the father replied, I had rather a physician called him so a hundred times than a judge on bench once." It is an anxious, and by no means an easy problem in medical ethics, to determine the period when the sentence of 'no recovery' ought no longer to be withheld.

"(As testy sick men, when their deaths be near,
No news but health from their physicians know:)
For, if I should despair. I should grow mad,
And in my madness might speak ill of thee:
Now this ill-wresting world has grown so bad,
Mad slanderers by mad ears believed be."

The 147th Sonnet is entirely medical, and so graphic, that explanation is needless. The description of delirium following fever, "frantic mad with evermore unrest," is thoroughly true to nature.

"My love is as a fever, longing still
For that which longer nurseth the disease;
Feeding on that which doth preserve the ill,
The uncertain sickly appetite to please.

My reason, the physician to my love,
  Angry that his prescriptions are not kept,
Hath left me, and I desperate now approve,
  Desire is death, which physic did except.
Past cure I am, now reason is past care,
  And frantic-mad with ever-more unrest;
My thoughts and my discourse as mad men's are,
  At random from the truth vainly express'd;
For I have sworn thee fair, and thought thee bright,
  Who art as black as hell, as dark as night."

The 153rd Sonnet undoubtedly refers to the use of some hot medicinal spring, perhaps to the bath which has given name to the city of King Baldud, as Steevens suggested. "The help of bath desir'd, and *thither* hied a sad distemper'd *guest*," certainly appears to support this view. The description of the spa, having a "dateless lively heat," and that it was "against strange maladies a sovereign cure," would also apply to the bath of Bath, the temperature of whose waters and the antiquity of whose reputation are of the highest. The 154th Sonnet refers more vaguely to the same.

" Cupid lay by his brand, and fell asleep:
  A maid of Dian's this advantage found,
And his love-kindling fire did quickly steep
  In a cold valley-fountain of that ground;
Which borrow'd from his holy fire of love
  A dateless lively heat, still to endure,
And grew a seething bath, which yet men prove.
  Against strange maladies a sovereign cure.
But at my mistress' eye Love's brand new-fir'd,
  The boy for trial needs would touch my breast;
I, sick withal, the help of bath desir'd,
  And thither hied, a sad distemper'd guest,
But found no cure: the bath for my help lies
Where Cupid got new fire,—my mistress' eyes."

The following lines, with medical significance, are from the LOVER'S COMPLAINT.

"As compound love to physic your cold breast."
"The aloes of all forces shocks and fears."
" Our drops this difference bore.
His poisoned me, and mine did him restore."
"O that sad breath his spongy lungs bestowed."

In concluding these pages, with whatever shortcoming of information or of ability the task has been executed, I trust that it will be admitted that I have discussed with impartiality the question propounded in the Introduction, namely, the extent of Shakespeare's knowledge of medicine, and the degree to which he was influenced by medical trains of thought. The enquiry has, of necessity, extended itself to the degree of Shakespeare's ignorance and errors of opinion on medical subjects, and to a comparison of his state of information with that of men living about the same time. The ignorance and error which then prevailed among all classes on medical subjects can only be conceived by the fullest appreciation of the fact that, before Bacon, natural science did not exist, and that, before the Reformation, the isolated facts of knowledge were obscured by the 'musty vapours' and 'rotten damps' of superstition. The printing press, moreover, was not active as it is now, and the march of knowledge was limping and feeble. Wunderlich records that the doctrines of Galen were yet popular in the middle of the 17th century, and that after Fabricius and Harvey had taught, such was the ignorance of anatomy, that two of the Heidelberg professors had a contention with the physician of the Margrave of Baden, as to whether the heart was in the middle of the thorax or on the left side of the sternum, and that they killed a hog in order to ascertain the fact, and to determine on which side of the chest they ought to apply cataplasms, so as to be over the Prince's heart.—*Geschichte der Medicin,* p. 121.

After a perusal of all the medical works of the period on which I have been able to lay hands, and the institution of a close comparison between them and the works of Shakespeare, I have arrived at the fullest conviction that the great dramatist had, at least, been a diligent student of all medical knowledge existing in his time. It has already been satisfactorily proved by the noble author to whom this work is dedicated, that he had been a diligent student of the law. If it be attempted to argue that Shakespeare had obtained his knowledge, either of law or of medicine, by any formal connection with either of these professions, it must be admitted that the arguments mutually invalidate each other; since the double event, say of his having been both a lawyer's clerk and a doctor's apprentice, is far more improbable than either single event would be. But if the argument only be urged that Shakespeare had been a diligent student both of medicine and law, not for professional purposes, but for the sake of increasing his general information, it would seem that the evidence of diligent study in either department of knowledge would fortify the evidence of such study in the other department; for the great hungry mind, which had an appetite for all accessible knowledge, in one of the large divisions into which the knowledge of cause and effect may be separated, would, in all probability, be far from satisfied without appropriating to itself the counterpart of such knowledge from the complementary department.

In claiming for law and medicine so wide a dominion as the extent of the knowledge of nature and its laws, I, of course, only do so with reservation, and for the purpose of expressing the undoubted fact that the one is founded upon the moral, and that the other is founded upon the physical law, and that, as professions, they practically apply these laws to man's welfare. Whewell speaks of civil law and medicine, as "two of the leading studies of those times (the middle ages) which occupied much of men's time and thoughts, and had a very great influence on society ; the one dealing with notions, the other with things ; the one employed about moral rules, the other about material causes, but both for practical ends."—*Inductive Sciences*, vol. 1, p. 330.

But it has been said that, granting the validity of the proof of Shakespeare's knowledge of medicine and law, he was also acquainted with many other subjects; thus, he wrote of "lavoltas high, and swift corantos," and might therefore have been a dancing master; he wrote of "tackle, sail, and mast," and might have been a sailor. Doubtless there are few subjects which might not be, incidentally, thus illustrated from the writings of our author. My learned friend, Dr. Copland, has communicated to me an anecdote which tells on this point. He was present at a dinner party with Haslam, of Bethlehem Hospital, a man of great reading and infinite wit, and Mr. Jerdan, editor of the *Literary Gazette ;* the former, having stated his opinion that there was no possible subject which could not be illustrated out of Shakespeare, the latter expressed dissent, and the wager of a dinner for the party was laid between the two, that Jerdan could not name a subject to which Haslam would fail, within fifteen minutes, to apply from memory a Shakespearean illustration. Jerdan named the Tread-mill which had been recently invented, to which Haslam almost immediately applied the words from *Lear*, "Down thou climbing sorrow, thy element's below," and was adjudged to have won the wager.

But it is not upon any ingenious perversion of meaning, nor even upon real but insignificant references, that the proof stands of Shakespeare's study of those great departments of knowledge in which the theories of ethics and physics become concrete and practical. Speaking on my own subject of investigation, I refer to the cumulative evidence collected in the foregoing pages as unanswerable proof that his mind was deeply imbued with the best medical information of his age. If, however, it be thus established that he diligently worked the champion lodes of knowledge, it is not therefore to be assumed that with indiscriminating avidity he followed every small branch and leader of ore.

49914

ST. MARY'S COLLEGE OF MARYLAND
ST. MARY'S CITY, MARYLAND